DP

Europe's Displaced Persons,
1945–1951

THE DISPLACED
PERSONS' EUROPE

Occupation Zones,
Representative Camps,
Major Cities 1946

DP

Europe's Displaced Persons, 1945–1951

Mark Wyman

PHILADELPHIA
The Balch Institute Press
London and Toronto: Associated University Presses

Associated University Presses
440 Forsgate Drive
Cranbury, NJ 08512

Associated University Presses
25 Sicilian Avenue
London WC1A 2QH, England

Associated University Presses
P.O. Box 488, Port Credit
Mississauga, Ontario
Canada L5G 4M2

The paper used in this publication meets the requirements
of the American National Standard for Permanence of Paper
for Printed Library Materials Z39.48-1984.

Library of Congress Cataloging-in-Publication Data

Wyman, Mark.
    DP : Europe's displaced persons, 1945–1951.

    Bibliography: p.
    Includes index.
    1. World War, 1939–1945—Refugees. I. Title.
II. Title: Europe's displaced persons, 1945–1951.
D808.W96   1989   940.53′159   88-70152
ISBN 0-944190-04-9 (alk. paper)

PRINTED IN THE UNITED STATES OF AMERICA

For my Parents

Who helped me see that
each person is important
and has an
interesting story to tell

CONTENTS

PREFACE

THE displaced persons came into my life one day in the late 1940s. They came from their world of war, and wandering, and debates over diplomacy and borders, into our children's world of football, campouts, and arithmetic. It must have seemed provincial to some of them, although they never acted as if it was; and I have a feeling they were glad to be done with international issues for a while. At any rate they soon settled into life in a small Wisconsin town, and the DP children quickly became part of our group.

But when we later went our separate ways my curiosity about them remained, and it has gradually increased as those years recede further back in time. Finally I decided to seek out my old friends—and eventually dozens of other former displaced persons, in Canada and the United States, from all major nationalities involved—and piece together their story. And so this is a history that is also a memory, utilizing some of the tools of the historian and some of the listener who draws examples from the recollections of participants.

I know that memory can become dimmed, that tales of what occurred can become burdened with nostalgia, that unpleasant incidents can be forgotten. But I have learned that dramatic, crucial events are usually recalled in vivid detail. And contemporary accounts and records have provided a way to measure the accuracy of recollections. Drawing on interviews and English-language sources and translations, I have tried to present a true picture of the displaced persons. I hope they—above all—will find this book both accurate in detail and honest in spirit.

ACKNOWLEDGMENTS

To write on the displaced persons is to build up an enormous debt to those who have opened their memories to an outsider. I am deeply grateful to the dozens of former DPs and former UNRRA, IRO, U.S. government, and voluntary agency workers who took the time to sit down with me and remember details of their lives from thirty-five to forty-five years ago. High on this list would be my former classmate, Aija Kancitis Vikmanis, and her husband Vilis; Bernard Warach; Ben Kaplan; Prof. Howard and Sally Wriggins; Prof. Leo Srole; Dr. Rudolph Susel of *Ameriška Domovina;* Alexander Squadrilli; and my Illinois State University colleagues Drs. Olgerts Počs and Sol Shulman.

Personnel of many libraries, historical collections, and archives went out of their way to assist me. Chief among these were staff workers at Milner Library of Illinois State University, especially Helga Whitcomb, Garold Cole, Marian Carroll, and Joan Winters; Jack Sutters of the American Friends Service Committee Archives in Philadelphia; Howard Hong of the Lutheran World Federation Service to Refugees Collection at St. Olaf College; Jack Belwood of the United Nations Archives in New York; Susan Grigg and Halyna Myroniuk of the Immigration History Research Center in St. Paul; University of Illinois Library staff members, especially Dmytro M. Shtohryn of the Slavic and East European Library; Helen Wajda of the Polish Museum and Archives of America in Chicago; Irma Kopp Krents, director of the William E. Wiener Oral History Library of the American Jewish Committee, New York; the staff of the Lithuanian World Archives in Chicago; and the staffs of the National Archives Photo Division and the U.S. Army Center of Military History, both in Washington, D.C.

These persons also gave extra, much-appreciated assistance: Emilian Basiuk, director, Ukrainian National Museum in Chicago; Dr. B. I. Balinsky; Myron Momryk, Public Archives of Canada; Birthe Myers; Prof. Lawrence Walker; Prof. Alfreds Straumanis, and Prof. Alvin Goldfarb.

Some eighty interviews were conducted for this project, in person and by mail. In some cases the interpretations of these persons varied from mine; at any rate, interpretations in these pages are my own. Many of those interviewed wished to remain anonymous, and their wishes will be respected. Thanks are due to them as well as to these interviewees: Dr. Edgar Anderson, Rev. Vytautas Bagdanavičius of *Draugas,* Rev. Msgr. Louis B. Baznik, Jerome Brentar, Jan Cieslar, Wanda Cioth, Eileen Eagan, Marek Gordon, Alfons Hering of *Gwiazda Polarna,* Orest Horodysky, Dr. Visvaldis Janavs, Miro Javornik, Ilmar Kuljus, Msgr. Andrew P. Landi, James MacCracken, Fernanda U. Malmin, Juozas Masilionis, Joseph Melaher, Lydia Palij, Bohdan Panchuk, Prof. Edward and Ursula Peterson, Arnold F. Pikre, Milko Pust, August Raja, Oscar Ratti, Prof. Valerian Revutsky, Matej Roesmann, George Sadomytschenko, Mr. and Mrs. Ivan Sadomytschenko, Gertrude Sovik, Mr. and Mrs. Mate Szedlak, and Vasilije and Zlatka Vuckovich.

1
A CONTINENT IN RUINS

Europe is on the move. The exiled peoples are going home. The roads are filled with men and women of a score of nations trudging back hundreds of miles. Frequently they pause and rest in the warm sun, for the end of the shooting finds Europe not only injured but very tired.
>   —The *Times* (London), 18 May 1945

IN the last week of April 1945 a long, slow-moving mass of humanity made its way out of northwest Yugoslavia into Italy. It included many people who had fled their homes with only an hour's notice, as Tito's Partisans began closing in following the German retreat and the collapse of home guard forces.

It was a movement typical of those hectic final weeks of World War II across Europe. Most of those fleeing went on foot, so crowded into the narrow roadways that those with bicycles could only walk with them. Some attempted to use wagons pulled by horses or oxen, and German soldiers occasionally traveled in trucks that could proceed only fitfully amid the crowds moving toward Italy.

Near Gorizia they met the British. The encounter came after they crossed the Soca River, which rumor had pointed to as the stopping point of the eastward-pushing Allied troops. Better, then, to cross the Soca. A journalist accompanying the British soldiers reported that they met "a sombre trail of bewildered peoples." In that mass of humanity were representatives from all Europe—Slovenians and Slovaks, Italians and Rumanians, Frenchmen and Jews. One participant recalled the scene as evening crept over the weary travelers gathered by the military into a dusty open field:

Orthodox priests with long beards were there, waving their hands and getting people together. There was a proliferation of religious

15

groups—with nothing material to have, people were hanging on to religion. Through the smoke of the campfires we heard singing coming from many points of the encampment—Jewish songs, Serbian chants, Frenchmen singing popular numbers. There were violins, fiddles, flutes, clarinets, an accordion.[1]

The mood of this congregation of the homeless and dispossessed, fleeing territory torn by the clash of opposing armies, was in sharp contrast with the jubilation erupting elsewhere as word came of the end of the war. Cheering multitudes appeared among the victors—dancing around hastily built bonfires across England, pouring into massive celebrations along Paris's boulevards, hearing King Christian of Denmark announce in Copenhagen, "We are once again able to raise our ancient flag." When John Deane arrived at the U.S. Embassy in Moscow the afternoon following the German surrender, he found the city center still celebrating after twelve hours of revelry. The Russians joyfully seized Americans and tossed them like corks on upraised hands above the crowd, giving prolonged cheers to anyone appearing at an embassy window. "The day was cold in Moscow," Deane wrote, "but my heart was warmed by the spontaneous spirit of friendship being shown by the thousands of Russian people in the square outside my window."[2]

In areas left behind by the fleeing refugees, however, the celebrations were mainly confined to Allied bases. No shouts of exhilaration broke the eerie silence of the bombed-out cities, many of which had virtually lost their identities. "Pforzheim doesn't exist anymore," a traveler reported incredulously as he entered a familiar area in Germany.[3] Cologne's cathedral could still be viewed from afar, but persons nearing the city center found only a "white sea of rubble, faceless and featureless in the bright sunlight," like "the sprawling skeleton of a giant animal." When General Eisenhower visited Berlin he confided to a friend, "It is quite likely, in my opinion, that there will never be any attempt to rebuild Berlin."[4] The devastation was as bad to the east, where in addition to Poland's urban ruin a sixth of the farms were out of operation and three-fourths of the standard railroad trackage was damaged or unusable. Some cities of the Soviet Ukraine had sustained 90 percent destruction; to the north in Byelorussia, Minsk's 80-percent destruction was comparable to Warsaw's. In Yugoslavia, too, the land had been laid waste by invasions and bombings in addition to civil war. One heavily contested area of Yugoslavia could show no building still standing along a 125-mile stretch of highway.[5]

Amid this barren countryside that marked much of the continent of Europe, with odors of corpses rotting in bombed basements and washing up along the shores, survivors haltingly began to poke their way.

Military planners tried to prepare for these refugees, since the total of those running from battle zones had been growing long before the climactic final struggles of 1945. This was noted in 1943 when the tide of war changed and the Western powers and their Soviet allies began to push toward Germany from the east, south, and west. A former resident of Gdansk recalled going shopping one day in 1943 and suddenly encountering a seemingly endless train of horse-drawn wagons and carts moving wearily through the city, filled with refugees escaping the war to the east.[6] Allied armies advancing up the Italian boot in 1943, and inland from the Normandy beachhead in 1944, faced the problem of handling the massive numbers of refugees they encountered. By August 1944 a center had been set up near Cherbourg to care for some 1,000 mainly non-French refugees, and within two months 50,000 of these—mostly Poles and Russians—were collected at locations across France.

The front had been pushed far enough toward Germany by January 1945 to make way for a hundred assembly centers in France, Belgium, Luxembourg, and the Netherlands that housed and fed some 247,000 persons. By then each major Allied advance brought a crescendo of refugees. Soon after Hamburg finally fell in early May of 1945 its 1.5 million population was swollen by some 500,000 of the homeless. Allied officers were instructed to make preparations to care for more than 1 million Allied nationals by war's end, a third of them liberated prisoners of war from Allied armies, the rest civilians. The eventual totals were far above these predictions.[7]

Most estimates placed almost 7 million civilians on the move in western Europe during the early summer of 1945. Like those the British met at Gorizia, these were fleeing, or heading home, or searching for family members, or simply trying to survive. Another 7 million traveled in the Soviet Union's areas of control in central and east Europe, while Italy reported at least 95,000, and Norway, 141,000, on the road. Thousands of others escaped being included in the statistics.[8]

There were others who would soon join this slow-moving mass— some 7.8 million German soldiers who were held by the Western Allies at war's end and another 2 million who were interned by the Soviet Union. These Wehrmacht veterans had often rushed to surrender in the closing weeks, throwing their weapons into piles as they marched by Allied checkpoints. In the British area of control

Soldiers to the front, refugees to the rear. U.S. infantrymen near the Erft Canal at Bergheim, Germany, pursue the Germans while liberated French civilians move home again on 4 March 1945. *(National Archives photo.)*

in northern Germany enemy POWS were being released at the rate of 22,000 a day by mid-May. The Allies everywhere found it was too difficult to maintain them for long.[9]

Occasionally the victors uncovered strange groups within the Wehrmacht, 15 to 20 percent of whose forces were non-German. Guarding the passes in the Austrian Alps were thousands of Cossacks, bitterly anti-Communist, who had joined the German cause during the occupation of the Ukraine. A *Times* (London) reporter who happened upon one group of 24,000 Cossack men, women, and children, moving along the Gail River toward Oberdrauburg and Lienz, described the scenes as "no different in any major detail from what an artist might have painted in the Napoleonic wars." Here were peasants with horses and wooden wagons, "like a convoy of prairie schooners trekking onwards." It had taken them nearly a year to travel to northern Italy from their beloved country of the Don; now, bewildered and apprehensive, they joined the new lost army of the road in liberated Europe.[10]

This conglomeration of moving humanity—Cossacks and French, Serbs and Belgians, Silesians and Ukrainians—provided scenes of chaos in the spring of 1945 that few participants will ever forget. One family journeyed across the Rhineland on a camel "liberated" from a German zoo. A Croatian general fleeing from Zagreb in the final days recalled that "so thickly packed together were wagons, tanks, oxcarts, carriages, automobiles, trucks, and vans of all descriptions that at many points no ground could be discerned between them." It was a mass migration like that of the Ostrogoths some 1,500 years earlier, he said. Women, children, old people, and all kinds of animals mingled with Croatian, German, White Russian, and Albanian troops. A journalist watched this human flotsam that seemed to move in all directions:

> Here is an emaciated man in striped pyjama clothing, plodding down the road to Aschaffenburg, a poignant reminder of the horrors behind the beautiful facade of the countryside. Then some parties of men and women pushing a piled-up hand-cart bearing a Luxembourg flag. . . . The French pass in American lorries, the Tricolor fluttering bravely beside the United States driver, the sides garlanded with branches plucked from the roadside, the men and women seeming too dazed to display their native vivacity.[11]

Others worried over the refugees' future when they compared the kilometers still to be traveled with the physical condition of the travelers. And all the while overworked, underfed oxen and horses strained to pull decrepit wagons and carts. A *New York Times* reporter was present when a horse collapsed and fell to the side of the clogged roadway, where its owner quickly removed the harness and cut its throat; immediately "a swarm of people, all with murderous looking knives, appeared and cut off hunks of meat for their next meal" while the animal still lived. The horse "was a near skeleton with his head untouched" in less than an hour.[12]

Despite their handicaps, the bulk of the Western European refugees moved quickly to their former homes. Of the 1.2 million French found in Germany at the surrender, for example, only 40,550 remained by 18 June. The Western Allies reported that 3.2 million refugees had found their way home by 2 July, mainly to the USSR, France, Belgium, and the Netherlands; many were sped on their way in Allied trucks and airplanes.[13]

But just as the crowds on the roadways of Germany began to show signs of thinning in late summer, a new group of refugees appeared—the ethnic Germans or *Volksdeutschen* who had resided as their ancestors had in areas of Poland or other central European countries now freed of Nazi control, or who lived in regions of Germany transferred to Polish sovereignty by the Potsdam Agreement. Perhaps 12 million of these "expellees," as they were sometimes called, entered Germany in the two years immediately following the war.[14] In a single week some 200,000 arrived in Berlin, many with tales of having received thirty minutes' warning before their forced departure, or of Gdańsk evictions being carried out street by street.[15]

The *Volksdeutschen* could call on other Germans to look after them. That was a crucial difference, for although there were enormous strains in this situation these refugees were, in the end, settled among their own people, speaking their own language. Most of the German prisoners of war were also able to leave the fenced-in detention centers soon after the war and return to their old neighborhoods and to sympathetic countrymen. This was true as well for many of the foreign laborers, especially the Dutch, Belgians, French, Norwegians, Danes, and Italians. Confidently, Allied planners looked forward to rebuilding Europe without the refugees in the way.

But this was not to be. As the masses moved along the roads, observers reported that some groups were not rushing home. They were, in fact, heading in other directions. A reporter watching the exhuberant Western Europeans pass along the highway in throngs noted that "a sadder sight is presented by the Poles." In contrast with the others, the Polish current "sets toward the West" instead of toward Poland, he wrote. "The problem of their repatriation is more complicated than that of the Belgians and Dutch, or even of the Italians, who with the Russians make up the balance of this human flotsam."[16]

Where did they come from? What twisting paths of war had decreed that these people would end up "displaced" after V-E day? The first steps along that pathway often came very early, even ahead of the blitzkrieg attacks that plummeted Europe into war.

Hitler's rise to power in Germany in 1933 set off an ever-mounting exodus of Jews, of his political and economic opponents, and of others who were under increasing pressure from the Nazis. Some 17,000 German Jews and 8,000 Austrian Jews found refuge in Britain during the war, part of the total of over 114,000 refugees residing there for most of the duration. Ninety percent of the 55,000 refugees in Switzerland in early 1945 were Jewish. One group of Jews made it to Shanghai, China; 10,000 of these were allowed to cross the Soviet Union on the Trans-Siberian Railroad, where they waited out the European war while being drawn into the Far Eastern conflict. Some 400,000 Jews had fled from Germany, Austria, and the Sudetenland by May 1939. A total of 63,000 emigrated to the United States and 55,000, to Palestine; the rest scattered over the globe—many to other European countries where they were again caught by the Third Reich.

Their tragedy became apparent as the Allies probed into the reality of the Third Reich. Some five hundred concentration camps and satellite work camps were soon uncovered, and later estimates put the human totals held in them during some part of the Nazi years at 6.6 million. The *Konzentrationslager* was often a death camp; 6 million of the inmates were killed or died, three-fourths of them Jews.

The story of the concentration camps has been told often, and in grisly detail, but it must be noted here because of the camps' long-term impact—if only (in Malcolm Proudfoot's words) "because terror of these camps was a part of the grim background of every displaced person in Hitler's Europe," and care of the camps' survivors became one of the most important tasks facing the conquerors.[17]

The numbers killed by direct or indirect causes in the concentration and extermination camps are still only capable of estimate. And there were "other holocausts" as well that brought death to millions of others, Jews and non-Jews, outside of combat. What is not debated on the realistic level is the existence of horror the world had never before known—the piles of hair, eyeglasses, and shoes found by the invading armies; the mass graves and stacks of emaciated bodies—testifying to "the depth to which the national debauchment has gone," as a British reporter put it. An early visitor from the outside to the Belsen camp reported that when he entered with a military team in mid-April of 1945,

> there were approximately 50,000 people in the camp, of which about 10,000 lay dead in the huts or about the camp. Those still alive had had no food for about seven days, after a long period of semi-starvation. Typhus, amongst other diseases, was raging . . . the very air was poisoned. . . . The British have supervised the burial by SS and German PW, of some 23,000 of which approximately 10,000 or even more lay unburied when they arrived here on 15th April, 1945. The daily death rate has been terribly high, but it is steadily decreasing. On 30th April, 1945, 548 people died. 97 died on 17th May, 1945.

But the report noted that the end of Belsen was imminent, for a final ceremony and burning of the structures was scheduled for 21 May 1945.[18] One of the participants in that ceremony told of someone placing a huge photograph of Hitler upon Block 44, at which time a British colonel stepped forward. "The Colonel fired a shot from a fire-pistol into Hitler's photograph and the old camp was set on fire. This symbolized to us the end of Nazism."[19]

No, the *fact* of the concentration camps is not debatable. General Eisenhower made sure of that when, having learned that some Germans were denying knowledge of the camps, he ordered American military police to escort a thousand citizens of Weimar through Buchenwald, located only some six miles from their homes. The people of Weimar, as well as the rest of the world, now knew of Buchenwald. And it would not be forgotten: huts could be knocked down and fences removed, but the fact of Buchenwald would remain a nightmare, a symbol of the Nazi years. A United Nations representative who came to see Dachau in mid-1946 discovered that the smell of burnt flesh still hovered over the area, fourteen months after the ovens last burned human beings. Just before fainting, the UN man recalled where he had once encountered something like that odor: "It brought back a childhood memory of a visit to the Chicago stockyard."[20]

Paralleling the concentration and extermination camps' legacy of horror was the Nazis' exploitation of some 8 million foreign workers, who comprised 29 percent of the Reich's industrial labor force and 20 percent of the total labor force by May 1944. The term *slave labor,* widely used in referring to these workers, is perhaps inaccurate when applied to all 8 million, but it was wretchedly true for many. As revealed by Edward Homze's study, the system was one of shifting, contradicting policies and unpredictable turns, of volunteerism and wage offers as well as threats and beatings. Its origins lay in a variety of sources, especially the long prewar tradition of annual migrations of foreign agricultural workers into Prussia and other areas at harvest time and Germany's memories of the First World War's frightening labor shortages.

Nazi racial philosophies became part of these developments as well. The Jews and east European *Untermenschen*—the subhumans—were to be treated differently than German workers or those brought in from the conquered lands of western and northern Europe. Forced labor recruitment by Nazis was harshest in the Ukraine, Poland, Byelorussia, and adjacent areas as manpower shortages worsened. Analysts have concluded that these manhunts played a major role in turning initially receptive local populations against the Germans.

The foreign labor policy began to take form soon after the fall of Warsaw in 1939, when some thirty recruitment offices were set up in Poland to hire Poles for paid work in Germany; 110,000 civilians were signed up by October. But this was still inadequate, and

300,000 Polish prisoners of war helped harvest the 1939–40 crops. By the spring of 1942 there were 1,080,000 Poles employed in Germany. Some had been recruited under pressure, while others had volunteered for lack of a better alternative.

Still more were needed. Children as young as ten years of age were recruited. Early successes on the Russian front brought in a flood of 3.5 million Soviet prisoners, but the desire to treat them as *Untermenschen,* along with poor German planning, resulted in an enormous death toll among them from inadequate food, clothing, and shelter. Over 5 million Soviet prisoners of war were eventually held by the Germans, but this total was reduced by starvation, disease, desertion, and recruitment into German forces to 1.053 million by the spring of 1944; some 875,000 of these were then laboring for the Reich.[21]

Contracts between workers and Germans were often forbidden or closely regulated. To make them readily identifiable, Polish workers wore an insignia with a large "P" on a yellow square, while Ukrainians and Russians wore an "O" for *Ost* (east) on a blue square. Some 22,000 foreign labor camps housed two-thirds of the foreign workers by 1943, but others were kept within concentration camps or private dwellings. German industries competed for them, lobbying among Hitler's aides. The I. G. Farben synthetic gasoline plant was installed at Auschwitz, and 55 percent of its employees were foreigners, over one-quarter of them concentration camp inmates. Living conditions of the foreign workers were not uniform but were generally poor, and they deteriorated sharply in the closing months of the war. Homze concluded in his study of the foreign workers that their life "was one long, continual nightmare of hard work, insufficient food, inadequate quarters, personal discrimination, and cruelty."[22]

They worked in more than factories, and often outside the borders of prewar Germany. An Estonian recalled being taken by Germans to a farm labor camp with a crew almost entirely made up of Estonian fifteen- and sixteen-year-olds, French POWs, and Poles. Wheat and barley were the main crops, the farm's operators treated them decently, and there was enough to eat. But when the front collapsed the tolerable situation suddenly ended: "The Germans didn't quite want it to end," he recalled; "they took our leader—an old man, an Estonian—away and killed him." An American in Italy in mid-1945 encountered 250 Hungarians who had served in a German railway labor battalion, holding jobs from dispatcher to track walker. With them was a group of Hungarian orphans who had also worked in a Nazi labor gang; their ages ranged from ten to fourteen. Foreign workers built Wehrmacht fortifications, airports, the Atlantic Wall, and similar structures for Germany's *Organisation Todt* (named after its founder, General Fritz Todt). These "Todt workers" were soon known for their high death rates as well as the enormous amount of defense construction they accomplished.[23]

Among the large groups leaving their countries and eventually falling into the classification of displaced persons, the Polish soldiers led by Lieutenant General Władysław Anders deserve major attention. These men had been captured by the USSR during its advance into Poland in the autumn of 1939 and were imprisoned in the Soviet Union until 1941, but were then allowed to go to Iran and the Middle East where they reorganized as the fifty-thousand-strong II Polish Corps and fought with Allied troops up through Italy.

The II Polish Corps' most famous battle—one that has merited an important page in World War II history—was the final, successful assault on the German-held monastery at Monte Cassino in May 1944. The Germans' Gustav Line, which blocked the main road leading to Rome, ran across the peninsula along the Garigliano and Rapido rivers, with the abandoned Benedictine monastery above Cassino providing an observation post crucial to German control of the area.

After repeated shellings and a final massive barrage the evening of 11 May, troops of many nationalities began the final onslaught on the Gustav Line, with the Polish Corps picked for the final attack on the monastery. On the morning of 18 May, the third Carpathian Rifle Division raised the Polish flag over Monte Cassino, a symbol of the Allied success in opening the road to Rome. The corps lost 860 men in the assault, and another 2,822 were wounded. General Anders climbed over the pockmarked mountainside, viewing the splintered tree stumps, shattered helmets, and pieces of uniforms, encountering corpses of Polish and German soldiers "sometimes entangled in a deathly embrace." But he also found the slopes covered with red poppies, "weirdly appropriate to the scene." A cemetery was later prepared on the Monte Cassino slopes, its marble spire telling the story of these men whose longing to return home had taken them from Totskoie camp to Yangi-Yul, Pahlevi, Gazi, and now to Italy:

We Polish soldiers
For our freedom and yours
Have given our souls to God
Our bodies to the soil of Italy
And our hearts to Poland.

Although the 1941 Polish-Soviet agreement had stated that "at the end of the war the army will return to Poland," Allied war strategies and the postwar political situation in Eastern Europe prevented this. Polish army veterans were eventually placed in the ranks of the displaced persons. And although Anders ordered them to "remain a closely-knit, militant body," they were eventually widely scattered. Anders's II Polish Corps made its way to Britain, where it was demobilized in 1946; some twenty thousand other Poles who had fought for the Allies turned up in France; and large numbers of Poles made their way to the Middle East. It was an epic, an odyssey of wartime, but for the time being it ended in a displaced persons camp.

Other Europeans also escaped to the Middle East and North Africa, eventually finding refuge at camps in Aleppo, Syria; near Gaza in Palestine; and at Moses Wells, El Shatt, Khataba, and Tolumbat in Egypt. One group of Poles spent the war years in Mexico. They had been taken to Siberia by the Soviets in the aftermath of the Nazi-Soviet invasion of Poland in 1939, but because of Allied pressure they—like Anders's army corps—were allowed to leave, going through Iran and eventually reaching a camp near Guanajuato, Mexico.[24]

Legal classifications of displaced persons drawn up by Supreme Headquarters, Allied Expeditionary Force (SHAEF), included evacuees, war or political refugees, political prisoners, forced or voluntary workers, Todt workers and former members of forces under German command, deportees, intruded persons, extruded persons, civilian internees, ex–prisoners of war, and stateless persons.

There were human beings behind these legal terms. Something of the diversity—and precariousness—of the wartime routes that eventually delivered refugees into the classification of displaced persons can be seen in the personal histories of four individuals, a Pole, a Ukrainian, a Slovenian, and a Latvian.

For Jan Cieslar, the pathway toward becoming a displaced person began at Gdynia, a Baltic seaport near Gdańsk, where a special seminar for Polish teachers was winding up at the end of August

1939. The seminar's final speaker was Karol Irzykowski, a well-known poet, who informed the audience at the outset that he had planned to lecture on "Tragedy in Literature." Sadly he continued, "I'm sorry—but the tragedy has already begun. And you will be the actors in this tragedy." His prediction was soon proven correct, as Poles met the crushing impact of invasions from west and east, starting only days after he spoke and continuing over the next six years.

The seminar at Gdynia broke up immediately, participants rushed to catch transportation to their homes, and Jan Cieslar eventually made it back to his teaching job in a small town. Civil defense work was already underway, and he was awakened early one morning by shouts: "Teacher, get up! The war is on!"

It was indeed on, that first day of September 1939. The village was bombed by German planes and residents fled into the surrounding forest, escaping toward the east until they learned the Russians were invading from that direction. Eventually German soldiers captured Cieslar and put him in a prison camp at Kielce. Released in two weeks, he then helped his parents until friends urged him to flee in the spring of 1940. The Gestapo learned of his escape plans, however, and put him in a prison for eight months before taking him to a concentration camp with a truckload of others. This was the infamous *Konzentrationslager Auschwitz,* and he wore the "P" insignia on a red background, classifying him as a political prisoner.

The presence of a camp doctor who by chance was from Cieslar's hometown was probably crucial to his surviving illness and injury at Auschwitz. Memories of those years remain vivid—the cruelty, the depression, but also spots of brightness that still shine through memory. Cieslar described a Christmas concert by the camp orchestra, made up of musicians from various areas overrun by the Nazis, which included carols, a tango, and Schubert's *Unfinished Symphony*. After the music, Cieslar drifted off to sleep, dreaming he was not in Auschwitz, not ill, not hungry, not a prisoner. For some magic moments of the Auschwitz Christmas he was spiritually back home, close by his family for the holidays.

But then there was another move, this time to the concentration camp at Mauthausen-Gusen in Austria, where he went in mid-April of 1943 as part of Nazi retaliation for escapes made by other prisoners. He remained in the Austrian camp, at work day after day, until the Allies arrived in early May of 1945. Like many other DPs, he remembered the moment of liberation in detail:

We were there in the camp until May 5, 1945, at five o'clock. It was a Saturday. The Nazi SS had fled some days earlier, leaving the Vienna police in charge for the last three or four days. On that day at the end of work we gathered for the head count. For the first time we didn't have to take off our hats as we filed by the guard.

Suddenly an American commander appeared at the gate. He announced, "You are free."

The first thing we did, we took our hats off, and we were all standing there—twenty thousand in the camp, mainly Poles. And we started singing the Polish national hymn. Even the guards sang, and somebody got a flag of Poland and it waved above us. We said the pledge: *Nie rzucim ziemi*—"We will not abandon the land of our forefathers."

Cieslar was transported by the U.S. Army to a sanitorium at Hohenfels in Bavaria, where he remained as a patient with some fifteen thousand others, mainly Poles. Deciding not to return to Poland, he was then classed as a displaced person, and lived and worked in various camps as a teacher and camp leader before landing at Bad Reichenhall near Berchtesgaden.

The odyssey that would make Daria Nahuievych (not her real name) a displaced person began one day late in 1939, when Soviet occupation officials criticized her because she had gone to morning mass before coming to the balloting area to vote for the single slate of candidates offered in an election, the first under Communist control. "Are you a teacher? You should be the first here—not go to church first." Shortly before that the new Communist school superintendent had told the pupils in her school, "No more *pani* (madame). But instead *tovaryschka* (comrade)."

That led to her decision to leave.

Daria Nahuievych's journey started in eastern Poland, under Soviet control after the dual Nazi-Russian invasion of Poland—but it was still the Ukraine. One of the world's less-understood regions, the Ukraine is an enormous land, stretching from the Don steppes in the east, to the Byelorussian marshes in the north, westward to Poland, Czechoslovakia, and the Carpathian Mountains, and southward to the Black Sea. Its frontiers are somewhat vague and have been frequently challenged over the centuries; the Ukraine's only unchallenged existence has been within the hearts of Ukrainians. To be Ukrainian is to speak Ukrainian and be part of the long Ukrainian cultural heritage, but generally in history it has also meant living under the control of another nation—whether the Austro-Hungarian Empire, Rumania, Poland, or the Soviet Union where most of the Ukrainian lands lie today. The history of the Ukraine, attacked and buffeted by its neighbors, has been laced with tragedy.[25]

This was the land Daria Nahuievych had to leave in 1939. Her first hurdle was to find a way into German-occupied Poland, the *General-gouvernement,* west of the San River demarcation line. With aid from local residents she and several others swam the San—only to run into the guns of watching Wehrmacht border guards on the western shore. At this time of German-USSR official friendship the guards tried to force the swimmers back; an older soldier overruled the others, however, and took the San River swimmers to the Ukrainian relief committee in a nearby town on the German side.

Living in German-occupied Poland meant freedom from the Russians and, for Daria Nahuievych, one more spot of brightness: she met and married another escaped Ukrainian, who had been captured by the Germans and released. Living among a group of Ukrainians, they felt a surge of national pride and expectation when, in the wake of the later German invasion of Soviet-held areas in 1941, a group of Ukrainians in L'vov proclaimed an independent Ukraine.* Hopes were high that the incoming Germans would permit this to become a reality, and many welcomed them as carriers of Western culture. German soldiers driving out Soviet troops were frequently met by Ukrainian civilians welcoming them with bread and salt; a Wehrmacht general recalled that women came "on to the very battlefield bringing wooden platters of bread and butter and eggs and, in my case at least, refused to let me move on before I had eaten." But Hitler's racial phobias won out. Ukrainians were downgraded as *Untermenschen,* and dreams of an immediate independent Ukraine were crushed by the rolling tanks and artillery of the Third Reich. But they were crushed only temporarily, for now the Ukrainian underground had a rallying point.[26]

Then came the German retreat. In midsummer of 1944 Daria and her husband decided they had to leave before Soviet troops arrived. This was the *pereselennia*—the westward trek of Ukrainians fleeing before onrushing Soviets, a movement that brought hundreds of thousands of people from east Europe into western areas near the close of the war. Daria and her husband were able to board a train carrying German soldiers and others westward, occupying a corner of a jostling flatcar with their newborn son held within a precariously placed packing box. At one point, crossing Czechoslovakia, Daria bent to pick him up—then moments later watched in horror as the box fell from the flatcar onto a steep boulder-strewn

---

*The current Soviet spelling of L'vov will be employed here to avoid confusion with other spellings for the same city: L'viv—Ukrainian; Lwów—Polish; Lemberg—German.

hillside below. Such incidents occur frequently in escape accounts, often indicating to the travelers that a divine presence guided them on their desperate journeys.

The train kept shifting directions—north, then west, bending north again and even eastward for a time—before Daria and her husband and child were forced off in Leipzig. In the final months of the war they traveled westward again, fearing a Soviet takeover, and made it to Hamburg short weeks before the British arrived and placed them in a camp.

Now they, too, were DPs.

Yugoslavia crumbled at the outset of the Nazis' southward expansion, and Tone Krim (not his real name) was quickly thrown into the role of rebel, outcast. His was a two-front war: seeking to combat the Communist Partisans while working for the overthrow of Nazi-allied local regimes. The Yugoslav monarchy had sought to maintain neutrality for some twenty months before March 1941, when it finally acceded to the Axis powers' demands for an alliance. This was then challenged by a military putsch, which in turn brought on a German and Italian takeover that came close to dismembering Yugoslavia by granting major portions of national territory to bordering countries.

Krim, mobilized into the military in Ljubljana in his native Slovenia in 1940, had been sent to central Yugoslavia at the time of the Nazi invasion. As the Royal Yugoslav Army fell apart, its members headed for safety and Krim walked the two hundred miles back to his hometown near Ljubljana.

The hometown he encountered had changed. Now German soldiers patrolled, forbidding people to speak Slovenian, placing schools under Nazi control, and expelling many persons to other areas. Krim's wife was assigned to work in Germany; he would not see her again for four years. In other regions, thousands were shifted to different communities, and Yugoslavia's age-old ethnic rivalries raged anew, especially the Croat-Serb bitterness. Blood flowed, with fighting between the Croatian Ustashi and their rivals especially violent; Jews were driven away and many persons were ripped from their homes in Macedonia (an area Hitler had promised to Bulgaria). Zagreb newspapers in April 1941 carried notices that Serbs had to vacate the city within twelve hours, and that persons caught hiding them would be executed. Many members of the Orthodox Eastern Church faced mandatory conversion to Catholicism.[27]

Unhappy with the Croatian Ustashi and their cooperation with the Nazis, Krim joined the Chetnik movement led by the rebel general Draza Mihailovic. Various local armies were active in Slovenia—some Slovenians joined the Partisans, the pro-Communist guerrilla army led by Tito (Joseph Broz); many others preferred one of the branches of the strongly anti-Communist and pro-Catholic *domobranci* (home guards). The latter fought the Partisans and sometimes received German assistance, while trying to expand their influence in order to control the region after the war.

The Gestapo learned of Krim's activities and placed him under arrest, scheduling his execution for the following day. But Krim escaped and spent the next three years with Chetnik forces in the steep mountainous country of northern Yugoslavia, staging hit-and-run attacks on German outposts, challenging the Partisans' control. Sometimes the Chetniks worked against the Partisans in cooperation with German or Italian troops.[28]

But the future belonged to Tito's Partisans, who received major aid from the British and Americans. The reasons for this aid are still debated, but evidence from wartime statements indicates that the Allies were led to believe that Tito's was the only group consistently and effectively battling the Nazis—and defeat of the Nazis remained the Allies' dominant war aim, to the exclusion of questions about postwar power among competing groups.

As the end drew near in the spring of 1945, the position of Tito's Yugoslav opponents suddenly turned desperate. One Chetnik leader attempted to negotiate free passage for his 10,000 followers across Croatia to Slovenia and Italy, but he was refused, and his men had to battle Ustashi troops all the way into Carinthia in southern Austria.

"If they would catch us they would exterminate us," Krim said, "so we had to leave." It was a quick decision, and his unit of five hundred moved rapidly through Slovenia to Austria and the British lines. Then the British transferred them to Italy, Krim and his men leaving in the first transports. His unit made it into Italy; as will be discussed in chapter 3, many later groups were shifted back to Yugoslavia into the hands of waiting Partisans.

In Italy Krim found mainly discouragement. Sent first to Forli, then to Eboli, he discovered that he and other Chetniks were considered prisoners of war. His unit's shelter consisted of two small tents with empty biscuit boxes piled along the sides. The Chetniks' rising anger at this point stemmed also from their feeling that they had, after all, given aid to the Allies: "At the end of the war we were caring for twelve British soldiers who had escaped from Crete, and two American pilots," Krim argued.

But he still had one hope—that he could find his wife. Through various sources he learned that after spending much of the war peeling potatoes for a Wehrmacht mess hall, she had been shifted to a factory at Kupfumburg where tanks and large guns were manufactured. It had been bombed heavily in her four months there, but she had escaped serious injury and at war's end made her way into Austria. Krim reached her there after crossing the Alps illegally—not difficult for a veteran of five years of guerrilla fighting—and brought her back into Italy with him. This time he wore a British uniform and showed border guards "official" papers.

At least they had each other as their lives as displaced persons began.

To the north, the seesaw of war brought different agonies to the Baltic peoples and directed them along other pathways to becoming displaced persons. Olgerts Počs recalls the sudden end of his idyllic life as a child growing up along Latvia's eastern border, where he lived with his parents, brother, and sister in an old revamped castle that housed the county grade school and several families of teachers. Počs's father was the principal and his mother was a teacher.

Počs's homeland was—again—the victim of its neighbors. The Soviet takeover of the Baltic states in October 1939 ended the brief twenty-one-year period of independence that Latvia, Estonia, and Lithuania had gained when the Bolshevik Revolution and the end of the First World War opened the way to self-rule. That independence had been won and maintained only with difficulty. Bolsheviks invaded at the outset, Germans attacked in 1919, and there were continuing controversies over the years with the USSR, Germany, and Poland. The split between Lithuania and Poland was so severe that rail, highway, telegraph, telephone, and diplomatic links were broken in 1920; they were not restored until Poland issued an ultimatum in 1938 as it sought to parry threats of German encirclement.[29]

The German attack on Poland in September 1939 opened the final act in the drama of the Baltic nations' struggle for independence, and there would be many tragic scenes before the curtain fell. Initially desiring control over the Baltic states, Hitler in those months of German-USSR alliance finally turned them over to the Soviets in exchange for Poland's Lublin province. The Soviets then demanded "treaties of mutual assistance" with the Baltic nations late in 1939; incorporation into the USSR was "requested" by the three states' puppet assemblies in August 1940.[30]

The Soviet takeover brought disruption to the Počs family along with thousands of other Latvians. Počs's parents were transferred to another, distant, school, which meant the family had to leave its castle home. Within schools the changes were more drastic: The Communists ended religious instruction, brought in Soviet text-books, and planted spies among the pupils. (An Estonian school principal recalled that in those months of Communist control she was required to attend gatherings where "upon the instigation of two or three rowdies, the mood of the whole meeting would change. . . . All at once a resolution would be passed that such a province, or such and such a region, desires incorporation into the Soviet Union.") Church property was nationalized, as were farms, factories, and rural co-operatives.

But for citizens of the Baltic states, the horror of living under Soviet control reached its climax in the early morning hours of 14 June 1941, when the secret police began deporting thousands of persons it considered dangerous, including much of the intellectual and administrative leadership of the Baltic countries. Many were given only minutes to gather clothing for the journey that would take them to Siberia, Kazakhstan, or other areas of the Soviet hinterland, a one-way journey for all but a few. Estimates are that the Soviets deported or killed 131,500 Balts during their period of control lasting less than eighteen months.[31]

This helps explain why the Počs family, and most residents of the Baltic states, welcomed the German invasion that began on 22 June 1941, just over a week after the Soviet mass deportations. The Germans gave Počs's parents their former school positions, while much private property was restored initially and many confiscated items were returned. Beginnings were made for some degree of self-rule in the Baltic states, fitting in with early plans of Alfred Rosen-berg, Hitler's minister for Occupied Eastern Territories. Rosenberg argued that the Baltic peoples were Aryans and should not be enslaved; they were to form part of the Third Reich's "Ostland" province comprising Lithuania, Latvia, Estonia, and the conquered Soviet state of Byelorussia.

The contrast was unavoidable for a people who had now seen two forms of dictatorship. "We preferred the Germans by miles," Počs recalled. "We were treated better—we got their ration cards, and were considered as eastern Germans. It was different than they treated Poles and Jews."

Indeed, the Nazis' actions toward some identifiable groups in the population quickly ended notions of benign rule. Some 200,000 Jews were killed or deported in Lithuania alone; thousands of young people were recruited throughout the three nations for *Ar-*

beitsdienst (work service) in Germany; 40,000 Balts were placed in concentration camps; and German troops massacred hundreds in reprisal raids (including all 119 residents of the village of Pirčiupis, Lithuania, after several Germans were ambushed nearby).

For the Baltic peoples, growing hopes for the end of the war included no realistic expectation of independence. True, the Germans were more lenient—but also more efficient. The Germans had shown mainly a desire to Germanize them, fastening an ever-tighter grip as Hitler's war machine called for greater output and obedience. Soviet propaganda, meanwhile, continued to refer to Latvia, Lithuania, and Estonia only as member states of the USSR.[32]

The Soviet breakthrough, after the Finnish front collapsed in early 1944, ended this respite from communism and confronted the Baltic peoples with the twin questions of when to leave, and by which route.

Members of the Počs family made their decision in early summer of 1944, finding neighbors already gathering outside their doorway to seize furniture as the family hurriedly packed, then left for the train station and what may have been the final train out. They traveled first to western Latvia, staying there two months, then headed to the Baltic port of Liepaja in October, when word came that Russian troops had cut off land escape routes to the south.

The Počses traveled in their exodus with another family that had formerly managed a creamery; with a case of butter it was possible to obtain crucial favors along the way—permission to board a German military boat carrying injured soldiers to Gdansk; tickets for a train in Gdansk that took the group to Berlin; further tickets on another train that ultimately left them in Oldenburg, north of Hamburg. Butter was also used to purchase food along the way, although in train stations old women and men gave out warm cereal, cabbage soup, and bread. Life on the trains remained organized, without panic, Počs said; cars were largely filled with civilians escaping the war zone, injured and cripped soldiers who were resigned to obeying orders, and party leaders without battle experience who continued to extol Hitler as the train rolled on.

In Oldenburg in late 1944 they stayed in two-room prefabricated cottages, hurriedly put up to handle the refugee influx. While the children gathered firewood and gleaned potatoes from nearby fields, within a week of their arrival the men were assigned to work for the fading German industrial machine. Počs's father made beer bottles at the local glass factory. But disruptions increased as air attacks became heavier in late spring, and then one day all the

German soldiers were gone and the city was without a military presence.

The silence did not last for long. Within a day new soldiers came—Canadians, moving on foot or in halftracks, who inspected all the dwellings, flipped through mattresses and opened cupboards, and even filched some clean handkerchiefs and an occasional pickle from a crock in an entryway. They left behind chewing gum, a totally new phenomenon.

The Canadian soldiers were followed shortly by Allied military administrators, who turned the local *Rennplatz*—a race track—into a displaced persons camp with temporary barracks. The Počs family was now part of the dispersed host of 200,000 Baltic citizens who had escaped into the western areas of Germany at war's end; some 30,000 others fled by boat across the Baltic to Sweden. Olgerts Počs and his family would stay at the Oldenburg displaced persons camp until 1950, their haven from war now their home for five long, uncertain years. [33]

Even accounts of such diverse wartime backgrounds cannot begin to indicate the wide variety of routes to becoming displaced. Those later classified as displaced persons also included thousands whose war years were spent with the anti-Nazi resistance—guerrilla units hiding in the marshes of northeastern Poland, loosely linked bands raiding in the Italian Alps, Ukrainians working on farms by day and sabotaging German rail facilities by night as part of the widespread operations of the underground OUN or UPA organization. Of the two major Polish resistance groups, the *Armia Krajowa* was considered the largest underground resistance unit in wartime Europe; it worked in loose alliance with various other groups, including some Polish Boy Scout units and several portions of the Jewish resistance. Many of these had political or philosophical alignments, such as with pro-Communist or anti-Semitic factions, which sometimes hurt their effectiveness. All provided large numbers of DPs in 1945. [34]

Even the closing of prisoner of war camps proved more complicated than originally thought by Allied leaders. One reason so many POWs became displaced persons was that the Wehrmacht was not entirely a *German* army. At least half a million men from the Soviet Union alone were reported serving in German forces by war's end. These were the *Osttruppen,* usually organized into *Ost-bataillone* units within the German army. Other nationalities were also found within the Nazi military apparatus—captured Poles, groups such as the Russian Defense Corps of Serbia (made up of older Russian émigrés) and Balts who served in units such as the "Latvian Volunteer Legion."

The most famous of these non-German units was the *Russkaia Osvoboditelnaia Armiia* (ROA, or Russian Army of Liberation), formed late in the war by General Andrei Andreevich Vlasov. Vlasov, a rising Soviet general praised for his heroics in the defense of Moscow in late 1941, was captured the following summer near Leningrad. Harboring a longstanding bitterness against the Stalinist regime—which had seized his father's land earlier—and angry over what he felt was abandonment of his forces in the swamps near Leningrad, Vlasov urged his Nazi captors to permit him to organize other prisoners from the Red Army. His aim was a partnership with the Wehrmacht to defeat Stalin and set up a new, non-Communist regime in the Soviet Union. Vlassov emerged as the single leader of this German-encouraged, anti-USSR army after several other attempts in German prisoner of war camps came to nothing. Diversity and antagonism between various USSR nationalities plagued these efforts, including Vlasov's.

Formed at a time when defeat of the USSR still appeared possible, the Vlasov army drew on longstanding hatred of the Soviet leadership among thousands of members of the Red Army. Most probably considered themselves true patriots. (An émigré serving in the Wehrmacht wrote to a Russian-language newspaper in Paris, "This war is not terrible for us, Russian patriots, but only joyous; for the Bolshevik Yoke over our motherland will be ended. . . I consider myself a warrior of Christ.") Recruits poured into the ROA in 1943 and 1944, especially after Vlasov yielded and promised self-determination for national groups—such as Ukrainians—following the predicted victory over Stalin. Despite the worsening military situation for the Third Reich, by late 1944 enlistment applications from captured Soviet troops rose to a million, perhaps encouraged by the earlier Soviet edict that falling into captivity was considered treason. The increasing possibility of a Soviet victory made that edict more threatening, more perilous.[35]

With such a wartime history, the ranks of POWs, both German-held and Allied-held, furnished thousands of members to the lists of displaced persons.

As month followed month in that first postwar European summer, the factors that set the displaced persons apart from other refugees were coming into focus. They had become a stateless people, outside the people-territory-state condition that had traditionally been the basis of a nation. In Hannah Arendt's words, "Citizenship is no longer regarded as something immutable, and nationality is no longer necessarily identified with state and territory." To thousands of displaced persons, it became apparent in 1945 that the group controlling their homelands did not protect them in ways that other nations protected their citizens abroad. And these stateless people rejected that help; they feared that accepting it might mean they would be forced to return. Paradoxically, these same refugees fiercely proclaimed and defended their national identity.[36]

Finding a solution to the DPs' plight became one of the major policy issues confronting the victorious Allies. After World War I, the League of Nations issued Nansen passports to White Russians fleeing the Bolsheviks, and to others who were without the protection of a government. They retained these while living in France and other countries. But Nansen passports did not fit conditions after World War II, when many refugees waited and hoped for a change in their country's internal political control or wanted to emigrate to some other country that would change their stateless classification.

More than for most of the world's human population in 1945, the past guided and limited the present for the DPs. Thousands from the USSR, freed from Hitler's forced labor camps, reacted with disbelief, then despair—and sometimes belligerence—when they were informed by Americans and British troops in the closing days of the war that they would be returned to their homeland. The soldiers' announcements brought terror, for the Soviet homeland was identified in their minds with forced collectivization, the government-induced famine of the early 1930s, and Stalin's purges just before the war.

Some carried memories so searing that they would forever be unable to lead normal lives. The trauma of escape burned dates and scenes into their minds, so that thirty-five years later former displaced persons could sit at tables in Seattle or Toronto or Adelaide and recount specific details: Jan Ciesler's concentration camp internment ended at five o'clock on 5 May 1945; an Estonian couple fled the island of Hiumaa at 3:00 P.M. on 23 September 1944—a Saturday—and their little boat reached Sweden's shores at 11:00 P.M. on Monday the 25th. A historian who interviewed some fifty Volksdeutsche refugees in 1954 found it "surprising how many could give the exact date on which their Ortsgruppenleiter gave the orders to treck. Dates, places, and scenes seemed to be etched indelibly on the refugees' consciousness." Fear aids memory. And fear had been their unwanted but inescapable companion for months and years.[37]

Tangible signs further helped keep these memories alive long into the postwar era. The Nazis tattooed numbers on the arms of their workers, prisoners, and many of their other victims: eight numbers inside the forearm, eight violet-colored digits that spoke to the Reich's efficiency as well as its inhumanity. Missing legs, fingers, eyes—these were haunting reminders of the war years. The legs of a man encountered in a DP camp in 1947 had deep scars, gouged during the eighteen months he was shackled constantly—twenty-four hours a day—to an oven for his job cooking for SS troops.[38]

The greatest scars, however, were within. Dr. Paul Friedman, an American psychoanalyst, saw the task of rehabilitating the displaced persons as one with wider importance than simply curing individuals: "It is a project that has significance for the whole world; it is, indeed, a reassertion of our belief that the civilizing forces in man may yet win to victory."[39]

But with 1.8 million displaced persons piling up in Europe by the end of September 1945, these goals of human rehabilitation had to compete with more pressing concerns—basic concerns of food, water, shelter, sanitation—and with the vagaries of international politics. For such were the boundaries as the victorious Allies moved to care for these refugees who had traveled twisting, often torturous routes during the war and discovered at the end only that they had become displaced persons.

2
INTO THE CAMPS

[The displaced persons] are willing to go anywhere on earth except home. In the course of this suspended period of time, these people have turned into statistics and initials.
—Genêt, *New Yorker,* 30 October 1948

AFTER searching along twisting, cratered roadways for hours, the eight members of UNRRA Team I finally found their way to the former Wehrmacht tank casern near Neustadt early one warm April morning in 1945.[1] This casern, captured a month earlier as the Allies swept across the German Palatinate toward the Rhine, was filled with 2,500 refugees. It was the baptism for Team I, which served as the spearhead for the UNRRA (United Nations Relief and Rehabilitation Administration). The eight had crossed from London to Normandy some weeks earlier, then were called forward by SHAEF to handle the growing crowds of refugees uncovered as the Allies lunged deeper into the Reich. Crossing France into Germany, the team had passed through devastated cities and encountered masses of people fleeing the nearby front, from battles so recent that Nazi signs were still prominent everywhere ("Any Prisoner Caught Plundering During Air Raids Will Be Shot" proclaimed one poster, preserved in a UNRRA scrapbook). And finally Team I's four wheezing, dusty Leyland and Morris lorries rolled across the sun-baked maneuver field and drew up before a group of U.S. soldiers on duty at the Neustadt tank center. Now it was UNRRA Center Neustadt.

Despite rigorous and varied training, team members were unprepared for the chaos and debris they confronted. "There was a tremendous disorder," recalled Bernard Warach, the UNRRA Team I welfare officer. "It was a shambles. They had defecated all over. There were incredible scenes of people fornicating in the dorms—remember that the Nazis had kept men and women separate in the labor camps for years. At the start we just walked around and dished out C rations, talking with the people."

Housed haphazardly in the tank casern's extensive barracks and other structures, disorganized and grumbling, the predominantly Russian population was already worrying the U.S. soldiers guarding the camp. The official UNRRA report on the center buttressed Warach's recollections:

> This camp was in a state of chaos with regard to medical and sanitary conditions. The whole area of the camp had been fouled and litter and rubbish were scattered everywhere . . . the camp population were not habituated to the use of western lavatories. Lavatories and their surroundings were fouled, drains choked up, and conditions generally in a bad state. Further, many . . . had been using the surrounding buildings and ground as lavatories.

Cheerful feelings over the UNRRA team's arrival with C rations disintegrated rapidly, however. Trouble began when the army decided to move some three hundred Polish DPs into a separate building, hoping through this segregation to reduce tensions between nationalities. To carry out the transfer a U.S. Army riot squad was called in, with halftracks and machine guns at the ready. "There was a sullen air of hostility in the silence of the DPs," the official report admitted.

This inauguration for UNRRA Team I—of machine guns and choked toilets, of confusion and conflict—was to prove the norm in the coming months as care for refugees loomed ever larger among the tasks facing the liberators of Europe.

But the records speak well for Team I: by the time the Russians had been transported home two months later (and other refugees had been either returned to their western European homelands or shifted to other centers), the Neustadt camp had avoided a threatened typhus epidemic through repeated DDT dustings and lavatory repairs, while more food and required hot baths had improved the residents' health. A dental clinic, hospital, infant welfare center, and prenatal clinic had all been in operation.

At the completion of its first month under UNRRA leadership the entire appearance—human and structural—of the Neustadt camp had been drastically improved. A Soviet military official arrived and appointed various Russian refugees to leadership posts, so that UNRRA orders would be followed through a chain of command. Children now ran eagerly to school each morning at the sound of the bell (wearing red kerchiefs fashioned from Nazi flags);

the camp soccer team practiced daily, proud of its 1 to 1 tie with an RAF unit; and enough milk was obtained to provide children with half a liter per day. Lethargy was no longer so evident. Military drills kept some twenty-six hundred Soviet citizens busy for part of each day, while others formed various clubs and a theatrical group. The actors and actresses prepared a musical review, "Vodka Cocktail," which was presented in camp and at nearby Allied military centers (where the soldiers' whistles at first reduced the performers to tears: "Whistling in Russia is apparently a mark of disapprobation").

Military support remained crucial. During the Neustadt camp's brief existence in the spring of 1945, the UNRRA team relied on U.S. troops and their Soviet counterparts to keep peace from time to time within the camp, to move refugees in and out (and within), and to provide such things as medicine, boots, and double-decker beds. The army was both guard and transporter, source of DDT and Spam.

The military was not secretive about its purposes. Five years earlier, swarms of refugees had complicated Allied efforts to thwart the German invasion of France; because of that experience, by October 1943 the British were making plans for controlling civilian movements that would follow the shift of war back to the Continent. SHAEF set up its G-5 Division to control activities in liberated areas, with a separate Refugee, Displaced Persons and Welfare Branch. In the spring of 1944, a SHAEF plan warned that "uncontrolled self-repatriation" of refugees might result in pillaging in freed areas; it speculated that governmental authority could break down, perhaps leading to revolutions and revealing Allied incapacity to deal with Europe's ills.[2]

The Allies had earlier gained considerable experience in handling refugees, notably in North Africa and on the Italian Peninsula, where the need to segregate nationalities in the camps was painfully learned.[3]

Then came the entry into Hitler's Third Reich.

The sudden collapse of German resistance in the late spring of 1945 threw refugee problems to the forefront of military concern. The flow of people escaping the fury of battle became so great that bridges had to be blocked, even blown up, to stop or to control its movement. SHAEF set up refugee collecting points in rear areas and ordered trucks moving forward with military supplies to return with refugees—and none were to return empty. "We herded them into camps to clear the roads," one former GI recalled of those hectic days.

The sorting begins. As the Allies rolled across the Low Countries into Germany, refugees began to show up everywhere, transported by trucks and wagons, tanks and bicycles. An army truck delivered these refugees to a transit center in Verviers, Belgium. Soon they would begin to group together according to national or religious identity. *(UNRRA photo.)*

More than 400 separate clusters of non-German refugees were found when Hamburg was taken, 81 clusters in Linz, in a pattern repeated wherever the Allies advanced. Soldiers then consolidated these, so that the 128 scattered groups uncovered in Leipzig, for example, were first reduced to 86 groups and then placed in six collection centers that eventually held 30,000 persons.

These assembly centers, in turn, funneled refugees to other camps that were identified as containing mainly Poles, Russians, Dutch, or another national group. Still fearing the existence of Nazi "werewolves"—guerrillas preparing to attack isolated Allied positions—the Allies set stiff curfews for German civilians and kept close surveillance over the refugees, many of whom were presumed to be Nazis. Surprise searches of refugee camps were staged throughout the following year, and the military was frequently needed to restore order in many centers. A wild, undisciplined camp of Russian DPs at Châlons, France, was quieted by such a visit. A Soviet liaison officer suddenly arrived, lined up the inhabitants, and selected ten of the refugees at random to come forward. He shot each one. Discipline was no longer a problem in the camp.[4]

The military was present at every turn. A YMCA field worker who left his labors among prisoners of war to assist in the new DP

Forced laborers. The Germans used forced labor for a variety of tasks—from building airfields and coastal fortifications, to working in factories. These Soviet forced laborers were liberated near Châlons, France; they are preparing to travel to a refugee center. Many were soon transported back to the USSR, but some refused repatriation. *(National Archives photo.)*

camps admitted that although he and his co-workers were anti-militarists, they realized that "without the military then, it would have been utter shambles." For conditions were too chaotic, and war still too recent, for the military to be dispensed with. When the surrender was announced, the shooting stopped, but dangers remained on all sides. (Refugee children at Euskirchen, Germany, were forbidden to take walks in the neighborhood because of numerous undetected land mines "as well as stray hand grenades and ammunition.")[5]

On some occasions Germans were forced from their homes to provide shelter for refugees, an early plan put into effect again in some areas as winter approached in the autumn of 1945. In Hochfeld, workers' apartments had been transferred to refugee use in August; furniture and fuel were ordered left behind and all Germans had to be out by 8:00 A.M. on the day specified. The 1,100 refugees at Lampertheim, near Stuttgart, were later described as residing "in a normal, friendly community," in houses taken from German families. In 1948 there were 736 apartments in Augsburg still reserved for refugees.[6]

A wide variety of structures held refugees in 1945. Some 1,200 stayed in the modern Deutscher Ring insurance headquarters in

A camp amid the ruins. Amid the devastation of war no structure seemed inadequate to house DPs. At Heilbronn, Germany, the UNRRA moved refugees into a building hit just weeks earlier by aerial bombardment. *(UNRRA photo.)*

Hamburg; in Italy a requisitioned schoolhouse became the camp at Cremona, and at Reggio a former Black Shirt barracks held the refugees. In numbers of occupants the camps ranged from 200 in a converted Danish seaside hotel north of Copenhagen to more than 15,000 at the *Truppenlager* Wildflecken, a former SS camp containing sixty blockhouses and twelve kitchens strung along a mile-long street within its twenty-five-mile perimeter.[7]

Among the hundreds of types of refugee housing, three main classifications emerged:

1. Casern camps, usually former German or Italian military centers (such as the tank casern at Neustadt). These had many large,

permanent structures that could be converted for use by refugees. (One journalist apparently had these camps in mind when she wrote that DP camps "tend to be monotonously alike—modern, German military establishments. Typically, a camp is a quarter-mile square of harsh, four-story green stucco buildings that show signs of Allied bombings and DP repairs.")[8]

2. Barracks camps, including former forced-labor camps and concentration camps. Many were constructed after 1945 especially to house refugees and featured one-story wooden buildings or tents.

3. Dwelling-house camps, which were made up of entire villages, such as Meerbeck, Germany, or a section of a city such as the housing units inhabited by some 500 refugees in New Palestine, an area of Salzburg, Austria.[9]

Most displaced persons knew at least two of these basic types intimately, plus numerous variations that defied classification. A young Slovenian who escaped into Austria at war's end began his four years as a refugee in a plowed, muddy, tentless field outside Viktring, Austria, near Klagenfurt. From there his DP camp wanderings—sometimes encouraged by authorities, sometimes dictated by youthful whims—took him to an Austrian castle that had served as a wartime airplane parts factory but housed some 200 refugees in mid-1945; to a barracks camp at Lienz that was infamous for the poor quality of its food; to a large transit camp at Trieste; to a former Italian Air Force Academy camp at Forli, Italy; to a former military academy at Modena; to a converted railroad workers' structure at Bologna that housed student refugees; to a former cavalry barracks, also in Bologna; and finally to a resettlement center at Naples, before he shipped out to the United States in 1949.[10]

Once a site was designated, it quickly took on an ethnic identity, either through military fiat or simply through growth around a nucleus. Forty Balts were living in the barracks at Hanau, Germany, when it was first authorized as a DP camp, and they sent out the news through the refugee grapevine. Soon, according to a British official on the scene, "they began arriving in cars and trucks, on bicycles and on foot. They came in every way but by parachute," and the camp soon held some 3,300 Lithuanians, 1,700 Latvians, and 1,000 Estonians.[11]

Trucks appeared at camps at all hours of the day and night, depositing loads of refugees who had been rounded up along roadways or freed from forced-labor camps, or who had seen posted announcements. Kathryn Hulme, whose book *The Wild Place* re-

Early conditions. The first camps were usually primitive, and open-air cooking appeared frequently in the early weeks after the war. These women prepared meals at the Heilbronn DP camp. *(UNRRA photo.)*

A multipurpose room. This room had many uses for this family living in what was identified as a "refugee hut" at the camp at Cleverbrück at Bad Schwartau. The single room was a sickroom, nursery, workshop, kitchen, living room, and bedroom for a family of six. *(American Friends Service Committee photo.)*

mains the best description of day-to-day life in a DP camp, told of
meeting trainloads of Poles—up to 500 people a day—coming into
Wildflecken:

> The cars slid slowly by us, each car door decorated with wilted
> boughs which framed a still life of haggard faces shawled, bonneted,
> turbaned, or simply wrapped around with shreds of old blanket wool,
> each car door framing the same tight-packed composition varied here
> by addition of an infant at the breast, there by a crying child swung
> clear of the crush to ride on a man's shoulders, or at intervals by a
> graybeard or granny to whom chair space had been allowed in the
> precious footage of the open door.[12]

The occupying soldiers had only one major source—the
UNRRA—to turn to for help with the refugees.

The UNRRA's creation marked another step in the growing
concern for the uprooted of war in the twentieth century. After the
First World War this concern brought the birth of the League of
Nations High Commission for Refugees, organized in 1921 under
Dr. Fridtjof Nansen of Norway. It grew gradually, issuing the fa-
mous Nansen passports to thousands of stateless persons. In 1938
this developed into the Inter-Governmental Committee on Refugees
(IGCR), which worked mainly with Jews and others fleeing the
Nazis; Spanish Republicans were eventually aided as well. Then the
UNRRA was established in 1943 and provided a variety of services
for the next four years—food and mules to Africans and Chinese as
well as care for European refugees. Eventually it gave way to the
Preparatory Commission for the International Refugee Organization (PCIRO) in 1947, and the new IRO in 1948.[13]

The military began to look with more interest toward the
UNRRA as the Allies entered the Continent. Orders went out in
December 1944 to the UNRRA to prepare 200 teams of thirteen
members each, to help control the increasing flood of refugees as
the Allies pounded their way toward Germany. The first 4 spearhead
teams were brought to Granville, France, and in early April 1945
were sent forward to Neustadt, Homburg, and other German areas.
By month's end 30 UNRRA teams were helping the military run
assembly points, transit centers, and camps. This total grew to 322
teams in the field by the end of June, usually under a standard
pattern: the military set up camps and brought in supplies; the
UNRRA provided administrators with various specialties.[14]

Varieties existed within the UNRRA organizational framework.
Mobile units called "Flying Squads" were sent forward, stopping at

strategic points where refugees were massing by rail or roadway, to provide travelers with food and medical care. From France came 20 teams of women known as *Mission Militaire Liaison Administrative*, recruited by the Free French forces in London. These played a large role in DP care initially, when the UNRRA was still being developed.[15]

Official responsibility for administering DP camps in the American Zone of Germany was handed over to the UNRRA on 1 October 1945. By the end of the year the organization was running 227 centers in the western zones of Germany and 25 in Austria; this increased by June 1947 to 762 DP centers: 8 in Italy, 21 in Austria, 416 in the U.S. Zone of Germany, 272 in the British Zone, and 45 in the French Zone. The UNRRA workload was still increasing.[16]

Team members came from a variety of backgrounds. Teams recruited in Europe aimed for staffs of 60 percent Continental origin, to avoid a lopsided British or American representation. Early training was at the University of Maryland or in London and utilized a four-week course crammed with language training, field procedures, and policies. The Maryland center trained 2,585 persons of 38 nationalities, including many sent by such voluntary agencies as the Red Cross and YMCA. Many were transported quickly to the Middle East, where in May 1944 the UNRRA took over six camps operated by the British Middle East Relief and Rehabilitation Administration. When the Allies gained a foothold in Italy the UNRRA teams followed them there. By the winter of 1945–46 more than 5,000 UNRRA employees were involved in DP work in non-Communist areas of Europe, in addition to large numbers who delivered food and other assistance around the globe, Communist zones and countries included.

An average refugee center with 3,000 DPs was run by a thirteen-person UNRRA team, which ideally included a director and deputy director, clerk-stenographer, supply officer, mess officer, warehouse officer, medical officer, nurse, team cook, two welfare officers, and two drivers.[17]

Criticism developed from the fact that smaller military contingents had earlier run the same camps; the British noted that three of their soldiers—a corporal and two privates—had administered a camp later run by eleven UNRRA employees. A U.S. Army lieutenant and sergeant had managed a Wiesbaden camp containing 12,000 DPs. Observers conceded, however, that the military had run a holding operation, while, to UNRRA, camp work meant rehabilitation: physical, psychological, vocational. A corporal and two privates were generally not up to such work.[18]

The cubicle. Some 450 persons lived in cubicles like this in a camp near Weilheim, Germany. This Czechoslovak couple kept their surviving belongings here, plus a bed (not visible), a table, and some utensils. Others had even less space, and the contrast with the homes of the defeated Germans began to grate on the DPs. *(American Friends Service Committee photo.)*

Camp administration was complicated for the UNRRA teams by several factors. One was the constant arrival and departure of refugees, especially just before zonal boundaries were set on 1 July 1945 but in sporadic bursts of humanity throughout the first three years. Another was the fact that large numbers of DPs chose to live outside the camps. In Italy and Austria an estimated 50 percent of refugees receiving UNRRA aid at one point were such "free-livers," and when the new IRO reported in August 1948 that it was providing direct care and maintenance to 562,841 persons across Europe, it noted that 28,000 of this total appeared at camps for food or other assistance but did not live there, while another 113,148 free-livers only showed up from time to time for legal or other aid. (Several countries briefly ran limited refugee operations on their own, notably Britain with its Polish camps; Switzerland, which housed some DPs in "beautiful hotels" and assigned them large garden plots; Sweden; and Denmark.)[19]

Still another problem for camp administration was the fact that the UNRRA "accumulated the red tape of more than forty nations," and a Lutheran volunteer said he "almost wept at the red tape one must fight through even to exist in occupied Germany."[20]

These complications were worsened by language barriers. A DP recalled situations in which "a Slovenian talked to an Italian translator, who spoke then to an American or a British Army man. I wonder how much of it got across." And a director noted that while the main languages in his camp in northern Italy were Italian, German, and English, this system broke down when six Turks suddenly appeared who spoke no other language but their own. A Russian doctor who knew Turkish was found, and others speaking various languages were rounded up, so that questioning of the Turks "went from English to Hungarian, then to Polish, then to Lithuanian, then into Russian, and finally into Turkish. The process was then reversed."[21]

Initial camp activities for incoming DPs centered on immediate dangers—protecting the larger group from infections diseases and satisfying the individual's hunger. The UNRRA camp reception process began with registration, then shifted immediately to delousing, medical inspection, the first meal, and finally giving out soap, blankets, and cooking and eating equipment.

With hundreds, even thousands, of DPs coming and going overnight (Wildflecken said farewell to 1,500 and gained 10,000 in a two-month period), the problem of health loomed large. Rickets was "almost universal" in Bosnia, reported a British medical expert touring Yugoslavia, while dysentery and other intestinal infections, as well as tuberculosis, were widespread. Elsewhere, the major diseases among DPs were diphtheria, typhus, typhoid fever, small-pox, syphilis, and tuberculosis. Scabies and other skin diseases were common. Memories of the influenza epidemic that swept Europe after the First World War were still fresh in the minds of many governmental authorities, and their fears helped spur immu-nization and other health measures. A case of plague at Taranto, Italy, in 1945 sent shudders through the UNRRA medical net-work.[22]

Anticipating severe problems during the first winter, UNRRA brought two million doses of typhus serum from the United States in autumn 1945, and supplies of sulfa drugs were stocked for ex-pected outbreaks of pneumonia. By May 1946 the vaccination rate of DPs in the U.S. Zone of Germany was reported at 88 percent for typhus, 92 percent for typhoid fever, 91 percent for diphtheria, and 88 percent for smallpox. In addition, the water supply was 98 percent "perfect," according to an *Epidemiological Bulletin* survey, and kitchen and dining room cleanliness was 99 percent satisfac-tory. While the incidence of TB cases was still high—2.5 percent of all DPs in the British and French zones of Germany, for example— the death rate from the disease was low.[23]

Most DPs retain one bitter memory of the camps' health ac-tivities: the "dusting" with DDT powder in the delousing cam-paigns, aimed at blocking the spread of typhus. Dusting greeted them upon their arrival, was repeated in succeeding months, and continued until every nook and cranny of their living areas, clothing, and bodies were familiar with DDT powder.

They hated it.

One woman recalled that upon arrival her suede jacket was hit, and ruined, by the powder; others told of the indignity of being sprayed under their skirts. UNRRA Team 158 at Nammen, Ger-many, reported that ninety of every hundred DPs suffered the dusting "very unwillingly . . . or try to escape . . . and sometimes succeed. That operation is most unpopular." (On the other hand, only 10 percent at Nammen turned down inoculations, "except the Greeks, who refused formally the dusting and immunization.") Married women in a camp in Reggio, Italy, underwent emotional distress when examined for tuberculosis, because of their belief that having the disease classed them as prostitutes. Others resisted efforts to segregate them from the rest of the camp population when they were found infested with body parasites. Only the threat of force brought compliance.[24]

Doctors and nurses struggled to handle the situation. Team 158's

Dusting for lice. Fear of epidemics made health and sanitation problems immediate concerns in refugee populations. UNRRA Team No. 118 was in charge of spraying these displaced persons with DDT in a center located at the former Buchenwald concentration camp. A Polish DP holds his clothes to be dusted for lice, carriers of typhus. *(UNRRA photo.)*

doctor noted that supplies for sanitation at Nammen were scarce—especially disinfectant—and he lamented, "It is almost impossible to enforce hygienic principles on the DPs who, except the [former] soldiers, are completely undisciplined." Wildflecken camp knew the problem of shortages also: when the UNRRA team called for two thousand rubber glove–fingers to use in conducting VD exams, the army furnished only six. The six served for examinations of five thousand women.[25]

Somehow, the health measures worked. Rushed, inadequately supplied, understaffed, opposed by those they were trying to help, the medical teams still succeeded. By the spring of 1946 it was clear that the disease threat in the DP camps of Europe had been turned back. Louse control was put at 99 percent, demolishing the expectation of a typhus epidemic west of the Elbe-Adriatic line. Sewerage systems had been installed, and camp cleanliness was generally enforced. One survey expressed doubt "as to whether the population of any city in the world is receiving a similar amount of health services." And the UNRRA's official history accurately proclaimed the result: "No epidemics caught hold; the infant mortality rate was low; the veneral disease rate was lower than that among the German population or the armies of occupation."[26]

Complementing the attack on disease was the attack on malnutrition. SHAEF's policy was that since the Germans were responsible for the original importation of forced labor, Germany was therefore responsible for postwar care of those forced laborers and other refugees. Displaced persons were to be given preference over local Germans when supplies were short, although this policy was apparently not followed in Austria and Italy.

In addition to Allied military supplies, huge soup containers were taken from the Third Reich's foreign workers' camps, bread was baked using seized German flour, and other equipment and foodstocks were appropriated from German supplies—enough to attain levels of 2,000 to 2,500 calories a day for refugees during some months in the summer of 1945.[27]

But the dismal reality of European agriculture, transport, and distribution caught up with the optimistic goals of Allied planners: as late as January 1948 German food production was still less than 60 percent of prewar levels, and food riots were erupting across Europe. Calorie goals had to be modified. New goals of less than 2,000 per day were set but not often reached. During the IRO's first year of operation in 1947–48, the average daily calorie intake among European DPs was less than 1,600; by autumn 1948 this had inched up to 2,000.*[28] Food parcels helped make up part of the difference. Targeted initially for prisoners of war, Red Cross parcels from Canada, Britain, India, New Zealand, and the United States (which later sent CARE packages as well) provided such items as cheese, sardines, Spam, tuna, dried milk, shortening, a chocolate bar, and cigarettes. Camp administrators saw to it that the boxes were divided up and spread around—one or two per person each month. The black market also helped many DPs achieve a better diet.[29]

Food became, predictably, a major topic in the camps. Even today, thousands of days and miles away from the camps, the memory of it still rankles for many ex-DPs. A U.S. Army camp director reported that over half the complaints he received in his Italian camp centered on food—its quality, quantity, and serving

---

*Recent studies put the desirable calorie level for an adult male at 2,700 per day (Jean Mayer, "Nutrition," *World Book Encyclopedia* [Chicago, 1979] 14:466–70).

Initial requirement: food. Feeding the uprooted of war was an immediate task for the Allies, who sent mobile units to points where refugees gathered. Newly freed inmates of German prison and labor camps were predominant in this group at Bahnhof barracks in Bavaria, where the Red Cross served each a scoop of mashed potatoes and watery spinach. *(American Friends Service Committee photo.)*

size (servers were accused of giving more to members of their own nationality). The diet in that camp was based on British army rations and some local Italian items such as spaghetti; it was heavy on starch, but occasionally fresh vegetables were obtained locally in exchange for camp surpluses of dried beans and powdered milk.[30]

Horrible food seemed universal at times. Some camps became infamous for unpalatable provisions, and this reputation helped steer DPs away. By common consent, however, one frequent item in the UNRRA menu was so distasteful and so frequently offered that the mention of it today causes former DPs to wrinkle their noses: split-pea soup. Latvian DPs called it *Zalās Briesmas,* which translates as "green horror." One Latvian recalled that a major problem with split-pea soup in the camps was its lack of meat—there was usually no meat whatsoever. As they entered the dining area the cry went out: "Are we getting the 'green horror' again?" A Slovenian echoed this, remembering with disgust that split-pea soup was served twice a day in his camp for some time: "I said 'I will never eat that again!' "

Sometimes there were other items, such as cabbage soup, potatoes, and bread, but the usual problem was simply too much of one thing. That was one of the drawbacks with split peas, but it occurred as well with beans and corn bread, among other items. ("The corn bread would be weeks old; we had to soak it to use it. We would get nothing but cornbread for months; then all split pea.") Visitors said that such a diet could do nothing but maintain "a lusterless sort of physical life—it gives the DP look, which is not as gaunt and starved as it is tired and bloodless." One UNRRA worker complained that while the diet was meeting minimum caloric needs, it was inadequate for those coming from a background of starvation. The DPs' "strongest language," he asserted, "is reserved for the deadly monotony of the diet."[31]

Clothing remained a serious problem as well, although it improved sporadically due to donations from people who had escaped war's devastation. An Estonian recalled that he wore but one pair of shoes for the first three years after the war, and the touring UNRRA director discovered that leaflets distributed to refugees were not being read—they were used to patch clothing. Military uniforms and parts of uniforms were worn mismatched all over Europe, and DPs often looked like soldiers of some unknown, poorly fitted army. Military regulations required such apparel to be dyed blue before being worn by civilians, but in practice this was often ignored. Civilian-clothes distribution was not trouble-free either: UNRRA's

Hanau warehouse received fifty thousand identical items from Great Britain, only to discover later that what they were distributing as boys' knickers were really women's bloomers. Used clothing from drives in Canada, Australia, New Zealand, and the United States (where three large clothing campaigns in 1944–46 brought in over seventy-five thousand tons) also forced creative combinations upon the displaced persons while assuring that—as observers noted—at least no one went naked.[32]

But to many DPs, questions of food, clothing, and even health were secondary to locating their loved ones. For the war had done something else besides destroying cities—it had split families asunder.

Walls all over Europe were now covered with messages as wives sought husbands, parents sought children, nephews sought uncles. An American journalist found stairway walls in a UNRRA building in Bratislava, Czechoslovakia, heavily written over with names and questions. "One saw this kind of scrawl in every reception center in Europe. . . . Refugees wrote their names and home towns on every wall they came to with the hope that some friend of relative might see them." One wall in a DP school in Munich became known as the "wailing wall" because of its use as a message center for DPs passing through. Sometimes photos were attached: "This is my husband. I have had no word from him for four years. Does anyone know where he is now or whether he is still among the living?"[33]

Each newcomer to a DP camp was greeted with questions: Did you meet anyone from Tallinn? Was anyone from Nowy Sacz in your assembly center? Camps stationed persons to listen to morning radio broadcasts, which frequently gave names of DPs being sought by relatives; these names were then posted on the camp bulletin board. Camp newspapers devoted whole sections to the search. *Tevzeme,* published at the Hanau DP camp by Latvians, featured two full pages of such queries, which declined to one-third of a page by May 1947 as family members were located or searches were abandoned. Such notices took the place of advertisements, and one reader in the Jewish DP camp at Belsen called them "agony columns." Photos of missing persons were also shown at movies, and special radio programs were broadcast: one was for children who could remember their names and former addresses; another was aimed at parents still searching for their children.[34]

A variety of organizations rushed to help with inquiries. The International Red Cross and national Red Cross groups became the major tracing organizations, coordinating and drawing information

On to a new camp. Displaced persons camps remained transitory, for DPs moved frequently—either on orders from the authorities, as was the case with this group traveling to a camp at Oberammergau, or because they wanted to be with members of their own ethnic group. *(UNRRA photo.)*

from many of the smaller groups, relying heavily on the more than ten million names in Red Cross files in Geneva. A Slovenian DP told of his desperate but finally successful attempt to locate his family after he arrived in the camp at Graz, Austria. "Camp authorities worked with the Red Cross, and in six months they located my sister's husband, in Italy."[35]

Language training; a knowledge of geography, history, and nicknames; and a large dose of creativity proved essential in tracing lost persons during the chaotic postwar years. One success story involved a Jewish tracing agency that handled the problem of a Jewish child, Gustawa Stacka, left by her fleeing parents, Jehiel Stacka and his wife, with a non-Jewish family in Poland. Her legal documents were lost in the war. After liberation the foster family sent inquiries to tracing agencies, recalling in one letter that Gustawa had an aunt living in the Bronx. Meanwhile, the same agency had received an inquiry from the Bronx regarding the whereabouts of Geza Stack, seven, daughter of Chiel and Deborah Stack. The parents were presumed dead. The tracers recognized *Chiel* as a shortened form of the Hebrew name *Jehiel*. The agency noted the Bronx connection; they felt Gustawa might be Geza (both names began with the same letter, and one might have been a nickname or variation of the other). Further checking showed the Polish family's address as 2 Marzalkowska, Warsaw, while the Bronx letter mentioned that the Stacks had lived in Marzalkowska. "Stacka" was obviously close to "Stack." This reasoning proved to be correct, but the deciphering of clues was not always this direct.[36]

The UNRRA then established a Central Tracing Bureau that searched in Germany, Austria, and, briefly, in Italy, pooling cards from eleven inquiry centers to collect more than one million names. The bureau received more than 50,000 inquiries in its first four months. In a single month—June 1946—it received documents on 85,000 persons and sent out information on 18,000. The International Refugee Organization later formed the International Tracing Service (ITS), a permanent organization.[37]

The fact that DPs immediately began clustering by nationalities, and that official occupation policies also enforced national divisions, soon led to fears that camps would become staging areas for attacks to free the Soviet-controlled homelands. Communist officials repeatedly made such charges, and some DP accounts lend support to the view that dreams of this sort were kept alive in the camps.

These fears, in turn, meant that rising importance was given to the question of who should be allowed to stay in the camps: Anyone who showed up? All those displaced by war? Former Nazis? Those who in some way aided the Axis, even if only to avoid death? And once in a camp, what activities merited expulsion? Differing governmental controls confused the question also, for an Italian government existed in 1945 and signed a peace treaty in 1947; but Germany remained occupied by the military, which enforced different DP policies in each zone until 1949, when the three western zones were combined to form the Federal Republic of Germany. And the Allied High Commission continued to operate there until 1955. The Austrian state treaty was not signed until 1955, when military occupation officially ended. This meant that a DP's fate depended heavily on which country and zone he was in when the war ended.

Anyone appearing at a DP camp gate was admitted during the fluid situation of the summer and fall of 1945, however. In fact, large numbers of refugees tramped from camp to camp, searching for kin or others from their past. But as winter approached and supplies dwindled, while camp populations remained high, military and UNRRA authorities took a fresh look at eligibility. Attempts were then launched to draw up new questionnaires, locate translators, and set eligibility criteria. The lack of coordination between various branches and units meant that these sporadic efforts were sometimes contradictory, and usually frustrating for all concerned. Lt. Gen. Sir Frederick E. Morgan, the British military leader placed in charge of UNRRA operations in Germany, stated on 24 June 1946 that the UNRRA staff "and not the Military" would determine eligibility, "except for screening of war criminals, collaborators or traitors." But three months later UNRRA director general Fiorello La Guardia referred a group of Lithuanians to the military for questions "as to the citizenship and eviction from camps of Lithuanians." The UNRRA, La Guardia asserted, "has nothing to do with the screening, and has no control over determining citizenship. UNRRA does not expel displaced persons from its camps," he asserted, but left that to the military.[38]

In 1946 British Zone officials refused to give DP status to anyone showing up after 30 June of that year. American Zone officials put their cutoff at 1 August 1945, however, except for Jews and others persecuted for race or religion or those entering the zone "in an organized manner." Later, however, 21 April 1947 was set as the cutoff date for having entered the American Zone. Those turned away went to live on the German economy, then in dire straits.[39]

In such chaotic conditions, under changing rules, screening became a time of terror. A changed answer, a forgotten date, a charge of collaboration—any fact that nameless and faceless officials might seize upon became a nightmare for the DPs. Rumors began to multiply in the camps that a flat 10 percent were to be pushed out since room had to be made for new refugees, or that all camps were to be emptied. Added to this was fear of the ignorance displayed by the interrogators: Were they aware of the limited choices open to many persons in wartime? Looking back on it all, Lieutenant General Morgan wondered about the screeners' competence also:

> It seemed little probable that a newly commissioned American Second Lieutenant assisted by a coloured sergeant, both innocent of any language but their own, could make much sense out of a party of refugees from Bohemia with but a limited Czech vocabulary. Some had no documents of identity at all, others had each a whole pack of different passports. All owed their continued existence to their ability to confront and deceive real experts at "screening," those of Gestapo or NKVD. By 1945 the production of false identity papers in Europe had become almost a major industry.[40]

The time of terror in the Baltic camp at Hochfeld near Augsburg began in late 1946, when the UNRRA announced another screening. Automatic eviction was the penalty for those who refused to cooperate. A Lithuanian journalist's account of the fifty-seven-question screening claimed that it "was conducted in English, Russian and German exclusively, regardless of the lack of knowledge of these languages by the DP concerned. No interpreters were assigned," and the authorities ruled that if the DP had never been imprisoned he was not to be classed as a "persecutee." Addresses of DPs' relatives in the home country were required, although many feared this information might be leaked and endanger their loved ones.

This "perpetual screening," the journalist wrote, lasted nearly one year, "and became a source of mental suffering."[41]

Protests multiplied. Petitions with thousands of names were given to zone authorities, while DPs refused to take part and others walked out of the screening sessions. A four-day hunger strike was staged by some 2,000 Poles and Ukrainians after a screening team evicted 130 from their camp. DP clergymen took the lead in arguing with the army over the injustice of these acts. The United Ukrainian American Relief Committee (UUARC) received a frantic telegram from one of its workers:

DISTURBING NEWS RECEIVED 3500 UKRAINIANS SALZBURG CAMP AUSTRIA REFUSED TO GO BEFORE SCREENING COMMISSION BECAUSE OF SOVIET OR PROSOVIET PERSONNEL ON COMMISSION AND TYPE OF QUESTIONS ASKED STOP ALL MOSTLY POLISH UKRAINIANS STOP PEOPLE HAVE GONE INTO SILENT MOURNING WITH RELIGIOUS SERVICES AND HYMNS ARE PREPARED FOR MARTYRDOM AND WILL RESIST FORCE WITH FORCE. . . . CRISIS NOW FIVE DAYS AND MOST SERIOUS ALL NERVES AT HIGH PITCH.[42]

Eligibility questions were further complicated when a new influx of DPs appeared: East European Jews who were crossing desperately into the western zone, their numbers increasing to 3,000 weekly by December 1945. UNRRA reports suddenly began to note concern about these "infiltrees" piling up in Berlin and at other checkpoints. Should they be allowed into the camps?[43]

There was something festering here. That was evident from the fact that massive numbers of DPs showed no intention of returning home. General Eisenhower had seen by September 1945 that most countries would not take the DPs, leaving dispersal in western Europe as their only alternative. Care of these people, Eisenhower admitted, "may be a long-time job." The contrast with earlier Allied expectations was enormous: the British head of the wartime Inter-Governmental Committee on Refugees had once predicted that repatriation would reach 98 percent. But as 1945 ended there were still 737,375 DPs in Europe receiving aid from the UNRRA—almost 60 percent of them Poles—and this total ignored thousands of "free livers." The total receiving UNRRA aid by March 1946 jumped to 844,144.[44]

They were not going home.

And from this festering a truth was emerging and gradually becoming visible, something that some still could not, or would not, see. It involved a breakdown in the wartime alliance. DPs saw it coming, and UNRRA Center Neustadt confronted it at the outset of the DP era, as Welfare Officer Bernard Warach remembered.

One of the spearhead team's favorites among the thousands of Russians at Neustadt in the spring of 1945 was a man named Viktor, who had been captured by the Germans at Smolensk and was later put on forced labor. He was popular for his bright spirit and his ability to get the DP camp organized. When large-scale repatriation occurred in June, Viktor led the singing of the Soviet and American national anthems as the entire camp stood at attention before portraits of Stalin and Roosevelt. Then the Russian DPs and just-arrived Soviet officers waved their red flags again, gave a cheer for enduring Soviet-American friendship, and climbed into railroad boxcars for the first leg of their journey home.

Three weeks later at Neustadt, in the middle of the night, came a knock at the window. "It was Viktor," Warach recalled. "He was really disturbed." Viktor spent the rest of the night telling the team of the repatriation ride into Soviet-held territory. The DPs were stripped at the zonal boundary by the Russian "welcoming committee," their personal belongings were seized, and they were received as traitors rather than as long-suffering fellow countrymen. He escaped and returned to the West.

"We rubber-stamped papers to permit him to move on, and sent Viktor on his way to live on the civilian economy under a different name," Warach said.[45]

It was an ominous sign for a DP program based on the belief that when the war had ended everyone would go home.

REPATRIATION

Breaking the news to these families that they were to be repatriated seemed equivalent to delivering a death sentence.
—Denis Hills, British officer screening Soviet DPs for repatriation at Riccione, Italy, in May 1947

THE peace and quiet of two Baltic DP camps was shattered one day in late 1946 by the arrival of a Soviet officer. After his visit, the officer, a Major Chikmazow, issued an official complaint charging that "anti-Soviet propaganda was present." But a British lieutenant present attributed the whole problem to the visitor's wish to discuss repatriation, while the DPs of Schloss Gottorf and Venta camps were interested in "political questions."[1]

Major Chikmazow's presentation began simply enough. He explained how easy it was for DPs to repatriate themselves to the Baltic homeland: they were simply to report their intention to the British camp commander, who would direct them to Lübeck where they would embark on a ship that would transport them back. But at that point in the presentation, according to the British report, "the officer asked whether there were some questions in connection with his explanations."

There were.

Some of the DPs asked how they could return "if the Russian government acted as horribly as previously," noting that the Soviets promised much in 1940 when they first occupied the Baltic area, "but there happened quite different things." Why, for example, were old people and babies seized from their apartments?

Not true, the major said. Individuals might be punished, but the mass of people would not risk life or freedom. When asked whether democracy or dictatorship ruled in the USSR and Latvia, he replied that "he could not give answers to political questions," which set off a wild chorus of shouts and whistles. Major Chikmazow then warned the Balts that UNRRA aid would end someday, and all would be obliged to work. At that point a rough-hewn man suddenly jumped to his feet, held up his coarse hands, and shouted, "We are not afraid of work, we have worked and we will work in the future if only the freedom and life are left for us. In the Independent Latvia we did not see bread behind the heaps of butter but then came the Russians, and then the Germans and all was robbed away."

The reception given the Soviet repatriation officer at Schloss Gottorf and Venta was hardly uncommon in the stormy years following the war. Repatriation would not go away. It kept rising to the surface just when DP life seemed to be improving, tearing at the facade of cheerful camp existence, a continuing source of fear and tension. It brought ugly confrontations, set off contradictory policies on closing the camps, and drove many to desperate ploys to avoid being caught. Controversies over DP repatriation also helped weaken and tear the wartime bonds of Allied unity, fueling suspicions and mistrust that eventually were recognized as the cold war. Repatriation was all these things.

The Yalta Pact and the wartime Grand Alliance lay at the base of the problem.

Signed at Yalta in the Soviet Crimea in February 1945, the several agreements between Roosevelt, Churchill, and Stalin sought to put in place the basis for a postwar peace while forever preventing the rise of German power. Repatriation was but a small part of this. The agreements dealt mainly with formation of the United Nations, creation of occupation zones in Germany, joint protection of liberated countries, and shifts in Polish boundaries to give the area east of the Curzon Line to the USSR while transferring part of eastern Germany to Poland.[2]

Thirteen months after this tripartite meeting, the U.S. State Department revealed to the press a secret U.S.-Soviet agreement, signed at Yalta, on liberated prisoners of war and civilians; an identical agreement was signed between the Soviets and the British. Provisions included the statement that Americans and Soviet citizens "will without delay after their liberation, be separated from enemy prisoners of war and will be maintained separately from them in camps or points of concentration until they have been handed over to the Soviet or United States authorities." Furthermore, the agreement gave each side "the right of immediate access" into such camps, where the outside power could set up internal camp government among its own nationals; "hostile propaganda . . . will not be permitted."[3]

A U.S. Army training packet on the 1945–46 occupation revealed the interpretation given to this Yalta document: "Individuals identified by the Soviet repatriation representatives as Soviet citizens were subject to repatriation without regard to their personal wishes." This was implied as well in a later agreement between the Americans, British, and Russians signed at Halle, Germany, on 23 May 1945: "All former prisoners of war and citizens of the U.S.S.R. . . . will be delivered." The only exception to Soviet demands apparently was the Western powers' refusal to consider the Baltic peoples as "Soviet citizens," although the USSR had annexed Estonia, Latvia, and Lithuania a year earlier.[4]

Later criticism of the Yalta agreements has obscured their initial favorable reception. Allied unity was essential in early 1945 as the final drive on Germany began and as plans were put forward to conquer Japan—an operation that appeared to be many difficult months away from success. As George Fischer has written in his classic study of Soviet opposition to Stalin, Western opinion then rested on "the intense desire to prove our unqualified friendship for the Soviet government," along with the "blithe confidence" that Stalin also sought friendship and cooperation. General Eisenhower later wrote that in the crucial summer following V-E Day, he and his top aides believed that success in establishing joint government in Germany rested "almost exclusively" upon the West's success in overcoming Russian "suspicion and distrust." Yielding up the DPs sought by the Soviets was one way to help allay their suspicion and distrust. Moreover, there was great fear that if the Western Allies balked at returning liberated Soviet citizens, the Russians might do the same regarding captive American and British soldiers taken when Soviet armies overran Nazi camps.[5]

Beyond this was a widespread belief that returning home was what all liberated peoples desired, especially those whose war years had been spent in Nazi labor or concentration camps. Allied pilots over German-controlled France in 1944 dropped leaflets promising Soviet citizens held captive a "speedy return" to their "Russian fatherland"—a propaganda offensive that backfired, critics said. Polish general Władysław Anders charged that such promises meant that east European troops serving with the Nazis "fought desperately to the last man." They did not wish a "speedy return" home. The London *Times* stated hopefully in an editorial soon after the European battles ceased that the DPs presented "only formidable problems of transport and organization, since the policy, except in an insignificant number of special cases, can only be to return them to their places of origin." General Eisenhower scanned the millions of refugees piling up in the camps and worried about the cost of maintaining them. "The only complete solution to this problem from all points of view," he admitted, "is the early repatriation of these Russians."[6]

The summer rush seemed to bear out the expectation that all wished to go home. In nineteen days after the Halle agreement was signed on 22 May 1945, more than 1 million Soviet nationals were brought into the reception centers and began heading eastward at a daily rate exceeding 50,000. On 10, 11, and 12 June more than 101,000 Soviet citizens left for home each day; by the end of September over 2 million Soviet nationals had been repatriated from the western zones of Germany, Austria, and Czechoslovakia, while some 230,000 others had returned from France, Norway, and other west European countries. At the same time more than 200,000 Yugoslavs returned home.[7]

And most seemed to go without remorse. A public health nurse serving in Heidelberg described the departure of Russian DPs by train: "They go in a great fanfare of band music, flag-waving, pictures of Stalin, banners proclaiming Russian-American friendship, and decorations of green branches and yards and yards of red bunting which the American camp director requisitions from the Germans to keep the Russians happy. Twenty-five people travel in a boxcar with all the goods they possess."[8]

Amid such an atmosphere governments yielded easily to Soviet pressures. Sweden forced some 167 Balts to return to their USSR-controlled homelands in early 1946 because of their service in the German army. This came despite protests from clergymen as well as the Swedish soldiers guarding them, a hunger strike by the Balts, and several attempts at suicide by the prisoners. But Sweden's foreign minister called the Balts a foreign burden on the nation, belittled their achievements during their period of independence, and urged "that for their own good [they should] return home and participate in the reconstruction of their homelands." And a Swedish public opinion poll showed that 71 percent of those questioned thought that at least part of the thousands of Balts should be sent home.[9]

France allowed the Soviets to conduct manhunts for Soviet citizens on French soil for months, although the French Army of Occupation in Germany was much less cooperative. Soviet authorities throughout most of 1945 were allowed to freely visit DP camps in the western zones, and reception centers were installed inside the zones by both Yugoslavia and the USSR. On 8 July 1945, SHAEF ordered that citizens of the USSR identified as such by Soviet repatriation officers be sent home and "will not be offered any option on this score." In the first months after liberation such policies came naturally.[10]

But an ugly side to repatriation kept poking through the veneer of hopeful good will and patriotism. The British faced it in March 1945, even before the war had ended, when they sent home 6,000 Soviets captured in German uniforms. One hanged himself; another cut his throat. Two months later another group was sent from Liverpool, and as the men marched toward the gangplank one of the prisoners smashed his tea mug on the dock and slashed his throat with the remaining piece; Soviet officials insisted he be loaded onto the vessel. As the ship passed by Gibraltar another man leaped overboard, and several jumped into the Dardanelles as the vessel entered Turkish waters.[11]

The realization that many DPs did not want to return home and would refuse to be repatriated, even to the point of committing suicide, was to prove a continuing, nagging problem for the Western Allies. Studies by Nikolai Tolstoy (*Victims of Yalta*), Mark R. Elliott (*Pawns of Yalta*), Nicholas Bethell (*The Last Secret*), and Julius Epstein (*Operation Keelhaul*) have probed into newly released documents to make clear extensive American and British involvement in forcibly returning DPs to Communist control.

It is not a pretty picture. Certainly it is not so today, a generation after V-E Day, when the cold war seems a permanent fixture. But it was not pretty in the immediate postwar months either, when the Soviets were still allies and only soldiers, diplomats, and some refugees knew of many of the incidents. The job was distasteful, even though soldiers could justify using force against those who had fought with the Nazis in such Wehrmacht units as the KONR (Committee for the Liberation of the Peoples of Russia) or the ROA (Russian Liberation Army) of Andrei Vlasov.

The new studies reveal the Allies' record on forcible repatriation to be both long and bloody. In June and July of 1945 it included the return by the British in the Drau Valley of Austria of some 22,500 unwilling Cossacks and Caucasians who had fought for the Germans, as well as the suicides of three Russians at Fort Dix, New Jersey, when American soldiers tried to force them onto a waiting repatriation ship.[12]

And it took in the events of bloody August 1945, by which time refugees left in the camps were largely those who did not wish to return home. British soldiers surrounded 500 Ukrainians at Flensburg and dragged them off, aided by Soviet NKVD agents who killed one of the DPs. Ukrainians who had fought under General Vlasov were seized from their church at Kempten in Bavaria by rifle-swinging U.S. soldiers who left a trail of blood ("Shamefaced Americans saw their distinguished Negro compatriot, Dr. Washington, leaning against the church wall and weeping like a child," Nikolai Tolstoy reported).[13]

Many incidents still remain hidden in military records, although former DPs and camp authorities as well as Tolstoy, Elliott, Bethell, and Epstein have been able to present considerable evidence in some cases. An Estonian DP recalls in late 1945 at Thurigen camp he saw American GIs seize Ukrainian DPs for repatriation. "People tried to hide in the barracks," he stated. "They had to tear them away as they rounded them up. They were pulled away forcefully by the U.S. soldiers." And an American who worked in DP operations told of watching unhappy U.S. soldiers pursue refugees who were trying to hide. "I saw a woman throw her baby out of a building, to her husband," he recalled. "He tried to run, but U.S. soldiers caught him and his baby." (Ten years after the DP era, an American working in Europe encountered several dozen Russians in the Lienz area of Austria who had escaped the forced repatriations of 1945–46. Several were living in peonage under Austrian farmers— still afraid to protest for fear they would be turned over to the Soviets.)[14]

Large numbers of Slovenians were also forcibly repatriated, after fleeing Slovenia and entering southern Austria in May 1945. One of those was Mario Litrja (not his real name). He surrendered to the British along with thousands of other Slovenians who had served in the Domobranci (home guard), plus Serbians, "an emigration of the whole Croat nation" (in the words of one Croatian leader) and others. Litrja remembered the British as "very friendly."[15] He added:

> After surrendering we continued northward and reached Viktring on May 12 or 13. Toward the end of May we heard rumors that we were going to be transferred to Italy to join the other half of the Slovenian anti-Communist Army which had crossed into Italy. Tensions between the British and Tito's Partisans were reaching a peak at that time over control of Trieste.
>
> I was in the first transport of about three thousand soldiers that left on May 28, and we firmly believed we were going into Italy. We were happy. But when we got to Maria Elend, Austria, we were ordered out

of the trucks and surrounded by British soldiers, who searched us, seized our regimental papers, typewriters, and such, and detained us.

About four o'clock that same day we were transferred into railroad boxcars—forty men per car. The British then locked the cars, and immediately afterwards Partisans surrounded the train. After a short time the train passed through the Ljubelj underpass into Yugoslavia and stopped.

The Partisans immediately jumped into the cars and started to beat. They pulled out the officers, who were in the first boxcar, and led them into the nearby bush. They swore at us and spit on us. "Now you can see you are real traitors," they said. "Even the imperialist English did not want you and returned you to us."

The train went on, and stopped at every little village, and each time the Partisans opened the doors and jumped in. Frightened villagers were forced to gather around the train and demand our death. New soldiers came in and robbed us of everything we had. If someone among us had better shoes or clothes, these were taken. At Škofja Loka they crammed us into a convent and began to insult and torture us. They yelled: "Where is your Bishop Rozman? . . . Call Holy Mother Mary to help you! . . . Where is your General Rupnik?" This went on day and night for almost a week.

During the first week they already "sentenced" us, by simply dividing us into four groups: Number Four for officers and known opponents; Number Three for the majority of us, about eighty to eighty-five percent—and classification into numbers four or three meant an automatic death sentence. Finally, those fortunate underage repatriates (under seventeen years of age) were given Number Two or One; these were spared for the moment, but very few survived the two to three months of torture that followed.

Litrja eventually escaped with his brother but failed in crossing the border. He hid for three years before reaching Austria and eventually emigrating.

Thousands of others made the same journey into Yugoslavia in trucks or railroad cars, led by the British, believing they were going to Italy and safety. Death or prison camps awaited most. The tragedies at Bleiburg, Viktring, and other border towns in southern Austria remain as scars across the collective memory of thousands of Yugoslavs in exile. A DP's hold on this remembered past is tenacious, unrelenting. "I lost twenty-five cousins that day," a Croatian stated sadly in recounting the events.[16]

Such incidents became increasingly rare as time went on, however, and were mainly restricted to Soviet citizens who had been fighting in the Wehrmacht against the Allies at the end of the war. Many Soviet citizens escaped the British and American repatriation net by convincing the authorities they were Polish, Rumanian, or any other nationality but Soviet. Increasingly, the Allies permitted choice: just over three weeks after thousands of other Yugoslavs had been given over to the Partisans, some 2,400 Serbian officers—both Royal Yugoslav Army and Chetnik veterans—were allowed to choose which direction they would go from the train station in Mallnitz, Austria. Half moved to one side of the station and boarded a train for Yugoslavia, and half moved to the other side and were transported to a British camp. Later the residents of a large Yugoslav camp in Italy were allowed to vote in a secret-ballot election to measure repatriation sentiments: only ten of the 15,000 voted to go home.[17]

But not all had a choice. In February 1946, some 3,000 veterans of General Vlasov's forces held at Plattling, Germany, were turned over by Americans to the Soviets—after having been lulled into security by repeated promises that no repatriation was planned.

One year later, large-scale, forcible repatriation came to a close after British and U.S. soldiers took some 275 Soviet veterans of Wehrmacht service out of Italian camps in operations "Keelhaul" and "East Wind." As they were grabbed by their American captors the Cossacks repeatedly demanded to be shot rather than turned over to the Soviets.[18]

It was becoming too complicated—too complicated to hear USSR repatriation officers claiming that Poles were Soviet citizens when the Poles had grown up east of the Curzon Line in what had formerly been Poland; too complicated also when the Soviets tried to seize 2,100 German Mennonite DPs, whose ancestors had settled in Russia centuries earlier but who had fled westward during the war's final stages. In this case the American military chief finally intervened to protect them, stating that the Mennonites were "as much entitled to protection as the Jews who had fled from Poland." The changing East-West atmosphere now made everything more complicated.[19]

It was becoming difficult for Western leaders, raised on respect for the right of asylum, to continue to force citizens of Communist countries to return home—especially as understanding developed of what awaited them. In addition, the Geneva Convention said that captors were not to look behind the uniform. Russians in the service of the Nazis, therefore, were to be treated as German prisoners of war and, as such, could not be sent back to the Soviet Union.

Reluctance to forcibly handing back such persons spread among

Allied officers by late summer, after the masses of refugees had gone home. Now a hard core of DPs remained. By 30 September 1945, there were approximately 1 million Poles left in western Europe, plus some 170,000 Balts, more than 100,000 Yugoslavs, and 54,000 Soviet citizens. British field marshall Sir Harold Alexander refused to force Poles to leave his Italian command despite Soviet demands. General Eisenhower, who in mid-September of 1945 reported to President Truman that "a large percentage" of Balts, Poles, and Rumanians did not want to return home, in October banned the use of force in repatriation in the American Zone of Germany. On 21 December 1945, the American State-War-Navy Coordinating Committee forbade repatriation of any DPs who did not fit into one of three categories: (1) they were captured in German uniform; (2) they were members of the Soviet armed forces on or after 22 June 1941 and were not later discharged; or (3) the Soviet Union could prove they had voluntarily aided the enemy. Nikolai Tolstoy's study makes it clear that American commanders were revolted by forcible repatriation, and even when force could have been used legally they delayed and questioned the policy, yielding only on scattered occasions. One American who helped mislead the trusting Vlasov army veterans at Plattling was William Sloane Coffin, Jr. He later wrote that his role in the operation "left me a burden of guilt I am sure to carry the rest of my life."[20]

UNRRA workers faced the controversy as well. As they came into camps in the early weeks after the war, UNRRA team members worked diligently to prepare the refugees for their homeward journey. This brought them face to face with the reality of the repatriation controversy, as reported by one UNRRA worker in a camp of Russians:

> There were many people, particularly elderly men and women, who seemed extremely fearful of returning to the USSR, for religious or political reasons. They came to [the worker's] office, and whispering a request for an interview in privacy, fearfully asked if they could go somewhere else, other than back home. They stated that they would be done away with if they returned. These persons received the kindly but firm answer that under the laws of their own government they must return. They nevertheless tried time and again to see U.S. Army officers, and myself.[21]

These actions at the lower level of the UNRRA chain accurately reflected policies at the top. Repatriation had highest priority. Herbert Lehman, the organization's first director general, stressed in a

UNRRA Council session in August 1945 that Poles who refused for political reasons to go home "should no longer be taken care of by UNRRA." His successor, Fiorello La Guardia, once confronted a group of Yugoslavs who argued that they could not go home because they did not agree with communism. He told them, "That's no reason for refusing repatriation. I've disagreed with the government in my country for more than 20 years now—but you don't see me running away from America on that account." And in early 1946 both the outgoing UNRRA chief for the British Zone of Germany and his replacement emphasized the need for repatriation, "the pivot on which all UNRRA teams will revolve for the next few months" according to the incoming director, Sir Raphael Cilento. Cilento added in a confidential memo that at the beginning of spring all Poles should be told that if they failed to return home they would each lose their DP status and become instead "a voluntary settler in Germany or a political refugee." This was to be the policy "to the best of my knowledge and belief," he added.[22]

Although it went beyond both United Nations and occupation policies, Cilento's statement was not out of line with what other UNRRA leaders were asserting then. A year later, in 1947, the UNRRA's chief for DP Operations bluntly urged all refugees to go home. The UNRRA could not aid forcible repatriation, he admitted, "but to remain behind is to face the most dark and doubtful of futures. . . . Seize this opportunity—now," he exhorted. "Your relatives, your friends, your country wait for you."[23]

The new International Refugee Organization warned that DPs were not to exploit the new organization because they preferred "slothfulness" instead of helping to rebuild their countries, or because they wished to emigrate "for strictly economic reasons." As late as 1949 an IRO staff member found such pressures still present. "Superiors in the next headquarters up made sure we gave primary attention to repatriation," he said. "I felt that pressure." But in one year only three or four people were repatriated from his camp.[24]

Camp operations mirrored dissension at top levels. There, the Soviet Union and its partners increasingly tangled with Western representatives in the policy-making councils of both the UNRRA and the new United Nations. In September 1945 the UNRRA Council voted that the organization was to encourage repatriation of DPs "at the earliest possible moment," and a year later the notorious Order No. 199 was passed: it placed the UNRRA behind the "speedy return of the greatest possible number of displaced persons to their homeland as quickly as possible" and called for distributing Soviet literature and films, isolating antirepatriation DPs, and granting those who agreed to return "special status with UNRRA" regarding "stocks of clothing and amenity supplies." The order stated that "the skillful Repatriation Officer" would lead his camp to "acceptance of repatriation." The order drew a flurry of protests, however, and was revoked six weeks later.[25]

"Operation Carrot" had more success. This was a much-publicized program to grant each returning Pole a sixty-day ration of food. Launched by La Guardia in the summer of 1946, it built on a growing feeling in Europe that DPs were lazy (they often refused jobs in the local economy), freeloading (they ate better than many people living near camps), and undisciplined (some camps were stripped of light fixtures, furniture, even windows, when DPs were moved). Beginning in October 1946, the sixty-day plan seemed to have some success. The Polish repatriation figure was 23,500 in August 1946 and 32,579 in September, but shot up to 46,401 in October; after the program ended the total fell to 1,034 for January 1947. The contents of this sixty-day ration were put on display in camps and the offer was publicized by posters, bands, and proclamations telling of the friendly reception and jobs waiting for the DPs back in Poland. (Not all camp workers agreed with this. Kathryn Hulme described the fanfare at Wildflecken but added, "Gradually we forgot the secret shame we had felt when we had first stood beside the free food displays and had watched our DPs stare at the terrible fascination of the bait, thrashing, twisting and turning before they took the hook.")[26]

The plan was resumed in the western zones of Austria and Germany in April and May of 1947 and was opened to DPs of any nationality. Polish repatriation immediately tripled. The plan appeared once again in late 1948 with a twenty-day food supply.[27]

This "carrot" approach ran in tandem with another, harsher set of policies. "The gravy train is going round for the last time," an unnamed U.S. official told a journalist. Many UNRRA leaders, occupation authorities, and, increasingly, Austrian politicians pushed for reducing or eliminating any activities that encouraged DPs to remain where they were.

Even the continued existence of camps was questioned. Indeed, in March 1946 the U.S. commander in Germany, General Joseph McNarney, and U.S. secretary of state James Byrnes talked of the possibility that the DP camps would close in August for all but "persecuted persons" (mainly Jews). Those refusing repatriation, Byrnes said, "will have an opportunity to take their places in civilian life and obtain employment in our zones."[28]

Return to Poland. Repatriation trains generally left with great fanfare, with branches and flags adorning the cars, and songs competing with the rumble of the loco-motive. These Polish youths were typical of the joyful return. Some others went back apprehensively, however. *(UNRRA photo.)*

These policies were quietly abandoned. But authorities seeking new ways to drive the DPs home soon cast their eyes on another refugee activity: the camp schools. In Polish camps the Allies' transfer of official recognition to the Lublin (Communist) government in June 1945 brought new pressures on the DPs, eventually closing some camp schools. As viewed by critics, the schools were so popular that they encouraged the refugees to finish out the school year, then to start looking forward to the next session, rather than returning home. The UNRRA supervisor at Arnsberg in the British Zone complained of the impact of the well-developed school system in Lippstadt camp:

> With all this educational activity going on we cannot expect much in the way of repatriation from this camp. Parents will not leave without their children, neither will they drag them away from a free education to return to Poland where they would have to pay a high fee for the same service. In my opinion this free higher [sic] education is definitely a great hindrance to repatriation and I should be glad to know if anything could be done to keep it within bounds.[29]

To many, such threats and activities were evidence that the UNRRA was helping the Communists. Joseph Melaher, a former Chetnik officer in Slovenia who led his unit into refuge in Italy, watched in disbelief as a UNRRA screening commission badgered his fellow DPs. "A French woman was interrogating—she must have been left-wing. She said to an Anders Polish army veteran, 'You were all black marketeers and fascists!' I complained to the British commander, 'How can you allow that? The Anders group fought with the British all the way up the Italian peninsula!' Soon she was removed from the commission."[30]

Anti-Communists recoiled from Communist participation in repatriation drives, as when a Russian UNRRA employee blocked the escape of several Ukrainian Vlasov veterans in the Kempten incident. One of the most outspoken critics was Sir Frederick Morgan, who had pushed repatriation as the UNRRA chief in Germany but later charged that the organization was "honeycombed" with Soviet agents, who spread disaffection while seeking military information and collecting addresses of DP relatives. His charge received support when a group of Polish and Baltic DPs protested that a UNRRA screening team was asking for names and addresses of their kin; the UNRRA head for the U.S. Zone of Germany promptly ordered it stopped.[31]

Most UNRRA teams relied on other, more honest methods to

encourage repatriation, and the lack of alternatives for the DPs simplified their work. Team 87 was so successful in 1946 at Solingen in the North Rhine region that a description of the camp director's methods was circulated to other UNRRA teams:

> He has got the people to the meetings by merely having his Polish staff tell everyone that a meeting of vital importance to all the Camp is to be held at a given place and given time. In the meantime he does not mention the subject matter.
>
> He has started the meetings by saying "Good morning" in Polish. He has then brought up one or two camp matters in which he shows the people that he is interested in their welfare. One example of this is the arrangement he made to take all the children in the camp and the teachers to the circus at Cologne. He announced that he is going to the circus with them. By such methods he has established good feeling at the beginning of the meeting.
>
> He then has brought up again the 60 days ration plan and pointed to the samples in front of him. Secondly he has again told of the promises made by the Polish Government, and had the Polish proclamation read to the audience.
>
> He then has stated that it is very bad morally and physically for people to live in idleness having their food, clothing, and housing provided by others. He has especially pointed out how bad this is for young people.
>
> At his last meeting, he brought up the fact that two young couples had recently come to him with applications to be married. He outlined what he had said to these young people: that there was no future for them to make a family life in Germany, that their only assured future was to go home and help rebuild their own country and establish a real home, that they must not only think of today but also of the long to-morrow and that the time is coming when UNRRA will finish and nobody knows what will happen; that they will probably then become a part of the German population.

Then came questions from the Solingen camp audience, and a talk by the Polish repatriation officer. But a key part of this director's success, a visiting UNRRA field supervisor concluded, was his light touch. He "managed to bring considerable humor into his talks, e.g., he stated that he had provided some extra transport since the train at Wuppertal was cancelled and that he did not mind how much baggage they took provided they did not take the house."[32]

The results of such efforts were substantial, but they decreased after the massive summer rush of 1945. Under the UNRRA's aegis from 1 November 1945 to 30 June 1947, 202,037 DPs were repatriated from Austria; 741,987, from the western zones of Germany; and 18,021, from Italy. Most of these were Poles. Subsequently under the IRO, only 54,000 DPs returned to Communist-controlled areas in three years after mid-1947, most traveling to Poland.[33]

Those who elected to return home went for a variety of reasons in addition to the uncertainties of life in devastated Germany, Austria, or Italy. Concern for family land drove many back. A Ukrainian recalled a DP explaining his decision to return home: "If I don't, my sister will have the land, and I will never get my land back." Above all, the Ukrainian concluded, the incident demonstrated the extreme importance of land to the peasantry. An Estonian told of a woman who decided to return because she was apart from her husband, who had been drafted into the Soviet army. She presumed he was in Estonia, and she was returning to him. Such family separations figured frequently in repatriation decisions. A Briton who toured the camps in the early summer of 1947 for the Refugees Defense Committee chatted with passengers aboard a Polish repatriation train in Bavaria and found them "rather tired of Germany and its constant communal life of hopelessness and insecurity, and they had developed a wistful longing accentuated by demoralization which caused them to decide to 'go home and hope for the best.'"[34]

Officials from Communist countries showed increasing belligerance over repatriation, soon moving away from initial gentle words of assurance to threats and international pressure. At the beginning it was sweet talk, however, as when the Soviet High Command in August 1945 informed Soviet DPs in Austria that they were not disowned: "Even those who under German pressure and terror committed acts hostile to the interest of the Soviet Union will not be held responsible if, after their return, they fulfill their duty honorably." In fact, Americans who worked in the camps in those early months recall uniformly good relations with Soviet representatives.[35]

But threats, kidnappings, and the use of informers soon changed the tone of Soviet repatriation campaigns. DPs began disappearing from streets, and after several Ukrainians were seized in Vienna, presumbably by Soviet agents, an employee of a voluntary agency reported that "Ukrainian life in Vienna is dead, people terrorized." Only sharp-eyed U.S. Military Police stopped a Soviet transport at Nürnberg from carrying ten noncamp DPs into the Soviet Zone, and the *Lithuanian Bulletin* reported that "this incident encouraged the movement into Assembly Centers." France clamped down on Soviet repatriation operations after it learned that three French-born children had been kidnapped and were being held in the Soviet Union's heavily guarded Camp Beauregard near Paris. Police charged into the building in November 1947 and freed the captives, uncovered a substantial arsenal, and provided French authorities with an excuse to order repatriation drives reduced.[36]

The Belgrade government tried threatening the twenty-five thousand anti-Tito Yugoslavs in Italy to obtain their return in 1945, setting dates beyond which no amnesty would be offered: "If you will not appear until this time, you will have to support the responsibility and the consequences, and return to Yugoslavia will become very difficult for you. Death for the Fascism—Liberty for the People!" The dates were then progressively moved back, however—first to 16 April 1946, then to mid-1947. At that point Tito's regime warned the newly elected Italian government that future good relations depended on the return of the remaining Yugoslav DPs. Britain tried to force these refugees home by reducing food rations and ending military status for the soldiers of the Chetnik forces as well as the Royal Yugoslav Army. "We were told by the British, 'You are now displaced persons,'" one Serbian explained. Finally the Yugoslavs were simply transferred to camps in Germany, to clear the situation for the new Italian government.[37]

The Soviets placed similar pressures on Austria and attacked the Americans and British for permitting anti-Communist newspapers in the camps. Another frequent charge was that the Western Allies were blocking the return of DPs eager to come home. The Soviet journal *New Times,* published in Moscow, told the story of Nikolai Ivanovich Karpovich, who finally made his way home from the DP camps in August 1949, allegedly against great obstacles:

> He had three times intimated his desire to return to the Soviet Union, but all he got for his pains was to be kept in jail for three years. Karpovich was repeatedly interrogated and tortured by the British jail authorities. "I was made to kneel on peas with my knees bared and my hands stretched over my head until I lost consciousness," he relates.
> . . . There are literally no lengths to which the camp administration will not go to frustrate repatriation.
> . . . When a Soviet repatriation officer came to Balondorf Camp 8/10 in February 10 of this year [1950] with newspapers for distribution among the Soviet internees, a British sergeant named Lewis flung himself upon him, armed with a rifle, and tried to tear the papers from his hand.[38]

In this atmosphere of worsening cold war tensions, camp visits by Soviet repatriation officers became even more unpleasant. But the Soviets pressed on. Their approach at the Baltic camp at Hannover was typical. They frequently held what the DPs came to call "Russian Days," when Soviet representatives put up signs and sat all day in a meeting hall. "Come Home—Your Country's Calling," the posters proclaimed. The Soviet spokesmen were met with jeers, sticks, and stones, a Hannover DP recalled; through it all, however, they remained "very friendly, correct."

Slovenian students at the University of Bologna were dismayed to learn that they would have to meet individually with a Yugoslavian official in their student hostel. One recalls it as only "mild pressure," however. They later learned that the meetings had been set up to pacify Communist officials who were charging that the Western Allies were not helping with repatriation.

A report from Schleswig-Holstein showed the deterioration in camp repatriation visits, at least at Grensstrasse. A Soviet major was making his way around the camp when a Latvian brought out a letter that, when read out loud, set off agitation in the crowd. The UNRRA director described what happened next:

> Somebody asked why so many thousands of Latvians were sent to Siberia. The Major answered, "They were enemies of the country." Somebody of the crowd then shouted, "Are children also enemies of the country?" This person got spontaneous support. The camp leader and I told the people to stop shouting. . . . While leaving the camp, some people tried to get near the Russian Officer's car, but they were held back by the Camp Police and the Camp Leader.

But this was not the end. The following day the major returned with a Red Army lieutenant colonel who said "he had heard from his Major that the people in this camp had been insulting the Russian officer. . . . [He asked] 'Why did not we arrest the man who had been reading a letter to the Major the day before?'"

The two Soviet officers then wandered about the camp, asking various DPs why they did not return to Latvia, finally addressing a crowd of forty or fifty in a small hall. "When we left the barracks," the UNRRA director reported, "the interpreter said to me 'that somebody had told the Colonel that they (the Latvians) would come back to Latvia, but not in the way the Colonel expected.' The interpreter gave me to understand that the DPs meant 'Come back with arms.'" After drinking some gin with the UNRRA team director, the Russians departed—but later issued a complaint that the British camp director was anti-Soviet.[39]

Behind their fears of repatriation, in the inner recesses of each DP's memory, were experiences under communism. Outsiders lacked such experiences. Trying to explain why there was so little repatriation from the Brauweiler camp in early 1946, a UNRRA team director said the main factor was "the predominating number of people from the East, who have experienced Russian occupation and will not face it again." The truth of this emerged bluntly when residents of a Baltic camp at Augsburg argued with their director over his plan to send a delegation to visit their homeland, to help them decide whether to return permanently. The director guessed the reason for their reluctance.

> *Director:* What do you suppose should be believed, what one sees with his own eyes, or what is printed in unofficial publications, such as "The Readers Digest?"
> *DP:* What one sees is more reliable than what one reads.
> *Director:* Well, then, why don't you wish to see the entire truth with your own eyes?
> *DP:* We saw enough of bolshevism in 1940 and 1941.[40]

And it was true that large numbers of the remaining adult DPs knew communism firsthand. Some of their knowledge reached back a generation; Hungarians encountered in northern Italy, for example, were afraid to return home because of what had happened to them in 1919 during Bela Kun's short-lived Hungarian Soviet Republic. One Hungarian who eventually escaped to Vienna with his wife and three children recalled his father's imprisonment during Kun's reign, when the family farm was confiscated. His father was released and the farm later returned to their control, but the village priest could not be brought back: captured, tortured, "they cut off his nose, his ears, poked through his eyes, and buried him in manure. They left him like this for a week. . . . When they were overthrown we found his body and buried him." Similarly, some Balts argued that their anger against the Russians predated 1917, for "the Soviets only legalized and formalized" the traditional cruelty of the Russian people, they said. Among Poles there were vivid, painful memories of life during the Soviet occupation of eastern Poland from 1939 to 1941 that included brutality, mass arrests, and such whispered incidents as the Katyn Forest massacre of some fifteen thousand Polish army officers. Their familiarity with communism did not come from the *Reader's Digest.*[41]

It was also true, of course, that the appearance of the "Iron

Curtain" sharply dividing East and West had an increasingly negative effect on repatriation. Many Poles initially planned to go home,
until the Soviet Union established its own Polish regime and spread
its control over the country, arresting returned officials of the exile
regime in London as well as leaders of wartime resistance. A
UNRRA report agreed that "it would be naive to deny that probably the single most important deterrent is a fear of the Soviet
Union and a distaste for what is believed to be a growing tendency
toward Communism and Totalitarianism in Poland."[42] Literature
given out to Polish DPs by the Warsaw regime tried to allay these
fears:

> *Q.* Is it planned to establish collective farms?
> *A.* The tales you hear about collective farms are only rumors. It is in
> the interest of the Polish State to have private holdings which are
> sufficiently large to be self-supporting. Collective farms are not being
> introduced anywhere in the country and will not be introduced. . . .
> *Q.* Is it not true that all Poles East of the Bug are sent to Siberia?
> *A.* No. Not only is it not true, but the reverse is the case. Two
> million Poles have already returned to Poland from East of the Bug
> and have been resettled in Poland. . . .
> *Q.* How much of what I bring will the Polish Government take from
> me (Customs)?
> *A.* Nothing.[43]

And when a Quaker working with the UNRRA accompanied a
repatriation train he reported that "each DP thought that he would
find a Russian behind every tree in Poland and they were all happy
when it didn't work out that way."[44]

The Baltic peoples, like the Poles, also feared conditions in their
homeland, due mainly to recollections of the early war years. The
Soviet Union had moved in on the three small nations in June 1940,
after first pressuring them to yield military bases. The USSR held
Lithuania, Latvia, and Estonia for a year before being driven out by
the invading Germans in late June and early July of 1941, as Hitler's
Operation Barbarossa began. But much happened in that year
under communism that would never be forgotten: farms and busi-
nesses were taken from their owners, dissent was crushed, and
thousands of persons in leadership positions were killed or forced
into exile in the Soviet Union—most during one night of terror from
13 June to 14 June 1941. The total killed or deported during the one-
year Soviet occupation has been estimated at 62,000 Estonians,
34,000 Latvians, and as many as 40,000 Lithuanians.[45]

DPs from Yugoslavia's feuding peoples also carried memories

into exile. Some of these were so fervent that it was said in an Italian camp that while Serbs were the most chauvinistic of any group present, they were almost totally united in refusing to return to the homeland they loved so strongly. The civil war between Croatians, Serbians, and the Balkan Peninsula's other peoples had been submerged by the Nazi invasion and the Partisans' victory, but the last of these events struck the most terror into the hearts of those who fled. Blood flowed in Yugoslav streets. A Vatican official in Croatia wrote in late 1945 of continued mass murders by the Partisans and lamented, "There is no one who does not mourn someone." Early promises of friendship did not long withstand the Partisans' push for total control, and by February 1946 a UNRRA worker in Yugoslavia concluded that "the honeymoon period of the Government seems to be over." The police system was being strengthened, schooling had become "highly colored," travel was closely supervised, "party block control committees are well organized, and the bite is being strongly put to the 'reactionary groups.' "[46]

Ukrainians, considered "the most nervous" about repatriation, along with Russians and Byelorussians, knew communism more intimately than other refugees. For Ukrainians the fight became one of proving that they were originally from the western Ukraine— Poland, Rumania, Czechoslovakia, Hungary. Those from the eastern Ukraine, part of the USSR, tried to obtain documents shifting their birthplace to Galicia and other areas of the western Ukraine so they would be recognized officially as Ukrainians rather than as "Russians" or "Soviets." Many showed considerable tenacity in this quest, and part of their success can be seen in a statistical change: while only 9,190 DPs were listed as Ukrainians in December 1945, this number climbed to 106,549 by June 1947. This perplexed screening teams, for the geographical naiveté of many UNRRA officers did not permit them to believe that Ukrainians could claim Polish citizenship and not be called Poles. An exasperated Ukrainian finally asked one American officer, "If you had a horse stable, and a cat went in the stable to give birth to kittens, are they kittens or horses?" Then the officer understood.[47]

Stories slipped out of the Soviet zones only added to the DPs' fear. A frequent report was that everything had gone well on the return home until the repatriate crossed into the Soviet Zone, when Soviet troops surrounded the DPs, stripping them of their clothing, suitcases, and objects such as bicycles and watches. They were asked why they had let themselves be captured, and when one homeward-bound Russian complained of the food provided in the holding camp, the guard told him the DPs "had feasted long enough on American rations and it would do [them] good to go hungry for a while."[48]

It is undisputed that the fate of many returning DPs was death. Western Allies learned little of this for years, although before the Mecklenburg area was transferred to Soviet control in July 1945 British soldiers observed the Soviets constructing an enormous gallows. Letters were secretly carried across the Yugoslav frontier and read aloud in Chetnik camps in Italy, giving details of the Partisans' vengeance. A Serbian officer in the Royal Yugoslav Army had been repatriated voluntarily after lengthy agonizing, and with the encouragement of his uncle. Two months after he had left the camp, however, a note was smuggled back saying that he had been killed in the train station when he arrived at his hometown.[49]

Recently the writings of Aleksandr Solzhenitsyn have revealed that the fate of thousands of these repatriated DPs was a lengthy term in a Soviet labor camp in the Gulag Archipelago. (As visits to Soviet bloc countries and the Soviet Union were increasingly allowed in the 1960s and 1970s, additional stories leaked out regarding the fate of repatriated DPs. A Canadian of Ukrainian extraction toured the Ukraine and met an ex-DP who had been forced to work in coal mines for twenty-five years; another had been ordered to live east of the Urals for a lengthy period.)[50]

The disaster these events brought to repatriation programs can be seen between the lines in frantic UNRRA appeals. A UNRRA report labeled "Secret" told of the return of a repatriated DP to the camp at Eller, near Düsseldorf, in late 1945:

> This man claims that the conditions there were absolutely horrible and no Poles should be influenced to return to Poland. There is no food, accommodation, coal and, what is worse, no work. He claims that the Russians have taken all the machinery out of the factories and farms and sent it back to Russia. Also that the Russian zone of Poland is policed by German Communist Police.
>
> This man is quite prepared to make this statement and sign it if necessary. He is not recognizable as the same man who left the camp at Eller . . . he is definitely making it his business to go round camps in the area informing DPs of the conditions in the Russian Zone of Poland. In his opinion it is absolutely wrong for these people to go back.[51]

As the cold war worsened—with Yugoslavia's shooting down of two American transport planes, the Czechoslovak coup, the Berlin blockade, and a string of other East-West flareups—the power of escapees' tales to discourage repatriation was magnified a hundred-fold. Repatriation officers could measure the decline in interest with each event in the developing cold war: the sharp dip in repatriation from one camp in March 1946, according to a UNRRA officer, was "entirely due to Mr. Churchill's recent speech." And increasingly the camps buzzed with another rumor: Americans and Soviets would go to war—against each other, this time.[52]

Opposition to repatriation thrived amid these uncertainties. It arose not only among DPs, but soon gained also among those who worked with DPs. Sympathetic Allied officers were quick to see that private agency personnel could help run interference around antagonistic UNRRA employees. This was apparent in Italy when an elderly British colonel appeared one Sunday morning at the room of Father Andrew P. Landi, then in charge of Catholic Relief Services efforts there. Father—now Monsignor—Landi recalled:

> "We have got a serious problem," he told me. "The Croats, in a camp near Bologna, are highly agitated because they heard they were going to be forcibly repatriated to Yugoslavia. This will mean their death."
> This colonel was sympathetic. He said they would have a riot unless someone they could trust would speak to them.
> I got a Croatian priest in Rome, who was already concerned with the plight of Croatian refugees in Italy, to go to the camp and quiet their fears. The colonel eventually arranged for them to be transferred to a camp in Germany, where it would be more difficult for them to be forcibly repatriated.[53]

Some of the voluntary workers' efforts were directed at higher levels. Canadians working for the Central Ukrainian Relief Bureau sent pleas to United Nations delegates, including Eleanor Roosevelt of the American delegation, urging an end to forced repatriation on humane grounds. Whether their efforts were responsible is unknown, but Mrs. Roosevelt took the lead in UN debates, tangling verbally with Communist bloc delegates on the issue.[54]

Catholic Relief Services helped lead an end run to help prevent closure of the DP camps as a means to force repatriation. One worker in the CRS DP program recalled that word was leaked in the spring of 1946 that the camps were to be closed. A British representative at the Fourth Session of the UNRRA Council in Atlantic City admitted that the only way such an event could be carried out would be suddenly, without warning, and he urged CRS to contact Secretary of State James Byrnes. Roman Catholic leaders went to

Byrnes and found him uninformed on the plight of the DPs. In later weeks Catholic workers helped focus pressure on the State Department, both through providing information and by threatening that any closings would be publicized. President Truman wrote to Byrnes on 17 April that the Catholic church and Poles " 'particularly . . . are simply going to have a spasm if we close out these camps without some sort of arrangement to take care of the people who can't go back.' " The result: Byrnes's plan was shelved.[55]

Because repatriation was the critical issue for their lives and futures, DPs themselves conducted most of the day-to-day fighting against it. Forging documents was one frequent recourse; suicide was another. Mark Elliott estimates that several thousand USSR citizens killed themselves rather than go back. DPs also pressured fellow DPs who were contemplating a return. When a Polish DP volunteered to be repatriated from Camp "C" near Ingolstadt— largely populated by veterans of a wartime resistance unit called "Saint Christ's Brigade"—his body was found the following day in a nearby river. No evidence of foul play or suicide was apparent, but officials felt he had been murdered because of his decision to go home. Black flags frequently were raised over camps as DPs left on their journey home to communism. To protect them from such incidents, camp officials placed returnees in isolation or transferred them to a distant holding center.[56]

Riots could not be avoided amid these tensions. Camp records are filled with cases of stone throwing, cars being overturned, jeering, shoving. A thousand Poles rioted in Wildflecken when seven Polish liaison officers showed up one day. Press accounts in May 1946 followed the trial in Wiesbaden of twenty-five Ukrainians who had assaulted two Soviet representatives:

> The Ukrainians, according to the charges, pelted the Russians with potatoes and stones, beat them and knifed one when they visited a Displaced Persons camp at Kastel near Mainz a month ago. The Russians were said to have been on a "routine visit" to explain the possibility of repatriation to the Ukrainians.
> Consternation swept through the camp. . . .
> Women wept and prayed, believing they were to be sent to the Soviet Union. A 24-year-old Ukrainian hanged himself, leaving a suicide note stating that his family had been deported to Siberia and he preferred death to falling under Soviet control.

In subsequent military court proceedings, two of the men were sentenced to ten years of hard labor, one received a suspended sentence, and charges against the rest were dropped.[57]

The most publicized case of DP violence over repatriation occurred at the Serbian Chetnik DP camp near Naples in early 1947. A witness recalls that when the Serbs learned that Vlatzko Glumchitch was the Yugoslav consul who would be visiting, they decided to act: they knew him for atrocities during the war. When he arrived with an aide to attempt to persuade the Chetniks to come home, the DPs threw themselves upon him, frightening the British escort into a corner and ultimately pummeling Glumchitch to death with bricks and rocks. Yugoslavia issued stern protests, but Britain ultimately did nothing to punish the Serbs involved; in fact, one version of the incident that was passed down in DP lore has the British issuing false papers to the man responsible for Glumchitch's death and sending him on his way.[58]

This was repatriation. It soon cast a pall over the V-E Day joys of liberation. It kept thousands of DPs constantly on edge, never quite feeling secure in the camps despite all they did to transform these into cheery communities.

One basic, searing question remains: Why did the Communist countries seek the forced return of so many DPs? Why was there such "extreme touchiness" on the issue among Soviet spokesmen, as Western diplomats noted even before V-E Day? If the DPs were so eager to stay in the West, why not leave them be—a continuing drain on the Western Allies' economies and a potential source of European disruption?

Several reasons for Soviet policies have been suggested. In the same way that many DPs drew on memories of the Soviet state, so, too, the Bolsheviks recalled that much of their opposition since 1918 had centered in exile communities beyond the USSR's frontiers. (Nikolai Tolstoy quotes a Soviet leader as confessing that Soviet authorities feared scattered bands of exiles because "that's the way we got our start!") And these refugees who stayed away were, in the words of Columbia University's Clarence A. Manning, "an uncomfortable demonstration to the world that all is not well within the Soviet Union. . . . They make plausible the seemingly fantastic stories of labor camps and of deportations that have come out of Moscow."[59]

More immediate Soviet needs appeared also. Facing monumental reconstruction challenges, the Stalinist regime fell back on a system it had used previously: forced-labor camps. One study examined the massive work to be done under the USSR's 1946–50 Five-

Year Plan and concluded that to fulfill it "under present Soviet conditions" required an expansion in the use of forced labor.[60]

A paranoid lives in constant fear of his opponents, and both Stalin and Soviet communism have suffered from paranoia. Marriages with foreigners were forbidden, emigration was blocked, the Soviet public was isolated from foreigners, and wartime posters warned: "Do not believe all returned soldiers." These fears could only have been increased by events during the war, when an estimated one million Soviet citizens went over to the enemy's forces (in contrast, a Nazi effort to recruit among captured British soldiers netted only thirty turncoats). It made the Soviets demand the return of these renegades, and, once in the motherland, made it essential to quarantine them to prevent contamination of the remaining loyal population. For these DPs had learned of a different way of life. As Nikolai Tolstoy devastatingly concluded, Stalin's was a system "whose rulers genuinely feared that a man whose knowledge of the outside world was confined to two years' experience of Auschwitz must necessarily be in danger of abandoning his socialist principles."[61]

It all fit into the worsening cold war—not as the prime cause, and yet more than a mere symptom, for Soviet anger over repatriation led to further hardening of attitudes between the former Allies. Perhaps Soviet and Western sensitivities were pushed to extremes on the issue because it symbolized basic differences between the two systems: the Western democracies looked on the rights of the individual as paramount, possessing liberties and the right of asylum, deserving care, while Communists saw the state as the supreme power, the sole arbiter of questions affecting individuals. From such sharply opposing philosophies, the issue of voluntary-versus-forcible repatriation could never be settled with a compromise.[62]

4

DISPLACED CHILDREN

I survived because I was strong enough to snatch food from
people who were too weak to keep it.
—Child from concentration camp

THE Hungarian girl was alone, only thirteen, and her wandering
drew the attention of camp officials at Reggio nell' Emilia in northern Italy. Under questioning, she described the events of September 1944, when Soviet troops neared her village of Pécs, and her
parents decided she must flee. They gave her two suitcases, some
money, and put her on the road to Austria, hoping the war would
not catch up with her. She avoided the final months' battles, and
after the Nazi capitulation traveled south to Rome, surviving by
begging. The girl was hitchhiking north when occupation troops
spotted her and delivered her to refugee officials. Her only possessions were the clothes she wore.

While the Hungarian girl's odyssey aroused the curiosity of the
camp director at Reggio, he admitted it was "to some extent typical
of a great number of children found in refugee camps."[1]

Such a judgment came naturally to anyone living in liberated
Europe, for the DP camps, no less than the Continent's streets and
roadways, provided constant reminders of the impact on children of
the horrors just past. Every spot freed by the Allies appeared to
contain its quota of younger victims—the 700 children "almost like
wild animals" discovered in the prisons of Łódź, Poland; half-
starved youngsters wandering in the woods of eastern Slovakia;
youthful beggars filling Athens and Rome; young searchers everywhere seeking news of their families from travelers and released
prisoners of war.[2]

Families were divided, communities destroyed. More than 60,000
Dutch children had neither homes nor parental care at war's end,

while estimates of the numbers of children who had lost both parents ran as high as 400,000 in Poland, 500,000 in Yugoslavia. But those orphans still had life; many others had not made it to war's end. One estimate was that only 60,000 of the 1.5 million European Jewish children west of the USSR survived the war.[3] When Yugoslav Partisans seized a concentration camp they found 1,500 children still alive among the unburied dead, but 500 of these youngsters died while being moved and another 300 perished soon after.[4]

Their stories were often difficult to piece together, for these children's memories included searing moments of terror and death that competed with a desire to blot out such horrors. Two young brothers found by the IRO had only vague recollections of what had occurred in the early portion of their lives. The older—apparently born in 1937—could remember a small farm with a well in front of the house and a woman and man who apparently were related and spoke a language other than German. "Much more vividly, however, he remembers his experiences during the war, when he moved from one place to another with a group of other children his age" amid bombings, fleeing to the woods, always running. The younger brother, born in 1939, had no memory of anything but war.[5]

Survivors had often learned the value of lying, of cheating, and the penalties for not doing so. Often that was why they survived. One boy hid for a year in the woods and fields near his home after his family was seized. When he found that former neighbors had moved into his house he went up to them and told his story, but was promptly turned in to the SS and spent the rest of the war in a concentration camp. A girl of ten told concentration camp officials that she was twelve, and was allowed to remain and work; her eleven-year-old sister reported her age honestly and was sent to die. A Czechoslovak woman doctor in a German factory taught children how to feign illness so they would be able to rest; she was not betrayed. Feelings had to be held back; if not, the results could be disastrous. When a child in Prague scribbled "Hitler is a fool" on a school wall, the Germans hauled away his headmaster, who returned crippled, his legs torn by dogs.[6]

Homeless, scarred, bitter, fearful, gaunt, begging, robbing, witnesses to terrible things—these were the children of liberated Europe. The International Red Cross asserted that 13 million children in Europe had lost their natural protectors, and the UNRRA had 50,000 unaccompanied children in its care a few months after V-E

Day. When the IRO took over the camps in 1948 it found that nearly a fourth of its DPs were under age seventeen.[7]

The plight of Europe's children was quickly placed at the focus of international concern, and a string of medical experts, psychologists, educators and others rushed to examine them. Europe's first postwar international conference, held at Zurich in September 1945, was devoted to "Children Victims of the War." France also convened an early conference on the moral rehabilitation of children affected by the war, and an international meeting on juvenile delinquency in Geneva in 1947 focused on the general topic of the children of Europe. The new United Nations became embroiled in controversy over the fate of the war orphans, the Soviet bloc demanding that its children be returned home from the "bandit nests" of the DP camps.[8]

Europe's children were at the center of world concern in the years following 1945 partly because the world had once more been made aware—painfully, tragically aware—of a basic truth: war was the harvest of seeds planted earlier. The children's physical rehabilitation and moral, emotional, and psychological readjustment, argued a French children's agency leader, "are essential to the reconstruction of the peaceful world we are striving for." Another writer wondered when the world's peoples would attempt to give real values and a real life to these young victims of the war—"now, while there is still time to make the hope of tomorrow's world; or with too little, too late to turn away the threat that they can grow into?" For they had only to cast a short backward glance to recall the Third Reich's emphasis on indoctrination of youth and Hitler's proclamation, " 'Wer die Jugend hat, hat die Zukunft' " (" 'He who possesses the Youth possesses the future' ").[9]

Some of their problems were readily apparent. Children were often pitiful-looking after years of hard labor, or hiding, or living on meager provisions—on olives in Provence, maize in Rumania, tulip bulbs in Holland, discarded scraps all across the Continent. Thirty Polish girls who had worked on Nazi farms were brought to a UNRRA children's center in a monastery near Dachau:

> Most of them were in rags, all showed marked effects of malnutrition and mental anxiety. Their hair was a mat filled with lice. All had skin infections, two so seriously that they were unable to wear shoes. Their feet and legs were wrapped in dirty blood-stained gauze. Some were so confused that they thought themselves German.[10]

Even outside the battle zones, however, the problems created by war were serious and long-lasting for children. Stunted growth was the most widespread visible effect, but tuberculosis and scabies also ranked high among the scourges of children. In Czechoslovakia, "every child is anemic," a doctor stated. "No children enjoy perfect health." Surveys found tuberculosis increasing by age among Czechoslovak children: 10 to 15 percent of the six-year-olds were infected, rising to 30 to 40 percent among fourteen-year-olds. Twenty-five abandoned babies found by the U.S. Army Medical Corps at Pilsen had tuberculosis, enteritis, ear trouble, or other serious infant health problems.[11]

As critical as these health problems were, potentially greater concerns existed. The harm done to children by the war "appears immeasurable," concluded Dorothy Macardle in her 1951 study, *Children of Europe*. Orphanages could be counted and weight loss measured, she admitted, "but there are other injuries which are imponderable. The hurt to the children's mental growth and nervous balance, to their faith in life and their natural feelings, cannot be estimated." They were called "children without a childhood."[12]

While many children slipped across borders during Europe's nightmare years, very few escaped the Continent to grow up in better conditions elsewhere. That had been a hope at the beginning of the war, but when a submarine sank the *City of Benares,* which was carrying British children to Canada in the fall of 1940, Britain refused to participate further in any such large-scale escape schemes. Fewer than 600 children were carried out of Europe from 1934 to 1943 by European Jewish Children's Aid, and the U.S. Committee for the Care of European Children managed to bring out fewer than 1,500. Escape was not possible for most, not for children, not for adults.[13]

And so they labored in the Third Reich's factories and farms, fought in its battalions, rotted in its concentration camps, hid, died.

Their age group pointed to an important fact: if they had been needed by the Nazis, they survived in numbers; if not needed, fewer survived. Sixty percent of the children in one DP camp of 5,000 inhabitants were between the ages of sixteen and eighteen; they had been useful to the Nazi war machine. IRO statistics in late 1947 revealed that 61.2 percent of its more than 600,000 DPs were between the ages of eighteen and forty-five, the working years.[14]

The Germans forced schools to indoctrinate pupils, and in some areas simply closed schools under various pretexts, then required children who were not enrolled to report to a labor exchange. Child labor in factories—a practice rooted out of Europe over previous decades—suddenly was reinstated across the Continent, and by

1943 the Germans were pulling in Polish children as young as age ten to become part of the forced-labor brigades. These were the *Ostkinder*. Many were seized as they arrived at school or were taken from farm jobs, then loaded into trucks and sent to quarries, factories, or road repair projects. A Ukrainian recalled the Gestapo surrounding his high school one day in 1944; all students were then forcibly taken away to Germany. Some of his friends went to an arms factory near Vienna, but he ended up near Dresden at a factory where barracks sections were constructed. "More often," he grimly recalled, "we were used to take away bodies of bombing victims, especially after the Dresden bombing."

But the Reich did not stop with high school students, as Kathryn Hulme discovered at the Wildflecken DP camp. When she admired how deftly the Polish children tore apart the Red Cross packages, so the contents could be distributed, one five-year-old explained, " 'Wie in der Fabrik' " (" 'As in the factory' "). She learned that his dexterity had been used and developed by the Nazis in a war plant.[15]

The Third Reich used them as soldiers as well. An Estonian looked back on his service in the Estonian SS Division, which began when he—then fifteen years old—and his father were seized as they fled from the invading Red Army. His military service was brief. "We retreated, trying to surrender to the Americans and British. Most of us had ditched our uniforms. . . . At the very end it was every man to himself." Earlier, in other areas, boys were forced to serve as auxiliaries to the German army, while girls from fifteen to twenty-five years of age were enlisted in the *Freies Militär Mädchen*.[16]

Many children participated in the Resistance, carrying messages for the underground, engaging in the hit-and-run attacks that marked most behind-the-lines opposition to the German invaders. Polish youths masqueraded as regular students while conducting training programs and operations for the Resistance, and when postwar Yugoslavia opened the ballot box to all who had borne arms against the Fascists, the electorate was found to include 10,000 children, ages thirteen through eighteen, who had fought for the Partisans.[17]

In the memories of many other children, however, the searing reality of the concentration camps pushed all else aside, and one phrase occurred over and over in their recollections: "went to the left." When the SS troops lined up parents, brothers, and sisters, they selected strong children and adults for labor but sent others "to the left," to the gas chambers. Labor assignments varied. Some children were harnessed to a hearse at Auschwitz, carrying bodies one way, returning with ashes; others were forced to cut down bodies from gallows, or they stoked fires for the crematoria, buried victims in pits, or laid out the dead in swastika patterns in fields. They knew what the smoking chimneys meant.[18]

A UNRRA worker encountered a Rumanian boy whose family had been seized in March 1944 and taken to the Oranienburg concentration camp. The father was shot to death and the mother and baby sister "went to the left." The four remaining children were sent to Auschwitz, then marched to another camp, but en route the two smaller boys lagged behind and guards made them stay back. "When the 15-year-old boy last saw his little brothers, they were huddled together on the roadside." His sister was separated from him at the Gleiwiyz concentration camp, after which he was moved back to Oranienburg, then to Flossenburg, and was en route to Dachau when American soldiers caught up with the column. Such odysseys were by no means uncommon, but most ended in other ways: only 800 children were found alive at Buchenwald; 500 at Belsen.[19]

As the victors sifted through the debris that covered Europe they began to realize that the Nazis' master plans had included not only the extermination of "inferior" populations—that was well-known by 1945—but also the massive plundering of the conquered lands' children, in pursuit of two major goals of the Thousand-Year Reich: (1) to impoverish and permanently weaken its neighbors, ensuring in the process that Germany would remain Europe's strongest nation even if it should lose the war; and (2) to maintain the German population despite manpower losses through battle. The achievement of both rested on seizing children from the rest of Europe.

Although in May 1940 Himmler had ordered the removal of certain Polish children to Germany, actual kidnappings were apparently only sporadic until early 1942, when they became so frequent and flagrant that residents of Czechoslovakia and Poland became aware that there must be a general policy behind them. Thousands between the ages of seven and fourteen disappeared from Łodz, Ozorkow, and other Polish cities, with reports of childhunts underway across Bohemia and Moravia. The Polish Red Cross would later find Nazi records indicating that 3,000 children were carried away from Silesia, 5,000 from Łodz, and 30,000 in the "Zamosc Area Action."[20]

Residents of Polish railroad towns soon were talking of the heavily guarded trains that passed through loaded with young children. Seven carloads went through Chelm, it was said; weeping trainfuls of children passed through Warsaw, and some local women attempted to storm the cars. Kidnappings were also conducted in other areas where the Nazi goose step was heard, though not as systematically or extensively as in Poland and Czechoslovakia.[21]

It was a turnabout: earlier, the Jewish-appearing children—dark-eyed, dark-haired, of darker complexion—faced the greatest danger from the roving Nazi kidnappers. Now it was the fair-haired, the blue-eyed, those who most closely fit Hitler's dream of a master race. A massive screening and sorting went on at the collecting stations, where "Nordic" types with the required intelligence and good health were picked for "Germanization." Children under the age of six were given new birth certificates dated from the *Lebensborn* maternity homes run by the Nazis; these children now belonged to the Reich. Those who fit a second classification, non-Aryan in appearance but strong of body, were dispatched to German factories and farms. The remainder were marked for extermination or laboratory experiments.[22]

Sometimes they vanished in droves, suddenly. A Polish nun described how officers expelled her and other nuns from an orphanage at Katowice, and 70 children disappeared from the building immediately, sent to Germany for assimilation. The nuns were then ordered to another institution, where some children were forbidden to have contact with them; the nuns were told those were the "more intelligent." The remaining group of 400 orphans was classified as "inferior" and designated for use as guinea pigs.[23]

Many were sent on to approved German families, after special schooling, and the families were paid to bring them up as Germans. With very young children these arrangements apparently were frequently as successful as regular adoptions, since strong bonds developed between the children and their new "parents." And the substitute parents were producing real Germans: one of the tragedies of the postwar era was the number of kidnapped children who lied in order to stay with their German foster-parents rather than return to their true parents of whom they knew little. One father finally found his son after the war in a home in Stuttgart, following months of desperate searching. But the son rejected him, believing the Germans' story that his father had murdered his mother and deserted. In truth, the father had been placed in a concentration camp, and the child was stolen from the mother, who perished at Auschwitz.[24]

As reports of such cases multiplied in late 1945, Allied officials began to realize that something more than an occasional kidnapping was involved. They had expected to encounter large numbers of unaccompanied children amid the ruins, and they did. But clues began to point to something more than this. Captured German documents first indicated that at least 50,000 children had been kidnapped, but the number of inquiries about missing children soon reached 65,000, and at the end of 1946 the UNRRA reported that more than 200,000 queries had been received by Polish welfare agencies searching for lost children.[25]

Confronted with requests from frantic parents, Allied authorities decided that standard location procedures were inadequate, and special child-search teams were formed. The first was launched in January 1946 and operated around Regensburg, Bavaria, an area to which many children had been evacuated by the Reich late in the war. By March the three-member team had located nearly 1,000 missing children. The program grew, and six teams with up to fifteen members each were active in the three western zones of Germany by July. Similarly, a group of Austrian women published pleas to foster parents to give up kidnapped children; eventually 800 were found through these efforts. By midsummer of 1946, some 10,000 lost and kidnapped children had been located through the tracing programs, a figure that climbed to 15,000 a year later. But for many, the search teams entered a "T" on the inquiry card— German for *tot,* dead.

Language skills proved to be crucial in the search. Twenty-seven languages were spoken among the six child-tracing teams at work in the autumn of 1946, and accounts of their successes point to the importance of these skills. One searcher went into a group of 150 supposed Germans, and by speaking Polish found 9 kidnapped youngsters. Another had difficulties with a child whose good German answers had almost convinced the visitor that this youngster was, indeed, German as claimed. But a final query brought the defiant reply, " 'Nein, nein, ništa' "—and the questioner immediately noted that *ništa* was Serbian, not German. That opened the way for a more honest discussion, and the child admitted that Germans had kidnapped him from his Yugoslav home one night when he was with his grandmother. After the war his German custodians had drilled him on the correct answers to give to the searchers' questions. Similarly, a group of German families declared to a Czechoslovak searcher that the children in their homes were really their own; he suspected that 5 of them were Czech or Slovaks. The children, however, supported the German parents' protestations. The searcher then set up a small camp nearby and asked the Germans to let the children come for a holiday. Within a few days the children were all speaking their native Czech again. In one town the *Bürgermeister* assured the tracing team there were no non-German children there; but when a passing nun was questioned, she led the visitors to a convent on a nearby hill that housed a large group of such children.[26]

The tortured road back for these hidden or unaccompanied children was revealed in all its hope and ugliness during the search for the surviving human remnants of Lidice, a Czechoslovak village totally obliterated by the Germans. The Nazis had taken revenge after earlier incidents—two young men from Lidice had escaped to England; later, Czechoslovak Resistance fighters coming from England assassinated a Nazi leader. That convinced the Germans of the need for reprisals.

At the outset of the German operation, relatives of the two men who had fled to England were taken away and shot, and a search of Lidice turned up some uniforms and food reserves. Then, on the evening of 8 June 1942, ten truckloads of German soldiers arrived. Women and children were placed in the schoolhouse overnight, then hauled away. Males over age fifteen were shot; 174 was the announced death total. The town was then systematically demolished by dynamite and bombs, and a Nazi radio broadcast gloated, "The very name of the village has ceased to exist." At war's end visitors found the site overgrown with grass.

Ninety-eight children were taken away from Lidice by the Germans. They were sent first to Łodz for racial testing, then classified for Germanization, labor, or extermination.

Three Lidice children whose later moves became known provide clues to the extent of the Nazi operations. As detailed by Dorothy Macardle, Anna, Marie, and Vaclav Hanfa were separated and given to different German families. When the war ended, Anna's German foster mother gave her some money and sent her away; a railroad worker at Dresden put Czechoslovak child-search workers in touch with her, and she was soon reunited with an uncle. Searchers eventually located Marie Hanfa in Berlin, but she initially refused to return, despite her maltreatment as a house servant; eventually she changed her mind.

Vaclav's case was more complicated. He had been given the name Wenzel Strauss by the Germans, but that clue yielded no results. And so searchers traced the rumors among villagers who had seen children kept in a castle near Łodz. A girl who had worked at the castle was found; she remembered that there had been a boy named Wenzel Hantz, whom she thought had been removed to a camp near Salzburg. Examination of the lists from children's homes around Salzburg, in turn, brought no success until the name Janek Wenzel turned up. "Janek," the search leader felt, might be a version of "Hans," and "Hans" might simply be an inaccurate rendering of "Hantz"; if so, first and last names could have been reversed, and "Wenzel, Hans" might have come out as "Wenzel Hantz." The similarity was close enough to investigate, at any rate.

But the boy Janek Wenzel was uncooperative and stubborn. Interviewing him in a Salzburg children's home, the search leader tried to break through his antagonism by telling stories and singing songs. Once when he relaxed she switched to a popular Czech nursery rhyme:

> I have horses
> I have black horses.

The boy finished it, laughing: "The black horses are mine," he sang out in Czech.

It was the moment of truth. Vaclav gradually told the story of his moves after leaving Lidice, his punishment for refusing to learn German, the beatings that left him lame, his transfers from camp to camp. Eventually the skill, perseverance, and patience of the search team had broken through his armor of Germanization. Vaclav Hanfa was one of only 15 of Lidice's 98 children who were found by searchers.[27]

The joy of locating lost children was often tempered by the realization of what wartime experiences had wrought. In response to a visitor's criticism that she and her friends were hysterical, a twenty-one-year-old Czechoslovak woman wrote to an English journal in 1946:

> We have to realize that the occupation which produced heroes produced cowards as well. During the years when young people were growing up, morals were inverted; evil was often shown to be more profitable than good and lies more profitable than truth. Those who grew used to whispering cannot speak out naturally now; they either shout or whisper. . . . It is not easy to expel fear from the hearts of the people from the Continent. This fear is seated deep in the subconscious minds of all of us.[28]

Her words found ready illustrations all across Europe—in DP camps, in towns buried under rubble, and in communities where homes remained standing and flowers bloomed. The German surrender, it was clear, did not magically wipe away practices of the previous decade. Gangs of children remained in the cities and soon formed in and around the DP camps, bent on stealing, robbing, even killing. Cunning, lying, cheating, had once meant survival; now they could not be suddenly jettisoned.

A psychological twisting marked many children, leaving some deaf and mute and others torn by guilt because they had survived. An American psychoanalyst, Dr. Paul Friedman, who surveyed DP conditions, found that all the children were filled with distrust and suspicion. Friedman visited a French foster home and met a Ukrainian-Jewish girl who could not cry; no tears would come. Reasons for this became apparent as she told of the days of the Nazi invasion when she was five. Since she did not look Jewish her parents sent her to help some Ukrainian neighbors, herding livestock. But some days later a Ukrainian boy showed her an identity card with her father's picture on it; the man in the photo, he said, had just been killed. " 'I wanted to cry,' " the girl said, " 'but I was afraid to cry because he would have known that I was a Jewish girl if I did. So I didn't cry.' " She went with the boy to a nearby wood where she saw the bodies of her parents, brothers, and others piled in a pit. Again she did not cry, to avoid giving herself away, but later when in hiding she did cry—only to stifle her sobs when some people approached. When Friedman encountered her in France she was still unable to cry, four and a half years later.[29]

Those who worked with Europe's children soon saw indications of the depth of psychological damage. The gangs that had formed in concentration camps would not tolerate being broken apart in a DP camp, even though no bonds of affection could be seen among their members. "They simply huddled together out of habit and extreme fear." One observer found that the loyalties within these groups were so intense that "they will fight, even kill, to protect a child of their group. Their families are gone. One another is all they have in this world."[30]

With others the psychological impact of the war came through only at specific moments. Outsiders felt the children were more subdued, less carefree. Some Yugoslav children would not put out their hands when food was offered because concentration camp guards had frequently tortured them in that manner. Another group receiving inoculations began to cry, and attendants finally realized the children thought they were being used for some evil purpose. At one Yugoslav center, children were strangely transformed when called in from the playground—their free-spirited exuberance ceased and they became robotlike, goose-stepping into the dining room. Another group, however, responded to the dinner bell by charging over tables and attacking the food like wolves. Their Nazi

Souvenirs of Hitler's war. The Germans left many scars on the children of Europe. Some of them, like these tattooed numbers, were physical. They are shown here by former concentration camp inmates housed in a center for stateless children at Vallombrosa, Italy. Soon the liberators discovered that these children had emotional scars as well. *(UNRRA photo.)*

leaders, it was learned, had made a sport of throwing crusts and watching them fight for each scrap. Suspicion remained strong, engrained, in these youngsters, and as late as Christmas Eve of 1946 a UNRRA party was dampened when the DP children refused even to taste the ice cream presented so cheerfully to them. They had never known it and were afraid it was something bad. No amount of coaxing changed their attitude. Another group of DP children refused to enter a bus for a camp excursion, for that vehicle was connected in their minds with a trip to the death camps. They boarded only reluctantly, and upon their return to the DP camp some knelt and kissed the ground. Lessons of the past died hard.

Adults who tried to help these children, to teach and rehabilitate, were sometimes overwhelmed. Czechoslovak teachers who were asked in 1946 to comment on the psychological needs of their pupils told of great aggressiveness as well as irritability, restlessness, and poor memories and powers of concentration. Some children had withdrawn into fantasy, they reported. At an English nursery the DP children "were like no other children that their nurses had ever known," Dorothy Macardle found. They managed all their own activities, expected no help or kindness from adults, and if a child stopped coming to the nursery the others commented, cheerfully, " 'Oh, he is dead.' "[31]

Perhaps because they were closest and saw the conditions first-hand, perhaps because they had the largest stake in the younger generation's development, the nations of Europe rushed first to help their continent's displaced children. Europeans opened their arms especially to the tragic children found in the concentration camps. Three hundred were flown from Theresienstadt to England in August 1945 and were joined soon by 150 from Belsen; all were taken to hostels in the Lake District. A Swedish Red Cross ship brought other Belsen children to Sweden for recuperation, while Buchenwald yielded up 350 children to Swiss care. Some 100 Dutch-Jewish children, most from Belsen, were taken to Denmark for convalescence. Yugoslavia's suffering children were moved about also—some 20,000 went for convalescent stays in neighboring Bulgaria, while others in the battle-scarred southern regions were sent for recuperation to areas of northern Yugoslavia where food was more abundant. In the twisted transport systems left by the war, it had become simpler to move children than to move food.[32]

Aid for children was also sent directly into the most devastated areas of Europe. The Swedes, for example, set up a children's soup kitchen in Vienna; the Swiss provided food and clothing rations regularly to children in Florence; and the Danish *Red Barnet* organization supplied school meals for 80,000 Norwegian children. The Danes also sent a Red Cross team to conduct tuberculosis tests and give vaccinations in Poland. Many similar programs were provided by other European countries.[33]

One of the notable institutions re-emerging in this period of deep concern for Europe's children was the children's home, which sometimes took the form of a children's center or village. A former Buchenwald inmate, Dr. Curt Bondy, sounded the call for more of these when he argued that "under no circumstances should the youngsters be forced to live in a system of barracks. They need to feel that at last they have found a home, their home, and that they are not in a camp any more."

Soon children's homes, villages, and school-towns sprouted. "The House of the Child" opened on three old estates near Gostynin, Poland, while Hungary had Hahduhadhaz Village, Holland created a Jewish children's center at Apeldoorn, and Belgium, Denmark, France, Italy, Yugoslavia, and other countries constructed homes or villages where orphans and other unaccompanied children could find shelter and understanding. A home for Jewish children was set up in the Warburg mansion at Blankenese, Germany. One of the most famous centers was Pestalozzi Children's Village, opened in late 1946 at Trogen, above Lake Constance in Switzerland. The UNRRA joined in, establishing fourteen children's centers in the British Zone of Germany by April 1946, six more in the American Zone and five in the French Zone.[34]

Schools were predictable responses to children's problems after 1945 in Europe, for they had served as centers of nationalism and resistance to the Nazis in many areas throughout the war years. One UNRRA veteran asserted that "in each DP camp, the first order of business was to set up a hospital. The second order of business was to open a school."

Little encouragement was needed. Children were underfoot in the camps; former teachers were unemployed; those with a vision of what was happening to their homeland saw that the national spirit had to be kept alive. Placing children in German schools meant assimilation—and eventual extinction of the children's national heritage. Education "was for the future nation," as one former DP put it. And German schools usually blocked the entry of DP pupils.

Many felt the call to help. A Pole received word from his father in late 1945 to come home and resume his former teaching position. But then he took a look at the DP camp situation and concluded, "I was single, and young, and I felt I had to teach these kids in the camps. They had not been allowed to go to school during the war." He stayed and became a leading educator in the Polish camps. A Lithuanian educator, Jouzas Masilionis, noted that "everyone felt that one year in Germany without schools—1944–45—was bad for our children." Moreover, the widespread idleness in the camps frightened many. "It was very bad to see kids without anything to do," Masilionis recalled. Very soon, then, children as well as parents and teachers were asking for schools.

Physical conditions were bleak at the outset. When Masilionis began teaching in the Regensberg camp, classes were held in a four-room house subdivided into eight rooms with blankets for walls. One Polish school was conducted in the open air at the outset. A Latvian woman, on the other hand, said that she had only to walk upstairs for her classes, since her family lived in a third-floor

School in a camp. Schools were among the first institutions created in DP camps, as adults worried about idle children and also the dangers of losing national identity. Paulina Rumbachs, right, a teacher from Riga, Latvia, taught this class at the Stemag DP camp at Lauf, Germany, in late 1945. The visitor at the left is Molly O'Donell, UNRRA Team 137 welfare officer. *(UNRRA photo.)*

apartment at Würzburg camp, and the camp's elementary school met on the fourth floor.

From such humble beginnings emerged elaborate camp school systems, based on traditional courses for each nationality, struggling and growing despite shortages of textbooks and materials. Mimeographed and typed books were common, but more common still was learning by rote. A Lithuanian experienced that approach in attending the fifth through seventh grade in the camp at Scheinfeld. "The teacher would tell us, and we would memorize what he said. We paid attention, so we could repeat it." Frequently no writing paper was available, but then one day there arrived a large supply of copybooks—already filled out, however, with writing by pupils at some unidentified American school. Lacking erasers, the Lithuanian pupils tried erasing by rubbing with bread, then finally gave up and simply wrote on top of the Americans' sentences. After a few years the situation improved as unused writing paper and some printed textbooks became available. There was even a traveling Lithuanian library that went from camp to camp.[35]

Just as the DP camps threw rich and poor together, former landowner and former tenant, the DP camp schools brought different social classes together in a democratic conglomeration that would have pleased Horace Mann and other nineteenth-century

Music class. Programs and projects of all sorts soon filled up the DP children's spare time—a music class in this case, at Wertheim DP camp. The girls were members of a Polish Girl Scout unit. *(UNRRA photo.)*

American public school advocates. One Ukrainian recalled that "some of the students of peasant background probably would not have attended the *Gymnasium* (grade school) it if had not been for the DP camps. And in the same classroom were children of Catholic, Orthodox, even Protestant faiths, of peasant, middle class, and upper class."

Religious and national goals were often present in this schooling. "We made all possible efforts to educate the children that they are Lithuanians," one educator-priest recalled. For more than language reasons, then, each nationality group usually had its own school. At the Reggio camp in Italy the Hungarians launched the first school, then expanded it to include several levels; others started operating during the next two weeks. Latvians and Lithuanians grouped themselves together in one school, taught by priests and young men who had been in college before the war; Poles were in another, led by Polish Red Cross representatives and two nuns from the Holy See. Other schools were inaugurated, until the Reggio camp eventually had nine.[36]

Soon the DP school systems began expanding beyond the one-room schoolhouse stage into a variety of levels and specializations. West German and Austrian education authorities gave them recognition. At the large Jewish camp at Landsberg, the system ran from preschool through college, with more than 700 high school students enrolled in training courses for carpenters, electricians, tinsmiths,

auto mechanics, dress cutters, nurses, and other skilled occupations. Evening adult courses enrolled some 500 persons, and the
system also featured a yeshiva, where 50 students prepared for the
rabbinate. Many other camps developed along similar lines, and
eventually the Lithuanians had a maritime academy at Flensburg
and the Estonians, an agricultural college near Lübeck. (Schooling
for adult DPs will be discussed in the following chapter.)[37]

Statistics revealed the extent to which schooling was important
among the DPs: ninety percent of the children from ages five
through sixteen in the American Zone DP camps were attending
camp schools, the army reported in April 1946.[38]

The DPs' creation of their own camp schools was further evidence of an important fact of the DP era: parents struggled mightily
to protect their children from the worries and fears of war and
displacement. Parents "were capable of tremendous sacrifices for
their children," the director of the Reggio camp observed. "They
would beg, steal, or sell their own clothing to ensure that the
children were well-fed." They labored to have schools developed,
holding dances and other fund-raisers, and the degree of their
success can be seen in the memories today of adults who were
children in those DP camps. "I look at it as a nice adventure,"
recalled a Ukrainian who was seven when the war ended. A Latvian
couple reminisced on their DP camp years but cautioned, "You
have to talk to older people. They suffered through it more than we
did. For the kids, the camps were fun!"

If camps were "fun," it was largely due to two factors beyond the
existence of schools: (1) these children had known no happy, carefree period earlier; and (2) camps provided a large number of youth
activities in addition to schools. Soccer and volleyball games ran
nearly nonstop in some camps, if DPs' recollections are at all
accurate. All kinds of clubs were encouraged, and twenty Hungarian boys at the Landeck camp in the Austrian Tyrol even organized a fire brigade, under the leadership of a Hungarian baron.
Children's music groups appeared in practically all camps, children's theater groups formed, and touring groups also put on concerts. Trips were scheduled—camping along the North Sea, going
to the zoo, visiting nearby cities.[39]

In these early months after the war a major impetus to such
activities came from voluntary organizations. Red Cross societies
rushed in early with help for children, as did the French-Jewish
OSE (L'Oeuvre de Secours aux Enfants), the American Joint Distribution Committee for Jewish camps, the National Catholic Welfare Conference, the YMCA and YWCA, and the American

Friends Service Committee (AFSC), among others. Each passing month brought new agencies into the DP field, most concentrating on aspects of aid for adults.[40]

One activity that gained popularity to a great degree in the DP camps was scouting, involving Boy Scouts, Girl Scouts, Girl Guides, and several national and religious variations. There were some 25,000 scouts in the U.S Zone of Germany by the spring of 1946, including subdivisions for various age groups. The Lithuanian camp at Seedorf had some 150 scouts: Sea Scouts, older and younger groups of Girl Scouts and Boy Scouts, Relief Scouts, and a fellowship of scouts at an orphanage. Scouts at the Polish DP camp of Lwow, in Darmstadt, put on campfires for the whole camp twice a week, with singing, speeches, and folk dances. An American soldier witnessed one of these evenings: "It was an impressive, touching spectacle. Several thousand people, young and old, remained on the athletic field until late into the night. For miles around, the glow of the fire lit up the horizon while the nostalgic melodies of Polish folk songs floated far beyond the camp gates."[41]

In Ukrainian DP camps many of these activities were carried on by the SUM—*Spilka Ukraïnśkoï Molodi,* or Ukrainian Youth Association—which was the cultural counterpart of the scout movement. Boy Scouts in the Ukrainian camps had their *Plast* organization, reborn in the DP era after having existed earlier as a Ukrainian nationalistic group (as such it had been banned in the Polish Ukraine). SUM itself was also a version of an earlier group, though it lacked direct ties to the anti-Russian group of the same name that was active right after the Bolshevik Revolution. *Plast* members went camping; SUM participants put on Ukrainian plays and choir concerts. The importance of these groups in DP life can be seen in the report of the Swallow Patrol of the Lesia Ukrainka "A" Troop, which won a "Good Deeds" Trophy for Ukrainian Scouting in Austria:

> Throughout the three months of keen competition they always showed themselves more than ready to volunteer for every type of special work in the D.P. camps . . . in the vegetable gardens . . . in flower gardens . . . the school . . . the barracks . . . etc. . . . They organized hospital visits to take comforts and reading material to the patients. During the summer camp on Lake Fuschl, they helped with the harvest and with many jobs in the village, and on one occasion saved a farmhouse from probable destruction by observing and putting out a fire that no one had seen.[42]

The nationalistic ties inherent in some of these youth organizations drew frowns from Allied leaders, especially when international criticism appeared. It was claimed that Polish Boy Scouts were being whisked secretly to Polish camps in Italy for training by General Anders's army. UNRRA officials worrried publicly in April 1946 over "the political complexion" of some of the DP camp youth groups, as well as the "militaristic trend of scout training in certain centers." The UNRRA sought some direction from the U.S. Army, "since all such 'national associations' have been banned by the 3d Army." These officials especially worried over reports that Polish Scouts used an oath that vowed, "We shall become soldiers who fight, who pour out blood, who kill"; these oaths also attacked the Soviet Union as the replacement for Nazi Germany.[43]

Part of the drive behind the scouting and school movements originated in the DPs' fears of other, alien, influences on their children in the chaos of postwar Europe. Sometimes they spoke openly of these fears, as when a woman in Schleissheim camp unburdened herself to an American representative of her fears for her children. Evil examples existed around the world, she admitted, but "nowhere are they concentrated in such a narrow territory as in a camp." The walls of her family's cubicle were of cardboard: "When the husband and wife in the next room quarrel one can hear very bad words and often blows at the wife and mother." Next day, the children "play the same quarrel in the corridor or out of doors." When a new woman came to live with two men across the hall, the children were full of questions, even more so after police took the woman away. At another time they saw a man stab another to death in nearby woods.

The DP mother asked, "Is it right for growing children to see such things?"[44]

In addition to attempting to combat the camp's bad influences through a school system and a multiplicity of clubs and activities, many camps created a juvenile court or made special provision for handling child offenders. A teacher who served on the children's court at Scheinfeld camp described the court's concern over keeping children out of the German judicial system, reputed to be extremely harsh on child offenders. Some cases involved children who had merely stolen apples or cherries from nearby orchards.

Juvenile court penalties in the camps were most often earlier curfews for the young offenders. The worst Scheinfeld case in the 1946–49 period occurred when a boy let the water out of an artificial pond used for raising fish. It was obviously a serious matter—it meant monetary loss to the fishery—and it led to lengthy discussion among the members of the court before they gave their order:

Services for children. Church played a crucial role for DP children as well as adults, and the connections between church and school were usually close in the camps. These Latvian young people attended Sunday children's service at Valka camp at Nürnberg. *(Lutheran World Federation photo.)*

the boy had to clean the camp's streets and sidewalks and help with general camp cleanup for three weeks.[45]

From such courts, and schools, and adult concern, the displaced children of Europe emerged from the physical and spiritual ruins of the Continent to make their way with new strength into the postwar world. As they did so they saw that adults were on the same trek and were finding some of the same solutions.

5
CAMPS BECOME COMMUNITIES

Now, of course, the people have been in camps for many months
(up to 19 months), and are deteriorating like anyone else who
remains in a camp for a long period without work. They recognize this, and the better ones among them constantly seek work
for their people and escape from this unhappy continent.
        —Letter from American Quaker, working in
        German DP camp, late 1946.

It happened every spring, as the blossoms and shoots of new
growth spread over postwar Europe, and again when the yellows
and browns of harvest time mingled with the ripeness of late summer and autumn. Through the gate of a displaced persons camp in
Germany walked an old man, an Estonian. He made his way to the
edge of a nearby farmer's field and stood watching the tilling of the
soil in the spring, the sowing; and again in the fall he hovered
nearby as the German farmer gathered in the crops. His vigil was
noticed by others in the camp, who could understand. The camp
newspaper reported that this old man who passed his days following the farmers' fieldwork went "always with the feeling, 'What are
the farmers doing now at home? How does my own field look
now?' "[1]

Others in the camp could understand the old man's actions because they knew his heart, knew the sense of being in a mistaken
place, part of some enormous error. For the jubilation of war's end
was giving way to the hopelessness of being displaced. "We knew
that after a war they have a peace conference and then everyone
goes home," a Lithuanian woman recalled. "But we finally came to
realize that we were not going to be going home." Many came to
that conclusion as month followed month in the camps in late 1945,
and a sense of futility began to drift like the fogs of European winter
over the scattered, huddled collections of DPs who remained.[2]

Visitors who expected to find enthusiasm continuing among these recently liberated peoples were shocked. Earl Harrison toured DP camps in late 1945 and met widespread apathy; residents of Mauthasen camp near Linz were "dazed and hopeless," he reported, "like prisoners whose spirits have been completely broken."[3] A British psychologist found them listless, and since all decisions over their lives were being made by others, many "remained in their barracks expecting UNRRA to provide for them . . . and unwilling to decide anything for themselves or to take responsibilities which could only make their situation more exasperating." An American visitor in 1947 lamented the pauperization that had left many DPs quivering in fear of antagonizing the outsiders who brought aid. Many former DPs who look back on those months remember being dispirited. Most of the camp inhabitants sat before the barracks and talked, endlessly talked, of the hopelessness of their situation.[4]

Part of this was simply the continuing impact of the war years. Many refugees had experienced the horrors of bombings, concentration camps, and treks, and were still psychologically reeling months afterward. One camp leader admitted that the war "often left them in a state that bordered on the animal." The UNRRA warned its new workers that because of the DPs' experiences they "are unbelievably acquisitive and possessive. They dread being parted from their belongings" and were to be moved only in the company of their possessions.[5]

And so the displaced persons struggled to find a private corner just for themselves in the spaces cordoned off by walls made of blankets. Some showed signs of fantasy such as writing letters to unknown persons; many quit smiling. Aggressive behavior became more common than before the war, and DPs showed a deep-seated distrust and suspicion of officialdom, especially when undergoing screenings or other investigations. A former Lutheran World Federation worker thought back on the era and observed that the behavior of DPs "was a strange thing, that one could not predict—because the same conditions would evoke a sort of transcendence in some people, making them even more glowingly aware of human values, and would bestialize others." Another veteran of the DP era, an American Friends Service Committee staff member, called it "a terrible uprooting. . . . How do you handle the problem of identity when all your familiar guides are missing?"[6]

Most ex-DPs interviewed agreed that camp life was hardest on the older workers with family responsibilities—those in their forties and fifties—while those under thirty (and especially under twenty-five) seemed most likely to accept the experience as an exciting challenge. The elderly, on the other hand, did not count on beginning new occupations elsewhere, so their sense of bewilderment over supporting a family was usually not great. "They sat around and talked about old times." The middle-aged DPs were generally those most given to despair, especially when their stay in the camp stretched beyond a year or two with no end in sight.[7]

And there was no end in sight in late 1945 and 1946.

The DPs followed many paths in attempting to escape the aimlessness, the hopelessness, of their lives. These ranged from fleeing, drowning their cares in drink, or embracing religion, to throwing themselves into work—any work. Many responded with a burst of creative energy aimed at filling their day-to-day lives with a wide variety of camp activities; others used the months of DP life to gain an education; others sat and cursed their plight.

A former Slovenian DP recalled his decision to escape. The camps he knew in Italy were "dehumanizing," he said. "You ceased to be a person, and became a number." When his number was posted on the camp announcement board he reported for a medical exam. "We got there in the morning, took our clothes off, and waited until noon. Then a nurse told us the doctor wouldn't come until the afternoon, so we put our clothes on and got lunch. In the afternoon the doctor opened the door, and asked, 'Are you all healthy?'—and signed the forms." The DP could take it no longer. In early December 1945 he put an extra shirt and tie into a small bag with a few books and walked out of the camp, heading for Milan where a relative lived. His DP camp experience was finished.[8]

Many others, watching listlessness spread among the camp populations, made this decision also. Authorities were thrown into a quandary about helping these "free-livers" who were technically DPs but who were not present in the camps to receive aid or announcements.

Alcohol provided another escape. At a temporary Polish camp on the island of Sylt, westward off the Schleswig-Holstein coast, only a hundred men worked in a camp population of one thousand. The remainder drank and played cards, hour after hour, day after day. Schleissheim camp's single men were criticized by a camp resident for wanting to "forget their sorrows in alcohol." Their only friends were fellow drinkers, she said, and they were "a sad sight in the camp streets," trying "to hide their wretchedness behind boasting and bragging."[9]

Much of the alcohol was purchased in nearby towns, but signifi-

Church in the open. DPs turned to religion as soon as they began to come together in the first days after the war, holding services everywhere, from dusty fields to dimly lit basements. Poles at Hanau constructed a Roman Catholic church in a former Wehrmacht cavalry stable. The overflow crowd was led in this service by a priest who had spent three and a half years in Dachau. *(UNRRA photo.)*

cant amounts were brewed or distilled on camp premises. At Wildflecken the approach of Christmas in late 1945 brought a vast increase in the numbers of schnapps stills run by Polish DPs, despite efforts of camp police to confiscate the copper coils. The stills ranged from large "corporation size" affairs to small devices operated in family cubicles. A special hospital ward was finally required to accommodate victims of Wildflecken's exploding homemade stills. Camp officials appear to have had little success in stopping these efforts, in any camp, among any national group. A Pole described his wedding in a German DP camp in 1946: "As a teacher, I knew some of the UNRRA people, and my fiancée was a beautician and so knew some camp officials. So we invited them. We had had some Polish vodka made for the wedding, using raisins, sugar, or grain. A few liters only. We served the vodka at our wedding. 'Where did you get that vodka?' they asked."[10]

The twin disasters of helplessness and hopelessness propelled others into a new-found concern for religion, and churches sprouted rapidly—in old barns and barracks, in former SS meeting halls, in schoolhouses. Materials for church construction were picked from rubble heaps and lovingly transformed by DP artisans. Latvians at a camp in Schleswig-Holstein built a chapel from discarded ammunition cases; when forced to shift to a different locale they

Creating a church from scraps. Ukrainian Orthodox DPs at Hersfeld, Germany, changed an abandoned barn into a chapel by cleaning, painting, and decorating it during one busy week. A nineteen-year-old artist did the paintings; scrap materials and tin cans provided materials for the candelabra, table, and altar, and the candles were dipped by hand. The "stained glass" window depicting Christ, behind the altar, was made by painting the window a frosty white and stretching a painted piece of gauze over the frame. *(UNRRA photo.)*

reconstructed the chapel in a garage. At another camp a half-timbered concrete structure that formerly served as a Wehrmacht training chamber for troops in gas masks became a church complete with pews and a small organ. A Lithuanian priest looked back on the religious rebirth that spread through the camps and observed that many of the DPs "were aware of a cosmic disaster." Their hopes had soared—now their dreams of an independent homeland were crushed. There was no new homeland in sight. When the priest, Father Vytautas Bagdanavičius, launched a Lithuanian DP Catholic newspaper, he named it *Naujasu Gyvenimas* (The new life), and its circulation shot up to twelve thousand.[11]

While some outsiders sought to serve the camps' religious needs, most of the DPs' spiritual leaders arose from among their own people. And these churches became rallying points for national identity. The Estonian Lutheran bishop J. Kopp argued that only a refugee could understand a refugee's troubles: "A clergyman speaking a foreign language not sufficiently a refugee, essentially ignorant of the refugee's sufferings, is hardly able to find a way to a refugee's, least of all to a young person's heart. They will forever remain strangers." This point was emphasized by a Catholic worker in the Polish camps who noted that "the priests I met there had all been deported during the war, all were graduates of Dachau, all had been tortured." The result was that "the people respected them, for what the people had suffered, they had suffered also." Fully 80 percent of Ukranian Catholic priests made it out to the West, one scholar has estimated, and many of these had worked among their countrymen during the war in forced-labor camps in Germany. In the DP camps they soon had 120 parishes, and a 1949 Vatican investigation found that three-fourths of the Ukrainian Catholic DPs regularly attended mass on Sundays.[12] Soon the camps were creating their own theological centers to train religious leaders, ranging from the Jewish yeshiva at the Landsberg camp to the Slovenian Catholic seminary at Praglia, Italy, which was moved to Argentina in 1948.

An American Lutheran worker got a glimpse of the importance of DP churches in providing unity and continuity when he attended a confirmation service for six children at a small Latvian camp in Hessen.

> From somewhere the girls had gotten long white dresses and the boys had black suits with the bow ties. . . . In the afternoon I visited the room of each confirmand. In every case there was a family celebration going. There was only one room but in each was a long table crowded with relatives and friends. They seemed so grateful for the personal visit, but as I left each room, I was sure I had received much more than I had given.[13]

In one religious rite the presence of the clergy was desperately needed in 1945 and 1946: marriage. The Third Reich had forbidden weddings in the forced-labor camps and concentration camps, but—as one writer has put it—"even the Germans could not prevent the young people from falling in love and waiting impatiently for the day when they might wed." The result was "wholesale weddings" in many camps, often with the couples' children standing by. The Belsen DP camp recorded twenty weddings a day after the initial months, and one American worker there said, "I was invited to attend more weddings than ever before in all my life." But it was more than simply catching up for wartime dislocation, for refugees were often lonely, torn from their family members, and they felt isolated. "People would meet, and five minutes later would ask, 'Are you married?'" one DP recalled.[14]

There was nothing unusual, therefore, when one day in 1946 a Polish priest with a delegation of Polish men approached Ben Kaplan, head of the UNRRA warehouse at Hanau, seeking white

cloth for brides' dresses and dark cloth for grooms' outfits—enough
for forty couples. "I had just received a shipment of white cloth, so
I gave that for the brides," Kaplan said. "But we had no dark cloth
for the men." The wedding day arrived, with Kaplan serving as best
man for all forty couples. The brides showed up in their white finery,
and the grooms suddenly appeared in handsome suits and high
hats. Curious, Kaplan learned that the DPs had "cleaned out the
German families in the area—they had taken the dress outfit that
each adult German man kept for special occasions." Another
American who attended several mass DP weddings reported that
even under austere camp conditions traditional rites were followed
faithfully. At one such event in a Polish camp the wedding party
refused to permit some visiting Americans to leave without attending the reception.

> To the strains of a wedding march played by a Polish orchestra, the
> guests were solemnly escorted inside the hall. The bride and groom
> welcomed the Americans with champagne, Polish sausage and wed-
> ding cake, which had somehow been conjured up from somewhere.
> No time was lost by the bridesmaids who promptly invited our
> officers to join in the dancing.
> The party finally broke up at five o'clock in the morning. . . . For a
> week all conversation revolved about Polish wedding customs. . . .
> Officers and men alike grew to like these victims of fate who had gone
> through hell in the past few years but who refused to talk about their
> sorrows and presented a cheerful face to the world.[15]

And if the seasons of life were commemorated by the DP church
and temple—upon birth, reaching adulthood, marriage, and death—
it was true as well that the seasons of the year were marked by
religious rites. Whether Passover in the Jewish camps or Christmas
among the Serbians, religious festivals helped provide a link with
tradition for uprooted people. An outpouring of food from the
outside world sometimes helped make such days special indeed, as
when four hundred individual CARE packages and eight hundred
ten-in-one CARE packages arrived to help Ukrainians celebrate
their Easter in the Austrian camps in 1948.[16]

But one thing was missing. No one could avoid noticing the
difference between celebrating a religious feast in a camp and in
one's native village. A Ukrainian woman recalled Easter in her
camp near Hamburg, where the traditional *paska* bread was made,
and people gathered at midnight in the Eastern Rite Catholic
Church for the priest's blessing. Then there was the walk home
before sunrise and the return to church for the 9:00 A.M. service,

followed by a large family dinner extending through the afternoon and evening.

This was a bit of home, a bit of the old life, for each of these events in camp closely followed Ukrainian tradition. But there were limits to how far tradition could be carried. On the Sunday following Easter back home in the village, she explained, everyone would walk to the cemetery, carrying a lunch of sweet wine, eggs, and cake, where they would spend the rest of the afternoon among the graves of their ancestors. This portion of the Easter tradition could not be followed in the camp. Trying to carry on the old ways, some of the Ukrainian DPs made the traditional cake on the Sunday after Easter, gave out decorated eggs, and then walked back to church. "But it was not the same," the Ukrainian woman recalled wistfully.[17]

Work filled out the days for other DPs—a fortunate few in the early months, whose numbers expanded as the UNRRA and IRO developed elaborate camp administrations needing large staffs, and as the German, Austrian, and Italian economies began to improve. Italy, however, forbade DP employment in the civilian economy.

"My salary is too small to deserve mentioning," a Slovenian refugee in Austria wrote, "yet I prefer hard work to the killing monotony of camp idleness." For most, however, "killing monotony" was the rule in the camps of 1945 and 1946, when DP unemployment of 90 percent was common. The UNRRA reported that morale was "not high" at five camps centered on Luisenberg in May 1946 "because of lack of occupation for population." Such reports were legion in those months.

The UNRRA increasingly hired DPs to fill out its camp staffs, recognizing that small UNRRA teams could not run camps of several thousand people and that more employment would improve camp spirit. DPs soon were on the payroll as internal police, firemen, and janitors, as well as teachers in camp schools and doctors and nurses in camp hospitals and infirmaries. DP workers also came to be relied upon for camp construction projects and secretarial help.[18]

Skilled workers began to come forward on their own, and in addition to schools and day care centers every camp soon had its shoemaker shop, its tailors and dressmakers, its hairdressers. Woodworkers, metalworkers, and jewelers created picture frames, scrollwork, and religious artifacts such as monstrances, chalices, and menorahs. DPs frequently found additional opportunities for employment outside the camps, usually with the harvest, occasionally in small shops or factories. By mid-1947 some 40,000 DPs were

A time of waiting. For most adult DPs, sitting and waiting were unavoidable for much of the era. Work was scarce, especially in the first years. Considering their situation temporary, they held back from putting down roots, but for many months chances to emigrate seemed nonexistant. Many former DPs today recall such scenes as this one at the Weilheim camp with some bitterness—the endless talk, the hopelessness, amid rabbit hutches and hanging clothes. *(American Friends Service Committee photo.)*

employed in U.S. Army labor-service companies. Employment inside and outside the camps was opening up then, and the UNRRA's official history claimed that 70 percent of the DP labor force in Germany was employed. The new IRO's statistics showed 242,406 DPs employed by 30 September 1947; major categories included 140,666 in camp, hospital, and central IRO administration; 2,942 with IRO-military projects inside the camps; 31,282 employed by the military outside the camps; 32,520 working for private employers outside the camps; and 28,786 receiving vocational training.[19]

Their pay was often in cigarettes. For postwar Europe was a cigarette economy, where DP schoolteachers were paid up to five packs a week, workers in the Hanau UNRRA warehouse got up to eight, and the Polish Government in Exile provided its camp representatives a munificent two cartons per week. With the German, Austrian, and Italian economies shattered, cigarettes became a focus of desire. The universal cry was "Zigaretten!"—mainly for

American brands, which were included both in army rations and in the thousands of prisoner of war cartons piled in military warehouses. But French, British, and other brands were accepted without question, for they all provided an alternative to smokes made of dried rhubarb leaves and other ersatz combustibles of wartime. And so armies of children searched the streets for cigarette butts; waiters collected their patrons' still-smoking discards; and everyone seemed prepared to pounce on the soldier's tossed "cig." A group of enterprising Serbians from a camp in Italy traveled to Sicily and acquired an entire truckload of tobacco leaves, which they then rolled into cigarettes and became rich beyond dreams. (But a disgruntled Slovenian charged that they mixed British tea leaves with the tobacco, carefully leaving pure tobacco at each end. With such wealth at stake, the temptation remained great to cut the tobacco with other substances.)[20]

An editor of the German newspaper *Frankenpost* (Hof) admitted that he had a Jekyll-and-Hyde life, for each evening he changed into old clothes and emerged into the streets to collect discarded cigarette butts. He especially prefered scavenging along the U.S. Army's through streets, "because frequently butts of very respectable length fly out of their automobiles and, under favorable circumstances, may lie in the gutter for up to 15 or 20 seconds." Back at home, the hour of triumph came when his dinner guest rolled a cigarette from the cleaned, loosened tobacco, "the origin of which he does not recognize," and then exulted as the first smoke rose to the ceiling, " 'Ah! How delicious!' and [added] as an afterthought, not without envy: 'Of course, if one has connections such as you have . . . !' "[21]

Cigarettes served "as well as gold ever did as a base for the economy," a UNRRA staff member recalled, noting that the price of a carton of American cigarettes rose to $165 in Berlin at one time "and at its lowest was sixty dollars." Tales were rife of what cigarettes would buy. A Polish DP purchased a German radio for twenty-five packs of cigarettes; Russian soldiers charged one pack of cigarettes per DP illegally entering Berlin; a Lithuanian camp teacher traveled by train from Regensburg in southern Germany all the way to Hamburg in the north for payment of a single pack. At a time when—as one German said—the "dream of all dreams was to have a bicycle!", the standard swap for a bicycle in Brunswick was six hundred cigarettes. When voluntary agency workers were unable to provide money to DPs, they sometimes could provide cigarettes instead, which were "worth their weight in gold," a Canadian reported.[22]

Those who did not smoke were in a buyer's market, for everyone cozied up to them in hopes of obtaining their unused rations. As Red Cross and CARE packages began to arrive in the camps, cigarettes as well as coffee powder and chocolates were available for trade, and a nonsmoking Hungarian DP couple exchanged their weekly two packs of cigarettes with a German farmer for a sack of potatoes, meat, and bread.[23]

Trading of cigarettes often took place in the *Schwarzmarkt,* the black market that mushroomed out of the shortages and governmental controls of Occupation. A Ukrainian DP recalled that "food was number one" in his camp's black market, with forays into the countryside to illegally barter with German farmers. The acquisition of bread, sugar, flour, vegetables, fruit, and similar items helped enrich the dismal diet of the camps. When investigations were conducted into black market activity at the Landsberg, Feldafing, and Ainring DP camps, the extent of illegal trade was discovered to be enormous. "Blankets issued to the refugees, food from their kitchens and articles of clothing . . . all find their way into the illicit trade," the *New York Times* reported in January 1946. Overcoats were going for a thousand marks and one refugee paid thirty thousand marks to a German for an automobile. Ainring even had its own illegal money exchange, at which German marks were exchanged for American dollars and British pounds. Hohenfels, a Polish camp, ran its "trade center" in a ravine at the camp each Saturday, where cigarettes from DPs' Red Cross packages were especially popular with the Germans, who were rationed to forty cigarettes each six weeks (twenty cigarettes for women).[24]

Efforts to thwart the illegal trading made little headway on a Continent where millions were participating in it—most notably the occupying troops. High-ranking Allied officers seeking vast riches were involved, as well as displaced persons trying to garner enough food for a satisfactory diet. UNRRA authorities were sensitive to the continuing complaints that DPs controlled the black market, and in November 1946 the organization's director ordered drastic steps to suppress DP black-marketing: "Any person trafficking in goods or currency in the black market—seller as well as buyer—shall immediately lose his status as a displaced person and be instantly expelled from our camps." Nine days later a raid on the Polish DP camp at Bamberg netted more than fifty thousand dollars worth of narcotics, military ammunition, and supplies; eighty-two persons were arrested. But some DPs recall only minor penalties for those caught trading illegally. One Ukrainian selling a pack of cigarettes in Hamburg was accosted by a policeman who searched him, hauled him to the police station for questioning—and then let him go.[25]

The DPs' busy involvement in the cigarette economy and the *Schwarzmarkt* gave evidence of their continuing movement away from the sloth and fear of the early months in the camps. "From the position of disinterested onlookers," the Reggio camp director noted, "they went on to take part in the camp activities," showing new pride in their appearance and asking new questions about their own futures. They soon were demonstrating that democracy could thrive even amid the rubble of war.[26]

Self-government was the order of the day across the occupied zones. Both the military and the UNRRA pushed democratic government among DPs from the beginning. SHAEF ordered that DPs "should be encouraged to organize themselves as much as is administratively possible," while the UNRRA stressed camp democracy on ideological grounds, "as a very practical *modus operandi*," and because experience showed it was best in such conditions.

Soon camps were being largely run by elected camp committees, and in many cases UNRRA leaders were only nominally in charge. The camp committee, sometimes including religious leaders, spoke for the camp's DPs in dealings with the UNRRA and the military and organized a host of activities within the camps.[27]

Refugees also elected their own judges, and a court system became a prominent camp feature. The UNRRA's official history would later admit that "the legality of this court was questionable, but the UNRRA officials were generally wise enough not to raise that question." Fear of the judiciary "outside the gates"—whether military or German, Austrian, or Italian—motivated many of the DPs as they rushed to set up their alternative system. In Italy, local police were frequently flexible and could be reasoned with by camp officials, but the national *carabinieri* were unbending on any infraction. A Polish DP leader in the French Zone of Germany said his people feared the French occupation police. "I saw a French cell once, after the interrogation of a DP. It was full of blood," he recalled with a shudder. The military ran penal farms for refugees convicted of serious crimes.[28]

Penalties varied in the camp courts. Arnold F. Pikre, an Estonian who was president of the court in the Baltic camp at Würzburg, recalled the judges' dilemmas in coming up with penalties for people who had little in worldly goods and whose lives had already been marked by forcible detention. Fights and drunkenness were common causes for arrest, and a prohibition on cigarette use a frequent penalty. One case Pikre recalled involved a DP woman caught stealing: a public hearing was held, she was convicted, and the court ordered her to clean the camp's toilets for a month, under guard.[29]

A Ukrainian described the visit of German police to his camp, when he and several other children were apprehended for stealing apples from a nearby farm. The boys had been spotted in the tree. The Germans, however, turned their young charges over to the camp court, which then held a public trial that resulted in a "verbal dressing down" for the offenders. The strongest penalty was suggested in the court's final warning: "If you want to emigrate, you can't have a criminal record." Parents used this threat over and over to keep their offspring in line.[30]

Much of the challenge facing camp committees, however was not to repress but to channel DP activity. Often little was needed to launch an enterprise beyond announcing a time and place for those with a specified interest. The committee at Reggio put on several dances, but then a group of DPs decided to branch out on their own:

> There was one large room that the soldiers had used for storage. Spontaneously, one night in early September, several of the young men and women went to this room and cleaned it. Then several musical instruments were produced: an accordion, a violin, and a balalaika; and a dance started. From this night forward dances were held and it was possible to see anything being performed from formal ballroom dancing to the "kosachok" and the "csardas."[31]

By a similar process sports grew to occupy the most prominent position among camp activities, drawing in everyone from young children through adults. Even chess tables were soon set up. Large camps usually had football (soccer), basketball, volleyball, boxing, swimming, track, and gymnastics, with DP leagues in operation and occasional contests scheduled against non-DP clubs or military units. At Leipheim the refugees built their own swimming pool. Baltic groups had their annual "Baltic Olympics," involving basketball, soccer, and track; over 750 Balts participated in the twenty-five events in the 1949 games at Funk Kaserne in Munich. A UNRRA report on the ethnically-mixed camps of Luisenberg, Windeby, Craigie, Estonia, and Noor in the spring of 1946 revealed something of both the diversity and the importance of sports in DP life:

> Greatest development has been in the sport field . . . 80 people at

Lithuanian camp are participating regularly in supervised sports; there is a program for men, women, and children at Estonia [camp], and the school-children from all Baltic camps have gymnastics all together twice a week in the gymnasium in the town. DPs are also using sport field in the town 4 afternoons weekly and tennis courts twice weekly. The Poles have been playing football with four teams (including one British) in the area and always they have been winners. A big sport festival for all DPs arranged with collaboration of the YMCA."[32]

One segment in each camp downplayed athletics, however. These DPs led their fellow refugees into a broad spectrum of activities and events that fit loosely into the category of "intellectual." Generally university graduates, often with previous careers in teaching, writing, law, or the performing arts, they transformed camp life and helped replace despair with creativity.

Some camps were well off in this regard. A Lithuanian who toured thirty of his countrymen's camps in September 1945 reported that intellectuals were the most numerous classification. Some 75 percent of the university, high school, and grade school teachers had fled Lithuania, he reported, as well as 80 percent of the doctors and "a large part of those who worked directly to augment our cultural heritage: writers, painters, musicians, artists, etc." Similarly, an American working in the Pfarrkirchen/Eggenfelden camp wrote home that among the camp's Ukrainian population it "seemed almost as though every second man was a 'pan magister' with a degree in engineering or law."[33]

Newspapers were usually the next endeavor of this group after the camp schools had been organized. At Spittal in Austria the Slovenian newspaper *Novice* (News) was launched in mimeographed form the second week after refugees arrived; it soon grew to three and ultimately, four pages daily. For two or three hours before it came out on Thursdays a line of customers formed, for on that day a weekly column of news from Yugoslavia appeared, based on accounts of newly arrived refugees. Scheinfeld's two-page daily, also mimeographed at the outset, featured international news compiled by a resident who sat listening to the radio much of the day, translating items into Lithuanian. Most camp newspapers also obtained information from nearby German, Austrian, or Italian journals and from such Occupation newspapers as *Stars and Stripes*.[34]

There was variety in this camp press, in form and subject matter. Latvian refugees in Sweden published two newspapers in the early

months and also a literary monthly, while the Lithuanian camp at
Seedorf offered *Daily Information,* which contained UNRRA and
camp announcements; a literary magazine named *Passes;* a satirical review, *Kirvarpa;* and poetry collections. The biweekly *Nizoz*
(The Spark), a Hebrew-language newspaper, originated in
Lithuania, went underground with the Resistance during the German occupation, and re-emerged with Jewish DPs in Munich after
the war. Many camps also had "wall newspapers," initially for
UNRRA announcements but soon presenting foreign news, camp
news, cartoons, and photos. Other camps ran a form of "radio
station," which broadcast only over the public address system. The
Landsberger Lager-Caytung, a semiweekly newspaper that circulated throughout the American Zone's Jewish camps as well as
among the five thousand DPs in Landsberg, sometimes ran to forty-
eight pages:

> It carries international, Palestinian, American, local, and DP news, of
> both general and specifically Jewish reference. It includes political
> commentaries, literary pieces, historical articles on the war period,
> pictures of camp life, essays on health and hygiene, and a page of
> "seeking kin" items. Except for a page in Hebrew covering Zionist
> and Palestinian matters, it is written in Yiddish.[35]

Newsprint scarcity rather than government censorship remained
the major problem faced by DP newspapers once they passed the
incubation stage. Due to the emphasis on democracy, or perhaps
because of a lack of personnel, the Occupation, UNRRA, and IRO
authorities did little to control newspaper content outside of occasional repatriation controversies. According to Alfons Hering, who
became co-editor of *Nowiny Obozowe* in the Polish camp at Land-
stuhl, "There was not prior censorship, but we had to tell the
UNRRA and the French what was in the newspaper. They never
said anything about the content." Especially among the large but
scattered Polish group, newspapers provided a way to spread news
that countered the Communist arguments usually carried in official
publications.[36]

The arts received much attention. Theatrical activity proceeded
on two levels in the camps: construction of auditoriums, which
could be used for a variety of purposes, and presentation of dramatic works by DP actors and actresses. At Hanau the Lithuanians
took the lead, aided by one of their architects, in changing the
Germans' riding school into a theater with seating for three thousand. At its grand opening in 1946 it featured violinists, a ballet, and

other performers drawn from the ranks of the Baltic DPs. A huge Wehrmacht parade hall became the theater in the Landsberg camp; workers used lumber from a demolished cavalry stable to make necessary alterations. Alexander Squadrilli, who held several top UNRRA and U.S. government positions in Europe, admitted he was somewhat overwhelmed by these cultural developments. "There was an invitation on my desk every week to a play, a ballet, a show, even banquets," he recalled.[37]

Many intellectuals worked to extend the camp school systems into adult ranks. "Folk universities" sprang up, and there was a vast growth of vocational training, with an eye to eventual employment abroad. A visitor to the Hanau camp in 1947 found that discarded radio parts were being made into new sets, a ceramic shop was in operation, and ladies' hats were being fashioned from rejected cloth. There was, he found, "no idleness at the camp. Everyone who had a trade is now teaching apprentices. In unheated sheds and former warehouses mechanics, carpenters, electricians and tailors are showing beginners how to help produce the goods and equipment needed by the community."[38]

At the peak of the educational pyramid were the DP universities, inaugurated by dedicated refugee scholars against great odds. There were major difficulties in acquiring equipment, books, and official permissions—difficulties, in fact, in every aspect except winning the enthusiastic support of refugee students and teachers. ("They were the best students I have ever had in my long life as a university teacher," concluded Professor B. I. Balinsky, who taught in the DP university at Munich. "Their enthusiasm and application were exemplary.")[39]

Refugees in the eighteen-to-twenty-five age group found life in the camps unproductive if their goal was to move into the professions or any career requiring specialized education. "We wanted to use this time to study," a DP emphasized, and soon the pressures mounted—on military authorities, on the UNRRA, on national universities—to open the doors of higher education to refugees.

Miro Kamnik (not his real name) was a young Slovenian student at the time. He had escaped into Austria and then traveled into Italy. In February 1946 he arrived at the University of Bologna, where the UNRRA was operating a hostel for the DPs attending the university. Some ninety Slovenians were there, as well as thirty Lithuanians, thirty Albanians, and smaller numbers of Latvians, Rumanians, Hungarians, Poles, and Serbians.

One early problem was documentation: What university would

take a student who could produce no records of his previous schooling? "Luckily," Kamnik said, "there was at the University of Bologna a professor who had been teaching at the University of Ljubljana during the Italian occupation." He helped many students, including Kamnik, by confirming to the Bolognese university administration their earlier studies at Ljubljana.

The hostel was run like a small, compact DP camp. The British and the UNRRA (later the IRO) provided food, and administration was handled by an English captain who was assisted by an American UNRRA worker. (The American woman was much loved, but lost her job with the UNRRA after she used "welfare" funds to help the DP students pay their tuition at the university. That aid was crucial, Kamnik said.)[40]

Italy only reluctantly opened the doors of its universities to DPs. DP students petitioned for entrance, and after intervention by the British, the Jesuits, and even Pope Pius XII, the universities began admitting refugees. The University of Graz in Austria also allowed DPs to register.[41]

Germany's western zones presented a more varied picture of refugee university life. Occupation authorities required German universities to reserve 10 percent of their enrollment for DPs, and these quotas were apparently filled. By late 1945 a Lithuanian publication was advising college-age DPs to take note of new openings: Marburg "already accepts application for admission to the Medical Faculty," and at Erlangen "dormitories are already provided for Lithuanian students." By May 1946 the DP enrollment in German universities neared 4,000 in the American Zone, 600 in the British Zone with 670 additional slots ready, and 600 in the French Zone. Being admitted to a German university did not mean a higher standard of living, however, for often the accommodations were primitive. Visvaldis Janavs, who was a Lativan medical student at Kiel, recalled that "the days went fast and we had some rather happy times—something to do, even if sometimes the ink in the inkstands froze, the bread was many times eaten dry, and it was not easy to steal firewood from German forests in the dark, cold, and snowy winter nights."[42]

Such conditions did not reduce the demand for education among DPs, and soon they took another bold step: they formed their own universities, research centers, and religious training institutions.

Ukrainians, in effect, carried two of their universities with them into exile. Earlier refugees had founded the Ukrainian University of Vienna in 1921, during the exodus from the Bolshevik Revolution. This institution was soon transferred to Prague, Czechoslovakia, and renamed the Free Ukrainian University. It was joined there by the Ukrainian Technical-Agricultural Institute of Podebrady, serving mainly Ukrainians in exile. With the upheaval of World War II these schools were moved again, following their students and professors into Germany. The Free Ukrainian University was renewed in Augsburg in the fall of 1946 and transferred the following year to Munich, which became the center of Ukrainian intellectual life in the German diaspora. The Technical-Agricultural Institute was moved there, joined by the Ukrainian Higher School of Economics as well as Orthodox and Catholic seminaries. The Ukrainian Free Academy of Sciences and the Shevchenko Scientific Society began publishing scholarly research books and journals in Munich.[43]

In late 1945 other stirrings were noted among DP intellectuals. Several former professors worked with the UNRRA in Munich to put together a new institution, known as the "UNRRA University." Housed in the old Deutsches Museum, which had been badly damaged, its first rector was Professor Mitinsky, a Russian from the University of Prague who taught engineering. Faculties were organized in 1946 in mechanical and civil engineering, natural sciences, economics, law, and medicine. Lectures were in German, the only language widely understood by the diverse student population. A touring American journalist called the school "a bright spot of color in a drab picture," and noted that the young DPs who "repaired the shattered walls" had no books but mimeographed their professors' lectures and helped acquire scientific apparatus.[44]

The latter activity pointed to one of the UNRRA University's major stumbling blocks, as described in a reminiscence by Professor B. I. Balinsky, a Ukrainian who chaired the Department of Histology and Embryology:

> It was my task to give the lecture course and to organize practicals for the students. For practicals I needed microscopes. To get these I made two trips, as head of a small delegation, to Frankfurt, to obtain a requisition order from the American Occupation authorities, and then to the Leitz factory in Wetzlar to collect the microscopes. I was successful, and was thus able to provide for my students both a practical as well as a lecture course.

Professor Balinsky had less success in obtaining materials from the University of Munich, then shut down. A personal appeal to the anatomy department there, for use of its vacant anatomical theater for dissections, met only rebuff.[45]

Despite problems, in 1946 the enrollment of DP students hit

DP university. One of the experiments in higher education in the DP era was creation of the UNRRA University in Munich in 1946. These students are shown working in the university's chemistry laboratory. DP students also studied in regular German, Austrian, and Italian universities. *(UNRRA photo.).*

1,400 (Ukrainians, Latvians, and Poles constituted the largest bloc) and both students and professors worked for the school's success as a permanent or semipermanent institution. But, as Professor Balinsky recalled and UNRRA documents emphasized, "While the internal life of the University proceeded very satisfactorily, its general status remained very precarious."

One major reason was its problem with military authorities. The university never obtained the clear backing of any portion of the American occupation establishment, and therefore no office was ready to provide support in crucial stages. Another problem grew out of conflicts within the UNRRA over the university's status. A Madame Gaszinska, welfare director of UNRRA Team 108, was its most vociferous supporter, even to the extent of alienating others. What was missing, however, was academic and administrative leadership from other areas of UNRRA. The UNRRA "obviously did not know what to do with the University in the long run," Professor Balinsky explained.[46]

And then, one day, it was over. The finish came when the Christmas–New Year's holiday had ended, just as the new term was

The DP as student. Baltic DPs, with aid from UNRRA, the Lutheran World Federation, and other groups, set up their own university at Hamburg, which was later moved to Pinneberg and renamed the DP Study Center. These students were part of a drawing class. *(Lutheran World Federation photo.)*

scheduled to begin in early 1947. Arriving one Monday morning, students and staff found the doors locked and a cordon of UNRRA guards blocking the way. A professor who managed to gain entry found "a chaos of destruction," Professor Balinsky recalled. "Cupboards which had been locked were broken open, and all the equipment which we had accumulated in our laboratories was removed."

The UNRRA gave out its official reason for the closing in the following month's *UNRRA Team News.* The UNRRA University was closed "as part of the Munich community's fuel conservation program," the newspaper stated. The U.S. Army found the Deutsches Museum heating plant too costly to operate, and UNRRA leaders also felt the "emergency educational institute . . . now has served its purpose." Other evidence, however, pointed to official opposition to anything that encouraged the DPs to remain in Germany.[47]

To the north, in the British Zone, another group of refugee scholars also dreamed of forming their own university. Even before the war had ended, Lithuanian teachers who had fled into Germany approached Third Reich officials on the question but were rebuked.

After V-E Day they tried again, this time with occupation authorities, as did a number of Latvian scholars. The British finally indicated they would look favorably on a joint Baltic camp and university in their zone.

In the months before the new university's opening on 14 March 1946, DP scholars from the three Baltic countries put together plans for eight faculties (medicine, chemistry, construction engineering, agronomy, mechanical engineering, natural sciences–mathematics, philology, and law), while students and UNRRA team members worked to acquire facilities and equipment. Briefly housed in the giant Deutscher Ring insurance headquarters in Hamburg, which held hundreds of DPs, the project was moved to the Museum für Hamburger Geschichte (Museum for Hamburg history), a badly bombed structure into which shopkeepers were already moving.[48]

"Scrounging" became the order of the day—in the best camp tradition—as DPs and UNRRA leaders under an American, Dr. Robert C. Riggle, set about to locate everything from nails to glass to chairs in the Hamburg area. Physics laboratory equipment, looted by Germans from the University of Vytaugas in Lithuania, had been traced by refugees and was brought into the new center. German factories and office buildings yielded desks, a secondary school gave up a chemical laboratory, and a herbarium that had been removed to Berlin by a University of Riga professor was later acquired by the new DP institution. As Dr. Riggle admitted, "Our University grew in a period of reckless adventure and we used pirate methods."[49]

As at Munich, status became crucial while the struggling "Baltic University" made its way through the military and UNRRA labyrinth. Minutes of a 31 July 1946 meeting between British military representatives, UNRRA leaders, and Baltic University administrators and student spokesmen reveal uneasiness over the school's name and its claims. One major argument was that "the DP Study Centre could not be regarded as a University with degree conferring powers on account of its emergency character and its limitation with regard to staff and equipment." The school was to be temporary; the German economy could not support such a project.

Students and faculty argued, however, that the level of teaching and student work was equal to that in prewar universities. Why not grant degrees, then? The students were especially concerned about recognition of their work when they transferred to other universities.

But in the end, the ruling was made: the Baltic University would be renamed the "DP University Study Centre," and it would be used mainly for early university career work, preparing students to transfer to established institutions. Nevertheless, enrollment soon topped one thousand.[50]

The DP Study Centre survived, but its road was rocky. In addition to the threats to its existence that came from the UNRRA and occupation hierarchies, hunger was a continuing problem. Sports activities had to be curtailed after an enthusiastic beginning, because "1,500 calories were not sufficient for the extra energy needed." The Lithuanian Red Cross found cases of tuberculosis among the students, all of whom showed weakness from undernourishment. The diet in the Study Centre barracks "is poorer than elsewhere in DP camps," one professor claimed. "During the winter colds, we are obliged to walk quite far, sometimes running to keep the blood in proper circulation when we visit our families in another DP camp."

In early 1947 the British moved the Study Centre from Hamburg to a former Luftwaffe school in Pinneberg, twenty kilometers away. While facilities were better at the new site, the status question was raised anew and the centre's future was brought into question. In June 1947 the faculty appealed to American authorities to transfer the entire institution, with teachers and students, to the United States. This effort came to nothing, however, and the Hamburg DP Study Centre closed on 30 September 1949, ending another attempt to create "an institution of learning in exile."[51]

The fact that these refugee institutions came into being—albeit only briefly—pointed to the crucial role of intellectuals in opening differing pathways within DP life. When a worker for Catholic War Relief Services toured DP centers in 1947, she was shocked at the contrast between camps. From the chaos and shouting of Wildflecken—then almost entirely Polish—she journeyed to the Baltic camps around Hanau. There she was immediately overwhelmed by the wealth of cultural activity: "They made such a good presentation. They would introduce you to this doctor, to that doctor, and there were banks of flowers, and a marvelous display of handiwork, painted wood, embroidery."

She admitted these differences bothered her, until she realized that the Baltic peoples escaped into exile "with a normal complement of the classes"—writers and lawyers as well as farmers and fishermen. The Polish camps, however, contained mainly peasants, workers, and young children, with relatively few professionals and intellectuals. Other observers were struck by this fact, but soon realized that Polish artists and intellectuals—in general, the edu-

cated class—had been active in the Resistance and had been killed
in large numbers. For them, escape to the West had not been an
option. The result was visible in the camp population.[52]

Many of the DP intellectuals threw themselves into political
activity. A worker in a Jewish camp said the conflicts between the
political and religious splinters were "as rough as the inner brawls
of the Nazi party." In some camps opposition offices were stoned
and burned and their flags were torn down. Most struggles were
political ("If you have two Croatians, you have four political parties," a Croatian sighed), but religious splintering appeared as well.
Ukrainians were divided between Catholic and Orthodox, but even
in camps with one religion, such as Judaism, divisions were rife.
Emphasis upon following the letter of the Law became the basis for
sharp religious controversies at Landsberg, a Jewish DP camp.[53]

But political groups fought most of the camp battles. Koppel S.
Pinson, an early worker for The American Jewish Joint Distribution
Committee, known as "Joint," argued that "the tendency in all DP
camps in the beginning was to prevent the development of political
parties in the camps." Newcomers were greeted with a sign at
Reggio: "Kein Politik!" (No politics!). The common front against
fascism that brought unity in wartime crumbled as old party lines
began to reappear. Often these groups sought to control the govern-
ment-in-exile as well as the camp. Ukrainian camps sometimes
presented twelve political parties, vigorously—sometimes
viciously—competing, which included middle-of-the-road democratic, nationalist, socialist, and monarchist groups. In addition to
simply reviving old party loyalties, DP camps provided the first
opportunity that many from the Soviet Union had ever had to live in
a democratic system, and they thrived in it.[54]

But sometimes they thrived too much. Bohdan Panchuk, a Canadian working among Ukrainian DPs, met repeated frustration when
political feuds upset camp events or endangered relations with
occupation authorities. Lysenko DP camp near Hannover, he wrote
in his memoir *Heroes of Their Day,* was "a political hotbed—West
Ukrainians against East Ukrainians, Orthodox against Catholic,
OUN Revolutionaries (OUNr) versus OUN Solidarists (OUNs) and
so on." Sometimes such a group would take over a camp's internal
government, then make the camp a center for its political propaganda. When Panchuk and other agency workers were trying to
urge emigration, some of the political groups called for DPs to stay
put and prepare to somehow "force their way back to their homeland."[55]

While most of the stimulation and organization for DP camp life came from the DPs themselves, an honest account of the era must mention one other important source: the voluntary agencies. These groups sent workers into the camps dispersing a cornucopia of amenities (toothbrushes, soap, cigarettes), equipment (musical instruments, books, volleyballs), instruction (in vocational skills, languages), and, above all, personal attention.

Outside Jewish organizations were generally first into the camps as the guns fell silent, and they maintained an ongoing system of aid that impressed other groups. The "Joint", receiving 95 percent of its more than $200 million from American Jews, rushed food and equipment into the Jewish camps, then helped in political and underground campaigns to move these remnants of European Jewry to haven outside Europe, principally to Palestine or the United States. The "Joint" cared for 140,000 of the 150,000 Jewish refugee children alive at the end of the war, and it set up loan banks and child care centers as well as camp libraries and cinemas.[56]

"The AJDC had money, it had people, it had personnel in good places," concluded a worker with the Lutheran World Federation. "The rest of us felt second-class." Several other Jewish agencies were active also, including the Hebrew Immigrant Aid Society and the Jewish Committee for Relief Abroad. The burst of activity from these groups lasted far beyond the initial harried months when Jews were emerging as near-skeletons from the concentration camps. The Preparatory Commission for the IRO reported in January 1948 that of the 710 workers with the thirteen voluntary agencies active that month in Germany, 60 percent were Jews.[57]

Other organizations moved in as well during the early months— principally the various national Red Cross agencies, the YMCA and YWCA, American Polish Relief, and some Quaker groups such as the British Friends Relief Sevice and the American Friends Service Committee. The Y's provided musical instruments and sports equipment, summer camps, and leadership training programs, the latter attended by some 4,500 DPs in Germany and Austria by August 1946. These DPs then returned to their camps to provide leadership for new programs among their fellow refugees.[58]

Soon many more organizations were active on a large scale, until at least twenty-eight were working with DPs in Europe. Many had already been working among civilians in the devastated areas and simply extended their operations to the DP camps. These other groups included the National Catholic Welfare Service, several other Red Cross organizations, World Student Relief, Church World Service, the Lutheran World Federation, the United Ukrainian American Relief Committee, and various other American and Canadian ethnic organizations. The UNRRA recruited many staff members from among the voluntary agencies' personnel. This effort reached its peak in March 1946 when 1,165 of the 6,276 UNRRA employees working with DPs in Germany were drawn from voluntary agencies. Other helpers came from Allied military ranks, such as the Ukrainian-Canadian soldiers who stayed in Europe to organize the Central Ukrainian Relief Bureau (CURB) in December 1945, which funneled aid to Ukrainian refugees while arguing with occupation authorities for recognition of Ukrainians as a separate group.[59]

The dedication of these voluntary agency workers impressed outsiders. But dedication in such an environment could bring difficulties such as burnout among workers who watched the months go by while basic problems remained unsolved. Many who were signed on by the UNRRA or IRO felt this especially keenly, for they were required to operate within strict guidelines. Among these was an American Friends Service Committee member who wrote home from his UNRRA post, "the tug between administrator and Quaker becomes daily more difficult. How one can mix in the world's necessary and dirty business and yet lead the life which I want to, still escapes me." Some of these workers treated DPs as members of their own family, rather than keeping their distance. "At times I envied the cold uncaring bureaucrats," recalled Oscar Ratti of the Catholic DP program. "But the people in the camp wouldn't go to them."[60]

These are the people who live on in DP memories today—the individuals who made a difference in refugees' lives because of their concern, their love. "The first person who treated me as a human was the American consul, who asked questions about my background," a Slovenian commented as he reminisced about the dehumanizing aspects of camp life. A Russian, Elena Skrjabina, took her son to an American doctor, who examined him and then gave them a package of food as they turned to leave. "How much human relationships mean in life," Skrjabina wrote. "The participation and help of this totally unknown person has completely reconciled us to the Americans. . . . Then as now it is this personal human relationship that gave one the strength to live and carry on." Others would recall UNRRA staff members, voluntary workers, and the caring persons among their fellow DPs who helped turn some of the most devastated spots of the Continent into centers alive with creative force.[61]

6

JEWS OF THE SURVIVING REMNANT

I felt free, without fear—freed from Poland, and from the concentration camp. That was the first time I felt like a free person without fear.

—Polish Jew remembering Feldafing DP camp

TRAINS were passing in the night across Eastern Europe in the spring and summer of 1946, carrying human cargoes with vastly different expectations. Rolling eastward from the zones of Germany were thousands of repatriated Poles, their trains decorated with leafy branches and Polish flags, their patriotic songs rising above the rumble of the cars as they moved toward repatriation.

But other trains were going toward the West. These carried Polish Jews, traveling across the continent to Germany and Austria in both legal and illegal journeys. These passengers sang, too, but instead of the Polish national hymn and Polish marching airs they chorused a joyful "Pioneers Prepare Themselves for Palestine." Their train cars were not decorated with Polish flags. An American journalist, I. F. Stone, rode with one Jewish group across Czechoslovakia and noted that sometimes an eastbound and a westbound train were stopped at the same time in a station, and Polish Jews and Polish Catholics got out on opposite sides of the platform to stretch their legs. There was no mixing, Stone reported, "no one shouted across the platform from one train to the other. Their mutual misery created no common bond between peoples who regarded each other as oppressors and oppressed. The hate and fear that flowed between us was almost tangible, like a thick current in the hot summer night."[1]

There was a momentous story in this. Groups were choosing their

131

futures: thousands thought, pondered, discussed, and made decisions that would direct the flow of their people for generations.

For many Jews, that decision came easily. Europe had become the graveyard of their people, its major monuments not the Eiffel Tower and Saint Peter's but the Nazi death camps where humans were turned into objects and plundered for their labor, gold fillings, hair. A newly arrived American serving with the UNRRA landed in Munich in July 1945 and made his way to nearby Dachau, one of the most infamous of the concentration camps. It had not yet been made presentable for tourists, and he could still see human ashes before the crematorium, fingernail scratches running down the gas chamber walls. The very silence shrieked.[2] Auschwitz in Poland was the leader in this macabre competition, its gas chambers killing from 12,000 to 15,000 each day in May and June of 1944, part of the camp's estimated 2 million victims, mainly Jews. Hitler's *Einsatzgruppen* (mobile death squads) operated at will over Poland and other conquered areas from 1941 on, as talk of a "final solution" of the Jewish question spread among the German leadership.[3]

Stories began to filter out. But the stories came into a disbelieving world, its credulity put on guard by the falsified Belgian atrocity tales of the First World War. The new stories told of the creation of *Judenrein* (Jew-free areas) in what were formerly Jewish population centers. They told of Nazi doctors experimenting with Jewish children, of mass murders. One story later passed on by an architect concerned his trip with a German Sixth Army Officer near Kiev one day in March 1942. As they drove by a ravine called Babi Yar, the architect suddenly saw the moist earth bubbling with small explosions. He was told that it was the thaw releasing gases from the 35,000 bodies covered there, the result of a two-day massacre of Jews. "Here my Jews are buried," the German officer explained. But some European Jews managed to elude the Nazis, hiding with gentile friends or in forests or melting unnoticed into the population; the earliest postwar surveys found 20,000 Jews left in Germany and 7,000 in Austria, with 80,000 surviving inside Poland (over 130,000 others had fled into Russia), 90,000 in Hungary, 100,000 in Rumania.

The war's death toll of Jews was finally estimated at almost 6 million, 72 percent of European Jewry.[4]

The impact of this Holocaust, as it eventually came to be known, was felt and continues to be felt in many areas of the world, on many activities and institutions. But in 1945 its impact was felt most severely by the *She'erit Ha-pletah*—the spared, or surviving, remnant of European Jews.

Like the tattoos that large numbers of Jews carried on their arms as permanent physical reminders of the concentration camps ("I saw few Jewish arms in Europe without a tattooed number," I. F. Stone reported), many of the psychological scars could also be observed readily. The *katzetler* or *katzetnik* (concentration camp veterans) broke into tears easily, fell apart at a knock at the door, froze when a black limousine stopped nearby. Some refused to enter ambulances being used to transfer ailing Belsen inmates to the ship for Sweden, because they remembered that the Nazis had used such vehicles, complete with Red Cross emblems, to carry Jews away to the gas chambers. And some would cry out in nightmares, shrieking "Deutschen!" They dwelt on the past, reliving it in their conversations again and again. Having seen small incidents of hatred in the 1930s lead to catastrophe in the Third Reich, they now became extremely sensitive to any hint of anti-semitism, generalizing from and exaggerating any such report.[5]

Many Jewish DPs lacked the capacity for anything sustained, as evidenced in their early responses in the DP camps. "They become fatigued after a few hours' work," one American worker reported. A newspaper correspondent in Austria encountered Jews resisting efforts by the American Jewish Joint Distribution Committee (the "Joint") to begin work projects. Some of the camp's DP tailors said they could make more money on their own, while "the rest of the people are too tired and indifferent to bother," the correspondent observed.[6]

One of the continuing effects of the war on Jewish DPs centered on their loss of close relatives. Receiving a tiny bit of evidence that a family member was still alive, they would travel hundreds of miles to track it down, usually returning only with additional details on the final hours of their loved one. Some fantasized against all evidence that one of the family had somehow survived, was still alive, waiting perhaps in another country overseas; they would meet someday. Continually frustrated in their search, they developed a fear of loving anyone, afraid they would lose that person and suffer again. Many developed guilt over having survived. An American traveling with a mixed group of Jewish and Christian DP children found that the Jews put "great importance on kinship; they valued a family tie, however distant."[7]

Outsiders had problems dealing with such people, for cynicism and suspicion were everywhere. Jewish DPs were often hostile, forcing some psychiatrists to give up their efforts in the camps because of a lack of rapport. A British DP official was flabbergasted at the refusal of a group of Jews to move into more commodious huts, but a Jewish writer later saw in the incident the problem of the "concentration camp psychology, which was ridden with inferiority complexes and resulting aggressiveness." Many Jewish DPs simply rejected the right of non-Jews to tell them what to do any longer.[8]

Placing the Jews of the *She'erit Ha-pletah* in the decrepit conditions of the first improvised DP camps created a volatile mixture. One problem lay with the victorious armies. Having just fought a war against an enemy who persecuted individuals according to their religion, the Allies were not willing to resort to such classifications in dealing with the refugees. A British official cautioned in 1944 that just because Jews could be "identified by certain characteristics," and because Nazi policies had inserted the Jewish question into world politics, there were still "not sufficient reasons for treating 'Jews' as a separate national category." As a result, Jews who struggled out of the concentration camps initially found themselves classified as "enemy nationals" if they originated in Germany, Austria, or other Axis nations; in some DP camps they were placed among their former Nazi guards and tormentors. General Eisenhower asserted in early August 1945 that his headquarters "makes no differentiation in treatment of displaced persons."[9]

Differentiation, however, became the goal of Jewish agency workers and DP spokesmen. The basis of their claim was that Jews had been singled out *as Jews* by the Nazis. "The fact was that we had not faced the Auschwitz crematoriums as Poles, Lithuanians, or Germans," one Auschwitz survivor stressed. "It was as Jews that we had become victims of the greatest catastrophe of our people." Although gypsies were killed, even slaughtered, by the Germans, not all Gypsies were ferreted out across Europe, and some were even protected; the anti-Gypsy policy was not the same as the anti-Jewish policy.

The refugee president of the Landsberg DP camp, Samuel Gringauz, noted that the Nazis' targeting of Jews had produced a sort of Jewish universalism not present before, under which Jews who formerly felt distinct from other Jews now felt one with them. He drew on his own concentration camp experiences:

> A Jewish tailor from Rhodes who could find no one in the camp to understand him, and a Hungarian druggist baptized thirty years before, lay in the same wooden bunk with me, shared their experience as Jews with me, and died only because they were Jewish. That is why the *She'erit Ha-pletah* feels itself to be the embodiment of the unity of Jewish experience.[10]

Conditions of Jews in the camps soon caught the eyes of journalists, Western officials, and Jewish spokesmen. As early as 21 July 1945, the World Jewish Congress appealed to the Allied leaders meeting at Potsdam to release the former concentration camp inmates from "conditions of the most abject misery." The WJC charged that Jews at the Lingen DP camp were housed in "indescribably filthy" structures, with inadequate medical and other supplies and personnel. Worse, the congress found that in some cases ex-Nazis had been placed in charge of their former victims and were "treating them with neglect and contempt."

The *Jewish Chronicle,* a London newspaper, compared American troops with Hitler's SS in reporting an incident in which Jewish DPs were driven from their huts by General Patton's Third Army. DP protests against this rough handling drew the response from the soldiers that " 'this was the only way to deal with Jews.' "[11]

These stories reached Washington. President Harry S Truman, only recently installed in office, soon wrote to the dean of the University of Pennsylvania Law School and asked him to investigate conditions in Europe, especially the situation of the Jewish displaced persons. The dean was Earl G. Harrison, who had been serving as American representative on the Inter-Governmental Committee on Refugees. After making contact with Jewish representatives in Europe, Harrison left the itinerary laid out by the army and probed into situations that, it seems likely, the military would have avoided. An inhabitant at the Belsen DP camp remembered Harrison visiting them, chain-smoking as tears streamed down his face. "He was so shaken he could not speak," the Belsen man recalled. "Finally, he whispered weakly: 'But how did you survive, and where do you take your strength from now?' "[12]

Harrison's report to Truman in early August 1945 was devastating. "As matters now stand, we appear to be treating the Jews as the Nazis treated them except that we do not exterminate them," he wrote. Harrison referred to the DP camps holding Jews as "concentration camps," where they wore the "rather hideous striped pajama" they had worn earlier when controlled by the Nazis (some were forced to wear leftover German SS uniforms), and existed on rations composed principally of bread and coffee, all the while guarded closely by American soldiers. Meanwhile, they could look not far off and see German civilians, "to all appearances living normal lives in their own homes."

Harrison's report, as might be expected, called for a vast improvement in food, clothing, and housing for the Jewish DPs. But he went beyond this to urge two sharp shifts in policy:

> The first and plainest need of these people is a recognition of their actual status and by this I mean their status of Jews. . . . While admittedly it is not normally desirable to set aside particular racial or religious groups from their nationality categories, the plain truth is that this was done for so long by the Nazis that a group has been created which has special needs. Jews as Jews (not as members of their nationality groups) have been more severely victimized than the non-Jewish members of the same or other nationalities.

This meant segregated DP camps for Jews, he stressed, with their own representatives to deal with the military authorities.

Harrison's second major proposal was for immediate help for Jews to leave Germany and Austria—through emigration to the United States and other countries if possible, but mainly through opening the doors into British-controlled Palestine. The Palestine issue "must be faced," he wrote. "For some of the European Jews, there is no acceptable or even decent solution for their future other than Palestine." The main solution lay, he stressed, "in the quick evacuation of all nonrepatriable Jews in Germany and Austria, who wish it, to Palestine."[13]

President Truman responded quickly to Harrison's report. He pressured General Eisenhower to improve conditions in the DP camps and sent a copy of the Harrison document to British prime minister Clement Atlee with the recommendation that British-controlled Palestine be opened for Jewish settlement. Truman commented later that year that the issue had stimulated the greatest volume of mail in the history of the White House.[14]

Eisenhower was stung by Harrison's findings. The general made his own inspection, then responded somewhat defensively and emphasized the army's enormous problems in Europe in the aftermath of the war. But he went on to authorize the creation of special Jewish DP centers, the selection of camp guards from among the DPs themselves, and an increase in the daily minimum caloric level to twenty-five hundred for "racial, religious and political persecutees." He also appointed a Jewish adviser and a Jewish liaison officer. In mid-November the British Zone finally permitted segregation of Jews within DP camps, although the new policy stated that "special camps exclusively for Jews will not be established."[15]

As a result of these changes, by early January 1946 the British Zone of Germany had one major heavily Jewish camp at Höhne (near the site of Belsen concentration camp) with 9,000 Jews, while the American Zone had twelve camps that were entirely Jewish, led by Landsberg and Wolfratshausen with more than 5,000 each, and

Feldafing with 3,700. In the French Zone more than three-fourths of the Jews lived in households taken from the Germans; no segregation was authorized. The Jewish camps soon were electing their own spokesmen, aided by the formation in July 1945 of the Central Committee of Liberated Jews, an umbrella leadership group for Jews in the western zones.[16]

These new Jewish spokesmen found the occupation authorities in Germany and Austria generally cooperative from late 1945 on. General Mark Clark, head of the U.S. occupation forces in Austria, instructed his assistants in October 1945 that Truman's orders were to be carried out "not only because they were orders" but because Clark believed the Jews' treatment during the war made them "entitled to first consideration." Jewish writers later referred to the months from late 1945 to mid-1947 as the "humanitarian period" of Occupation-Jewish relations. And in the meantime the Jewish DP camps emerged as the new centers of European Jewry, speaking for Jews, settling disputes, offering practical help and spiritual guidance. Remnants of the traditional Jewish centers in Hamburg, Lübeck, Bremen, and Düsseldorf now turned to the camps for leadership.[17]

The environment of the Jewish DPs began to change in other ways as well. The new political environment—perhaps *philosophical* environment is more accurate—flowed from two major developments, only slightly evident in the summer of 1945 but more apparent with each passing day: (1) a sharp upsurge in support for Zionism, the movement to re-establish Judaism's base in its ancient home of Palestine (Israel), and (2) the continuance and even the increase of virulent anti-Semitism in Poland and other areas of Eastern Europe.

These two changes in turn affected each other, and were essential ingredients in the growing international debate over the Palestine question. The DP issue, already frustrating to occupying powers and host nations, now took on new complexity.

Zionism's growth came from several factors. It was paradoxical that rising support for a Jewish homeland was accompanied by little or no increase in religiosity among the Jewish remnant—in fact, some argued that religious practice had declined from the thirties, because Orthodox Jews had been more noticeable and for that reason were more readily eliminated by the Nazis. But this new Zionism was not a religious movement: it drew strength from traditional Jewish beliefs, but only because they were given new relevance by events of the Hitler era. Koppel Pinson of "Joint," after working for a year among Jewish DPs, argued that Zionists "were the only ones that had a program that seemed to make sense after this catastrophe." The Palestine return became so identified with salvation for Europe's Jews, he emphasized, that "emotionally and psychologically as well as in a real physical sense it became dangerous to think outside this complex."[18]

This was because each week after V-E Day seemed to bring forth new evidence of the degradation and extermination of Europe's Jews during the war. And already whispers were heard of the probability of another war, between Americans and Russians, or even between Americans and the rumored underground Nazi movement. What would be the fate of the Jews then?

The head of the Landsberg DP camp's Jews, Dr. Samuel Gringauz, presented the argument for Jewish pessimism in the camp newspaper:

> We do not believe in progress, we do not believe in the 2,000-year-old Christian culture of the West, the culture that, *for them,* created the Statue of Liberty in New York and Westminster Abbey on the Thames, the wonder gardens of Versailles and the Uffizi and Pitti palaces in Florence, the Strassbourg *Münster* and the Cologne cathedral; but *for us,* the slaughters of the Crusades, the Spanish Inquisition, the blood bath of Khmielnicki, the pogroms of Russia, the gas chambers of Auschwitz and the massacres of entire Europe.

I. F. Stone encountered older Jews who put it more simply, as they told of their desire to go to Palestine despite not considering themselves Zionists: "I'm a Jew. That's enough. We have wandered enough. We have worked and struggled too long on the lands of other peoples. We must build a land of our own."[19]

In the recorded comments and letters of such people, and in reminiscences of Jews moving through the postwar period, the idea appears repeatedly that Palestine represented *home.* Virtually none had ever been there, but a return—*Aliyah*—to the land of Israel was a foundation block of their faith, repeated each year during Passover Seder prayers: "Next year in Jerusalem." Perhaps this image meant little in earlier years; it is not unusual for ritual to lose significance. But now, with all that had once meant home mixed with the dust, eliminated, destroyed, the thought came forward again. They still had a home. Children traveling on a cold train en route to a French port, to board a Haifa-bound ship, explained to concerned UNRRA workers, "Hardships? It is worth them all. We are going home."[20]

The symbol of Palestine the home also became a positive affirmation of Jewish existence. It was a way to finally show the world the Nazis had failed. Everything—even personal comfort—had to be sacrificed for Palestine. Plans to remove Jewish orphans to better conditions in Jewish homes in England were blocked by the Jewish Central Committee of the British Zone, which resolved that the children "who were with us in the Ghettos and concentration camps . . . must stay where they are until their Aliyah." The committee demanded that the first allocations for Palestine go to the children. At the same time in late 1945, delegates broke into tears as a Rome conference of Polish Jews voted for a ringing declaration to proceed "by all ways and means" to Palestine, despite British opposition. It was their last hope for survival, the delegates asserted, and they would go "because they owed such action to the 5,000,000 or more Jews of Europe exterminated by Nazism." UNRRA staff workers, trying to compile statistics on this phenomenon, distributed a questionnaire among 19,000 Jewish DPs and found that 18,700 listed "Palestine" as their first choice for emigration, but then 98 percent also wrote "Palestine" as their second choice. At the Fürth DP camp near Nürnberg, however, alert staff members told the DPs not to repeat "Palestine" for second choice, but to write another preference for emigration. One-fourth then wrote in "crematorium."[21]

An important difference in this new Zionism was that it temporarily overwhelmed divisions that had been rife among European Jews, divisions that earlier had left them almost incompetent to meet the challenges of the Hitler era. Earlier generations of Jews had debated extensively over Zionism—whether Jews should dream of resettlement at all, and even where their Land of Zion should be. At various times, Texas, Uganda, and the Argentine had been proposed, as well as Palestine. Britain's Balfour Declaration in 1917, supporting a Jewish national home in Palestine, stimulated the Zionists, although some sought only a federal arrangement with Arabs. Even in wartime, in the face of Nazi attacks, the different groups within Judaism had trouble working together; the antagonists included socialist bundists versus Zionists, Zionists versus assimilationists, the Orthodox versus the nonobservant, radicals versus capitalists, and socialists versus Communists. These and other divisions made a farce of the Third Reich's assertion that Jews represented a powerful conspiratorial group controlling vast areas of European life. In fact, no overall organization existed among the Jews of Europe, not even an information chain that might have kept them abreast of dangers.

That long-sought unity would appear only in 1945, and even then some outsiders might have missed it because of the multiplicity of political parties and organizations visible in the camps. The Belsen DP camp soon had elections fought out by General Zionists and Revisionists, as well as members of Hashomer Hatzair, Mapai, Mizrachi, Aguda, and Poale Zion. Several groups within the camp ran their own schools; most had their own newspapers. One participant called the Belsen DP camp not only a Jewish community but "an intense Zionist community. . . . I felt there as if I was back in my Lithuanian home town." But despite their differences these groups cooperated, he stressed. "It was based on a genuine compromise and an appreciation that, in the first place, they were all Zionists."[22]

The second major change in the Jewish DPs' environment arose out of events in the newly liberated areas of Eastern Europe. Release from concentration camps or forced labor was usually followed by a frantic search for family members, but for those Jews who returned to their homes in Eastern Europe the search was usually doubly numbing: not only were they unable to locate their kin, but former neighbors often turned upon them with a bitter anti-Semitism that recalled the recent days of Hitler's reign.

David Lubetkin's story will perhaps speak for thousands.[23]

David Lubetkin (not his real name) was liberated in Buchenwald near the end of the war, and a few weeks later, while scanning the names posted on a military bulletin board, he saw his two sisters listed as survivors in the concentration camp at Bergen-Belsen. Soon David and a friend headed off on bicycles to link up with their kin.

The next step was to return to Poland, to learn whether others of the family had survived. If three Lubetkins had made it through the war, why not more? David had high hopes for reuniting the entire family—parents and six children—who had been seized and sent away on 13 September 1939 after Germans overran their village.

The Russians also wanted David to go home. After taking over the Buchenwald area in midsummer of 1945, when zonal boundaries were re-drawn, Soviet officials encouraged all Poles to go back to rebuild their homeland. "Trains are prepared," they announced in the Buchenwald area. "Those who will not go on train, will have to go on foot." There was no other option.

And so David and his sisters boarded an eastward-bound train, heavily loaded with Buchenwald veterans who traveled with both expectation and apprehension. "It was not a joyful, singing trip," he said. Soon he joined with others, forming a group of eleven Jews from the same Polish town. At the German-Polish border they had to leave the train and wait a day for another to carry them into Poland. While the eleven prepared their night's shelter, however, a Polish border guard—Jewish, it turned out—talked privately with them. He showed some surprise at their return: "Why did you come back to hell? I'm looking to get away from hell."

That set them thinking. But they continued on, and two days later David and his friends received another jolt as they disembarked onto the railway platform in their hometown in central Poland. A local policeman, whom they had known before the war as the son of the village ice cream vendor, greeted them: "So many of you lived through the war? Why didn't they get you all?"

It was an ominous welcome. In one respect it should not have been surprising, however, for their village had been torn in the 1930s with anti-Semitic agitation. Warnings had been stenciled repeatedly on Jewish-owned shops: "Swoj do Swego" (Stay with your own) and "Zyd twoj wrog" (Jews are your enemies), among other slogans.

Despite this history of anti-Jewish acitivity the returning Jews were taken aback. "I expected they would have learned something from the war," David said. "I expected them to have changed in their thinking and ideas by then, due to the suffering they themselves had experienced." But such was not the case.

And so the few Jews making their way back to the village clustered together, sharing food and shelter and fears, welcoming the Jews starting to trickle in from the Soviet Union as well as the continuing arrivals from liberated Germany. Meanwhile, local anti-Semitism worsened as Polish nationalism flowered.

By November 1945, David, at his sisters' urging, decided it was time to get out. He and a cousin—the only surviving kinsman they had found—realized they had an advantage in their escape: they looked Polish. On the first leg of their train trip they sat next to a pretty gentile girl and listened respectfully to her diatribes against Jews.

It was a fortunate deception. On that day-long ride to Poznan they saw four Jewish passengers thrown out of windows while the train lumbered on, victims of roving bands of ultranationalistic *Armia Krajowa.*

The two cousins had chosen Poznan as their first destination because they knew trains left from there for Berlin. As luck would have it, a Soviet train carrying goods from Moscow to Berlin was then in the station, and by pooling their cash they bought two bottles of whiskey and several sausages, adequate to bribe a Russian soldier to allow them on board. Better than merely boarding, they were hidden in a baggage car filled with office furniture, which was not opened until the train entered Berlin.

At Berlin they made their way to the Zehlendorf transit camp in the United States sector, producing concentration camp release documents to prove they were Jewish. Later they were taken into western Germany, ending up at the Feldafing DP camp in early December 1945. Their next task was to plot the escape of David's sisters.

The experiences of David Lubetkin were repeated over and over across Eastern Europe in the first months after the war. Thousands of Jews returned home, including some 130,000 who had spent the war years in the Soviet Union. But they discovered that the defeat of the Third Reich was not the defeat of anti-Jewish feeling. Reborn anti-Semitism became so widespread that the new Polish regime finally ordered that attacks on Jews were to be punishable by death or life imprisonment.[24]

This anti-Semitism had both an ancient and a modern history. It had been woven into European tradition long before the modern era, but took on a viciously nationalistic character after the First World War and the rebirth of the Polish nation. Anything not identified as completely Polish was opposed vigorously in those years, which meant that Lithuanians, Jews, and non-Catholics could be depicted as enemies of the new Polish nation. One account stated that anti-Jewish disorders were "daily occurrences" in Poland by the mid-1930s. The Nazis later built on this hatred, encouraging divisions among the peoples they conquered. The invaders recruited warders among Poles and Ukrainians for Jewish labor camps, and in turn they used Jews to compile lists of Polish Catholics for deportation. The Germans also put a renewed emphasis on anti-Semitism in occupied Poland and added some new twists, such as a traveling exhibit called "The Jewish Contagion," which made its way from town to town. Small wonder, then, that some Polish Resistance groups opposed Jews, disarming them, driving them away. One ex-partisan admitted he hid his Jewish identity from his fellow partisans throughout the war; to do otherwise was to invite being shot while on patrol—by his comrades.[25]

The result was that anti-Semitism, so much identified in the outside world with Hitler, did not collapse when the Nazis retreated from Poland, and the first words heard by returning Jews were often such as these: "The one bad thing about Hitler is that he didn't kill all the Jews."[26]

Only two factors in 1945 were new amid this anti-Semitism. Many Poles had acquired property (buildings, jewelry, clothing) that Nazis had seized from Jews in 1939–40; now they feared it would be taken away and returned to the prewar Jewish owners. In fact, such returns were being authorized by the new Communist regime. Also, stories were circulating that Jews had helped the Soviet Union in its ultimately successful efforts to take over eastern Poland, and were now helping the Soviet-imposed regime.[27]

The latter argument appears to have been widely believed. General Władysław Anders stated in his memoir of the war that when the Russians invaded in 1939, "a number of Polish Jews, especially the young ones, who had made no secret of their joy at the entry of Soviet troops, began to cooperate" with Soviet officials. A book on Poland published in London after the war, *The Dark Side of the Moon,* noted the Soviets' inability to enlist Polish minorities in their cause. This was especially surprising in the case of the Jews, the anonymous author stated, for "nobody in Poland, they say, welcomed the Red Army in the same way as the Jews." (Thirty-five years and thousands of miles away, a Polish ex-DP thought back on those years and remembered that he had been told in the DP camps that when the Russians invaded in 1939, the Jews sided with them. "People resented that," he said.) In addition, several Jews were leading officials in the postwar Communist regime in Warsaw.[28]

There was no time to investigate and refute such charges amid the heated nationalism of 1945 and 1946. Attacks on Jews began even before the Germans were defeated. In the spring of 1945 a right-wing Polish group proclaimed it a sign of patriotism to kill Jews. A Polish government report stated that 351 Jews were murdered in Poland between November 1944 and October 1945, with anti-Jewish riots occurring during 1945 at Cracow on 20 August, in Sosnowiec on 25 October, and in Lublin on 19 November. But none held the terror of the incident at Kielce.[29]

It occurred in July 1946, when a Christian boy in the city some 120 miles south of Warsaw returned after a three-day absence with tales of a blood ritual. Jews had kidnapped him, he said, and took him into a cellar where he watched as fifteen other Christian children were murdered. As the story spread some five thousand protestors gathered around the Jewish community building. Men in Polish army uniforms brought the Jews out, then released them to the mob. Local militia, a Socialist factory director, even some members of the clergy took part in what rapidly turned into a melee. Forty-one Jews were killed at Kielce, and soon Jews were building stockade-like structures in various areas of Poland. The Catholic church's reaction surprised many: Poland's August Cardinal Hlond criticized Jews for increasing anti-Semitism by taking leading appointments in a government "that the majority of Poles do not want." When a Cracow priest denounced the riot, he was forbidden to continue ecclesiastical duties.

The Kielce boy's story was eventually revealed as a fabrication.[30]

In nearby countries anti-Semitism also became violent, as nationalism flared up in the aftermath of the German retreat and surrender. Anti-Hungarian demonstrations in Kosice, Czechoslovakia, were soon combined with anti-Jewish demonstrations, while in Presov five Jews were killed in what appeared to be a pogrom. German Jews in Prague, meanwhile, were attacked as Germans. Bucharest crowds screaming their support of king and country "fell to beating up all the Jews they could lay hands on," often with the thick staffs used to carry their Rumanian flags.[31]

The piling of murder upon murder, the shouts in the street and the rumors in the marketplace, all helped drive thousands of returned Jews out of Poland and neighboring countries from late 1945 on.

The impact of the Kielce killings in 1946 was immediate: some 16,000 Polish Jews fled the country that month; 23,000 more left in August (including almost 4,000 who crossed into Czechoslovakia one night), and another 23,000 left in September. A UNRRA official was on hand as fleeing Polish Jews arrived at the Zeilsheim DP camp near Frankfurt; he gazed out on

> what appeared to be an endless queue of refugees, packs and bundles on their backs, plodding up the path toward the camp. Never had I seen such a bedraggled lot of people. Mothers held infants to their breasts, clutching the hands of tiny youngsters who stumbled alongside them. As I watched, a group halted and, throwing their bundles to the ground, literally fell in their tracks from exhaustion, unable to make the last few yards to the camp. . . . They had arrived in the last few days from Cracow and Polish Silesia, more than seven hundred miles distant. Fathers, mothers and children alike, hitch-hiked, rode trucks, jumped freight trains, slept in the forests at night and somehow managed to reach here.[32]

Was this organized or unorganized?

Lt. Gen. Sir Frederick E. Morgan, briefly UNRRA's chief of operations in Germany, believed it was organized. This outflow from Poland, he charged, was "nothing short of a skillful campaign of anti-British aggression on the part of Zion aided and abetted by Russia." Although it was presented to the world by "Zionist propaganda" as being the "spontaneous surge of a tortured and persecuted people," Morgan held that it was really a well-organized drive by the American Joint Distribution Committee and related Jewish groups to pack the Jewish DPs into Germany. Their ultimate aim was to force the opening of Palestine for emigration—meaning "death to the British," Morgan charged.

The UNRRA officer was called on the carpet for such charges, restored to his post, then fired later by a new UNRRA chief for similar remarks.[33]

Other accounts challenged Morgan's claim that the movement was organized, for journalists found "infiltrees," as they were called, who had fled on their own and linked up with others as they headed west. In fact, soon after Morgan made his comments at a press conference in early 1946, a UNRRA investigator stated that "all the infiltrees with whom we spoke said that there was no organized program." Others noted that many people, not just Jews, wanted to leave their homes in Europe; a Netherlands survey estimated that even 20 percent of the Dutch population wished to emigrate.[34]

But organization was present; that became increasingly obvious. A probe by the U.S. Third Army in January 1946 discovered that a group of 250 Jewish refugees heading for Munich had been detoured at one point, then sent in another direction where better facilities would be available. Within two weeks of the opening of a new camp for Jews, the report stated, a new group of 200 infiltrees arrived there, without having passed through any other camp en route. The report said that Zionist committees along the way gave advice and assistance, and many trying to reach Italy were found in possession of forged passes. When the UNRRA ran an investigation in June and July 1946, interrogation of infiltrees at three major collection points confirmed that "the movements are fairly well organized, but . . . the fear of persecution is still the predominant motive." And that was before Kielce.[35]

Some evidence was also found for Morgan's charge that the movement aimed at pressuring the British. The western zones were obvious goals for anyone on the loose in Europe then, for few other spots were prepared to care for large numbers of refugees. But it is also on record that David Ben Gurion told the Jewish Agency in October 1945, "If we succeed in concentrating a quarter million Jews in the American zone, it will increase the American pressure [on the British]." This pressure would arise not through financial burdens, Ben Gurion added, "but because they see no future for these people outside *Eretz-Yisrael.*" A January 1946 probe by the UNRRA found a "strong impression" that one motive behind the organized flow of Jews was to "bring the questions of the future of the Jews and of Zionism to a head."[36]

The escape of one Polish Jew illustrates the mixed pattern of organized and unorganized flight that became common in late 1945 and much of 1946. Returning to her Polish hometown in April 1945, Chana Wilewska (not her real name) was met by the same apartment building janitor who had thrown out her family in 1939. Then, he had worn a large swastika badge; now he pleaded, "I didn't know what I was doing!" Gaining entry, she struggled in the ensuing weeks to regain family furniture and heirlooms, all the while overhearing anti-Jewish comments in the streets and rumors of attacks on Jews in nearby towns.[37]

Then came a letter from her uncle, who was serving with General Anders's Polish army in Italy. He told her to join him and sent forged papers with a fellow soldier who was returning to Poland for a visit. The papers were inadequate, however; two attempts to cross the border using them resulted only in two rebuffs.

Chana decided to work out her own plan. Since her mother had been born in Czechoslovakia, she went to the city hall and obtained a permit to visit her relatives in that country. The permit got her across the border in April 1946. Upon arrival at her mother's native city, she went immediately to the Jewish community center, where she met a visiting member of the Jewish Brigade who took her to Prague. It was in Prague that she was delivered to the headquarters of the *Bricha,* the organized exodus. (*Bricha* means "flight" in Hebrew.)

After several days' wait, persons running the Bricha center in Prague took her with a group of fifty fleeing Jews by train to the German border. All were given forged papers attesting to the legality of their trip in case they were caught. They were taken at night to a house, where they waited until 2:00 A.M. Three guides came for them, leading them in a two-hour trek over the mountains into Germany. (Chana believes that the border guards had been bribed, for the group of fifty traveled with no fear of capture.)

Early the next morning the group walked into a German train station, waited while their Bricha guides purchased their tickets, then boarded a train that eventually crossed into the American Zone. Most entered DP camps, as suggested by their Bricha guides.

Chana, meanwhile, elected not to enter a camp and instead registered as a German, which was easy to do since she had grown up in Polish Silesia.

Organized. Unorganized. At times disorganized. All three describe the massive exodus of Jews out of Eastern Europe beginning in late 1945. Undoubtedly many would have fled even without help, for a tenuous string of escape routes had existed sporadically in wartime. It is just as certain, however, that many were encouraged to leave by the knowledge that they would receive assistance along the way.

Yehuda Bauer, an Israeli scholar and expert on the Bricha, argues that despite what some Israelis would later claim, the postwar exodus from Poland received its early organizational drive from resident Polish and Lithuanian Jews—not from the special agents sent from Palestine, known as *shlichim* (emissaries). Ex-partisans first helped Polish Jews find the best border crossings, then forged Red Cross documents for them. Large numbers were assisted in traveling by train into Berlin, or down through Rumania into Yugoslavia or toward Italy.[38]

The most famous ruse employed in the early months of the Bricha was known as the "Greek bluff." Polish Jews who crossed into Czechoslovakia were given documents showing them to be Greeks who had been imprisoned by the Nazis and now were finally returning to Athens or Salonika. They were forbidden by their Bricha guides to speak Polish, Russian, or Yiddish, since the guards might recognize those as being something other than Greek, but they could talk in Hebrew because the men at the border would not know that. Since no Greek consulates were located in border towns, the travelers' papers could not be checked, and border guards were happy to speed the supposed Greek victims of Hitler on their way to a Hellenic homecoming. (The ultimate compliment for this ruse came when a group of authentic Greeks was arrested crossing into Czechoslovakia. Their documents were so different from those the guards were accustomed to view that they were charged with having forged papers.)[39]

Finally, in October 1945, the first emissaries arrived from Palestine, ten months after the initial groups of Polish Jews had escaped south into Romania and others had fled through Czechoslovakia and Germany. Now the Bricha became an established organization across much of the Continent, although local Jews continued to run most of the day-to-day operations in Poland. Members of the Jewish Brigade, a British military unit from Palestine that saw action near the end of the war in Italy, began to show up anywhere the Bricha needed them, helping Jews steal across frontiers, transporting them in disguised military trucks, carrying supplies, foiling occupation forces repeatedly. The Joint Distribution Committee provided food and clothing for many of the travelers.[40]

But six months after Lieutenant General Morgan charged that a well-organized, fully financed operation was moving thousands of Jews out of Eastern Europe, the reality was that the escape routes were being blocked, largely through British pressure and Soviet reluctance to go along with the exodus. And the truth was that the organizers were unable to cope with the mounting flow of refugee traffic.[41]

At that point a major shift occurred: the Czechoslovaks changed their minds. On 25 July 1946, the Czechoslovak cabinet officially recognized the Bricha, granting it permission to transport Jews across Czechoslovakia. The only proviso was that travelers were not to remain on Czechoslovak soil. (When I. F. Stone traveled with such a group, he found that a Czechoslovak policeman accompanied it to ensure that no one fled the train; in fact, his presence seems to have assured that none of the Jews would be harmed.) Poland then opened its borders also, so by late 1946 there was no legal barrier between any Polish Jew and the DP camps of Austria and Germany. The routes uncovered earlier that year by a UNRRA investigation were still in use, only now they were bulging with refugees:

> The movement into Berlin, for instance, has come almost exclusively on the rail route between Stettin and Berlin; the movement into Bavaria has been, first, on a rail route from Poland to Prague to Pilsen and to Hof in Germany, and second, along the rail route from Budapest to Vienna to Linz to Salzburg and to Munich.[42]

As this influx started to crowd western zone reception centers, Allied policymakers began to understand that they faced a new situation. The realization frequently came in a sudden confrontation, as experienced by Alexander Squadrilli, at that time displaced persons executive with the U.S. Army in Frankfurt. Squadrilli began to receive desperate pleas from officials in Austria, calling for trains to transport the infiltrees out of the vastly overcrowded centers there. Squadrilli dispatched empty train cars to Austria and later went to the camp sidings when they were due to return. "I was out there when the first train arrived," he said. "Some Jews were getting off with bundles and children on their backs. I would look into these people's eyes: it was as if they were seeing right through me—they had a hard glitter in their eyes, that told me they had reached the end of their tolerance—they would cut my throat if I did anything against them."[43]

Some authorities tried to block entry into their zones. But higher-ups intervened, ordering the infiltrees placed in Jewish camps and provided with regular DP food, shelter, and care; these officials also reversed an order that forbade organized groups from entering the U.S. Zone. In Austria the occupation forces quickly gave up efforts to block these "infiltrees"; they did an about-face and assisted them in moving through. "I could put a division up there on the line but it wouldn't stop the Jews," a high-ranking American officer told one correspondent. And the chief of British DP operations for Austria added, "I find it good policy to play along with the chaps who can turn the tap on and off. They buzz me and announce they have a thousand for my zone and I usually manage to settle for about 500." This became known as the "Green Plan," and it would be tolerated as long as the Jews were just passing through.[44]

In April 1947, however, the United States finally clamped down on the continuing influx. Nothing would be done to stop the infiltrees from coming into the American zones, the new order stated, but they could no longer enter DP camps. Private groups, such as the American Joint Distribution Committee and other Jewish agencies, would have to care for them.[45]

This loosening of occupation policy from 1945 to 1947 opened the doors to the West for thousands of east European Jews. Entering the American zones at rates of 2,000 or more a week, the Jewish population under UNRRA care in Germany and Austria jumped from 18,361 in December 1945 to 97,333 in December 1946; 167,529 were receiving IRO care on 30 September 1947. Thousands of others were not under UNRRA or IRO care. The influx into the U.S. Zone of Germany was so great that the expected decline in camp population from repatriation did not take place. More than 107,000 DPs were repatriated in the last half of 1946, and 16,000 other DPs were removed from the camps as ineligible—but total camp population rose by 8,000.[46]

The 1947 statistics on Jews receiving UNRRA care were dominated by the 122,313 Jews from Poland; there were also 18,593 from Romania, 8,445 from Hungary, 6,602 from Czechoslovakia, and 6,167 from Germany. By then, Jews accounted for 25 percent of displaced persons in Germany and Austria, a sharp rise from the 3.7 percent reported at the end of September 1945 (when many Jews were still classified by nationality).[47]

New camps for infiltrees were opened, a few of them luxurious—as at Bad Gastein in Austria—but most at the other end of the comfort spectrum. A visitor to the Zeilsheim DP camp near Frankfurt found four families crammed into a room measuring twelve by eighteen feet; he learned that a baby had been born that morning on the stoop outside the main office, and that there was no fresh milk for the camp's sixty new-born babies—while nearby German farmers pastured herds of milk cows. Visitors were appalled at the impermanence and squalor of these overcrowded infiltree centers. Various reasons for these conditions were advanced. One observer concluded that the refugees had a "burning desire to get out, and to shut out any implication that they may have to remain where they are for any serious length of time."[48]

As had happened with other DPs, it was this contrast of wretched overcrowding in the camps with well-housed Germans nearby that put bitterness into the hearts of many, and led some in the UNRRA and IRO to urge major shifts in priorities. This was behind the publicized resignation of the Landsberg camp's welfare director in December 1945 and the resulting army investigation.

The Landsberg director, Dr. Leo Srole, a sociologist, protested the overcrowding, underfeeding, and lack of adequate housing (some of which had been declared "unfit for German prisoners of war"), while expressing fear of impending epidemics, since outbreaks of cholera had been reported in Eastern Europe, source of most of the infiltrees. (In a recent interview, Srole, now of Columbia University, said the overcrowding in late 1945 held the potential for a serious crisis, based on a stalemate between the army and the powerless DPs. "In that setting, I tried to arouse action through that letter of protest, to break the deadlock." It worked. Reporters attending the nearby Nürnberg trials were largely responsible for the extensive publicity given to Srole's resignation.) The military made a quick investigation, and additional camp installations for the incoming Jews were ordered. In February 1946 the army ordered that infiltrees were to be housed and cared for according to the same standards applied to earlier arrivals.[49]

This chaos helped diffuse power in some camps. Much of the power was gathered by sophisticated DPs who organized quickly to protect themselves, to block unwanted actions by authorities, or simply to seek more supplies from the UNRRA or voluntary agencies. Sometimes the disorder was used by agency workers to gain influence, for many of them had access to great quantities of supplies. The situation at the Neustadt camp in March 1946 angered a UNRRA welfare officer in the British Zone:

There is no control of supplies distributed by the Jewish agencies. . . . They distribute it to whom they will and how they like, taking double ration for themselves. Occasionally food is given to Polish hospital patients, but only those who are friendly with the committee.

There is no satisfactory control of the DP population in the camp, consequently the food from Belsen is drawn on the strength of about 650, although the actual number of Jews in Neustadt is only around 400. There is constant movement of displaced persons in and out of the camp without any permit, which makes it possible for the same displaced person to be registered and collect food at Belsen and Neustadt at the same time.

The morale among the Jewish displaced persons is unsatisfactory. There is resistance toward any rehabilitative project and tendency toward isolation from the rest of the camp. The Jewish displaced persons, for instance, have not drawn any knitting wool because they would not accept the general scheme of control.

The present staff cannot cope with the situation.[50]

Less than four months later another UNRRA official complained of political infighting between Jewish groups—at Schwebda they were "fighting for the souls" of 150 unaccompanied children—and admitted that competent UNRRA personnel refused to leave jobs in stable Polish and Baltic camps "for the immense difficulties which confront personnel in infiltree centers."[51]

But this intense feeling, this anger at the outside world, also led to a burning desire to celebrate everything that was Jewish. The Joint Distribution Committee's supply network strained to provide enough kosher food for the Orthodox, although a donation of ten million pounds of kosher beef from the Irish Republic helped through a difficult period in early 1947.

A major need for special foods came during Jewish festivals, the succession of events that mark the seasons of the Jewish year. These were days when Jewish feeling was most concentrated, and they took on special meaning, special poignance, after liberation. For years Jews had met only secretly on those days, had passed messages, exchanged looks. Now they celebrated publicly and, as one escaped Polish Jew explained, "Jewish life began to exist again!"[52]

Several of the holidays were contemplative, sad events, bringing happiness after the war only in that they could now be commemorated openly again. But one holiday was sheer joy—Purim, the annual festival of the deliverance of Jews from a massacre planned

Matzo for the Passover. The first Passover after the war assumed great importance for Jews of the surviving remnant, and Jewish agencies worked to assure that Europe's Jews were able to celebrate the event wherever they were. Here a *Mashgiach* oversees the making of matzo at the Hanau DP center in early 1946. *(Photo courtesy of Ben Kaplan.)*

by Haman as related in the Book of Esther. Traditionally at that springtime event an effigy of Haman is ridiculed and attacked in a joking manner, to the accompaniment of noisemakers, hooting, and singing.

Purim 1946 became very special—perhaps the most special Purim for generations. It was the occasion when Europe's Jews finally threw off the worry and fear under which they had lived since the early 1930s and danced and laughed in the warm sunlight of freedom again. The DPs at Landsberg, one of the largest Jewish camps, turned the event into an exhilarating rebuke to Nazism—in the very city where Hitler wrote *Mein Kampf.* A recent study by Toby Blum-Dobkin dramatically presents the festival's importance in Landsberg in 1946.[53]

Camp leaders saw an opportunity to turn Purim week at Landsberg into rehabilitative activity that would spruce up the camp, help its Jewish residents shake off their despair and celebrate their joy at having survived. Streets were cleaned and buildings scrubbed all week long, while the DPs secretly planned costumes and floats, all to focus on a carnival on 24 March.

Haman's defeat was marked as Hitler's defeat: on the day of the carnival the grounds were filled with tombstones for Hitler, walls were decorated and ornamented, slogans and caricatures appeared everywhere. The camp newspaper reported:

> Hitler hangs in many variants and in many poses: A big Hitler, a fat Hitler, a small "Hitler," with medals, and without medals. Jews hung him by his head, by his feet, or by his belly. Or: a painter's ladder with a pail and brush, near a tombstone with the inscription: "P.N." (*po nikbar*) here lies Hitler, may his name be blotted out.

Groups from the camp paraded—the orchestra, sports clubs, unions, and kibbutzim—along with members of the trade schools, police and hospital staff.

But the day meant more than merriment. It also included the reading of a chapter from the *Megillah,* part of the traditional Purim service. And the speeches to the crowd also stressed the broader significance of Purim, 1946, in the DP camps across Europe:

> Hitler Germany was the embodiment of the bestial jungle. The Beast is conquered, not only for us, but for all of humanity. This is the meaning of the festival that we celebrate today. A year ago today, in the concentration camps, we did not imagine that the prophecy of the Prophet Ezekiel would be fulfilled: "dry bones" again become a living

people. We must rebuild our lives from the ground up and build our own home.

That night at the Landsberg camp they burned a copy of *Mein Kampf*—the chief testament of Adolph Hitler, who had warned in 1944 that unless Germany was victorious, "Jewry could then celebrate the destruction of Europe by a second triumphant Purim festival."

Europe had been nearly destroyed, because of Hitler, but some Jews he had tried to destroy lived on—and now commemorated their escape from both Haman's and Hitler's massacres. Europe was saved. And for the Jews of the *She'erit Ha-pletah,* Purim 1946 was a time of redeeming significance.

Thoughts of Palestine were quickened by these celebrations. The *Mossad le Aliyah Bet,* the underground group aiding emigration, sought to oblige, sending twelve ships illegally to Palestine with forty-four hundred European Jews between May and December 1945. Larger ships left in 1946, with elaborate strategies devised to outwit the British in European ports. The British were increasingly able to catch these ships en route, however. As in the famous case of the *Exodus* in 1947, many ships were forced to return to Europe or deposit their passengers in detention camps on Cyprus.[54]

But some Jews made it into Palestine despite British capture. One was Carl Friedman, who journeyed from a Nazi labor camp to liberated Bucharest and traveled from there into Austria using forged papers provided by the Bricha. He then gave up his wristwatch to purchase passage for his group of six Czechoslovak Jews over the Alps into Italy. Their next stop was a Jewish Brigade camp at Padua, from which they went to a new Kibbutz at Nonontola, where five hundred east European Jews gathered to undergo training for Palestine. Friedman recalled that the training even included methods to travel from the ship to the nearby shore.

> They told us all of the things that can happen, what the circumstances are, the chance to arrive or not to arrive. They had been building with barrels, empty barrels and they put wood around them to let us down in the middle of the water, because the ship cannot reach, to let us reach the port . . . 20 or 30 people can fit in it. To let them come ashore.

It was almost to no avail. Leaving with 950 others on the *Enzo Sereni* in December 1945, Friedman ultimately saw the ship intercepted by the British off Haifa; the passengers were forced into the British camp at Atlit but then released, apparently included in the shifting British legal admission totals. For Carl Friedman, Palestine—home—had been reached.[55]

World events soon changed the Palestine situation. In April 1946 the Anglo-American Committee of Inquiry called for admission of 100,000 Jews into Palestine immediately, and under mounting pressure the British turned the issue over to the United Nations. On 1 September 1947, the United Nations Special Committee on Palestine unanimously recommended that Britain give up its mandate on Palestine and partition it into separate Arab and Jewish states. This was approved by the UN General Assembly on 29 November 1947, and when word of the UN vote was flashed to Europe around midnight, the lights came on in the Jewish camps, DPs rushed out and the dancing and singing went on for hours. The British mandate would end on 15 May 1948. The state of Israel was born.[56]

By that time some 69,000 European Jews had made it into Palestine since the end of the war, or into detention on Cyprus. They were part of the estimated 250,000 east European Jews who had escaped into Western Europe through the Bricha. After the state of Israel was established, 331,594 European Jews emigrated there through 1951. Others, however, began looking elsewhere as doors began to open; 165,000 European Jews ultimately emigrated to other countries from 1946 to 1950.[57]

Why did they turn away from Israel? Many had relatives in America or other countries, but it should also be stated that opportunities for emigration began to appear by late 1947 that had not been present in 1945. At war's end only Palestine had seemed possible—that was the only "home." Malcolm Proudfoot, an early student of postwar refugee movements, speculated that the state of Israel might not have come into being if other countries had welcomed Europe's Jews earlier.[58]

The Bricha and the Jewish DPs' suffering in overcrowded camps must be counted as major factors in the rise of modern Israel. Armed struggle by the Haganah in Palestine was important, but, as Yehuda Bauer argued, the presence of Jewish DPs in Europe kept pressure on American opinion makers, while winning the world's sympathy, and ultimately helped swing the United Nations behind the partition of Palestine.

It all signified that DPs were increasingly being drawn into international politics, and their desire for better conditions, as well as their hope for emigration, would put them into more conflicts with their Western protectors as the cold war took on new intensity.

7

CULTURES IN EXILE

We are ready to go to the end of the world—beyond the oceans, into the tropical or polar countries, only not to return home—a phenomenon which is without comparison in history. . . . In such difficult circumstances of life, being at the mercy of foreign nations, and being temporary guests—we still create our culture.

—Yuri Klen, Ukrainian DP poet

We are the hope and blossom of our native land!
—from "God, Thy Earth is Aflame," by Andrejs Eglitis, Latvian DP poet

IN the city of Graz there was a Croatian consulate, a relic of Croatia's prewar and wartime aspirations to nationhood, and within it was a library of Croatian literature and historical documents. But by September 1945 the consulate was closed, and visitors were warned from its entryway by four authoritative seals: Russian, French, British, and American, representing the four powers occupying Austria.

Outside the consulate walls in the Graz area was a multitude of Croatian displaced persons, part of the two hundred thousand who fled north from Tito's Partisans in the closing days of the Yugoslav fighting. Soon they gathered in vacant buildings and hastily organized DP camps, where their thoughts turned to the uncertain future but dwelt also on the known, and loved, Croatian past.

It was the DPs' love for their past that brought the books in the sealed-up consulate to their attention. Within the camps were Croatians who knew of the books' presence there. Finally one of these DPs, a journalist, reconnoitered the building and found a way to break in. Several nights later he returned with a priest and several other Croatians, all carrying rucksacks. They stealthily entered the consulate, made their way to the library, loaded the books into their rucksacks, and made their escape. But as they reached safety the journalist turned to the priest. "Are we justified morally in taking these books?" he asked.

The priest held one of the volumes high. "These are the property of the Croatian people!"[1]

The incident at Graz in September 1945 had counterparts across Europe. For the DPs were a people in exile who still yearned for the tales, songs, and prayers of their native lands. Many were convinced in addition that they, in exile, represented the heart, the living soul, of their people. *They* were now the sovereign nation—they in the crowded camps, far from the hills, the coasts, the fields of home. If the authentic literature of the Croatian past, for example, was to be saved, it must be done by DPs; if the Latvian language was to be retained in its purity and beauty before being Russified, it must be through the lips of DPs; if traditions of the Warsaw Jewish theater were to remain for future generations, these would have to be remembered and carried on by actors of the Jewish surviving remnant.

Much had died with the war. That was gone forever. But much survived. It survived in memories as well as in the dusty, battered suitcases that came into the refugee camps. To protect and to build on these enduring fragments was to be the major task for many DPs.

A hostile environment confronted them, however. Not only were the overcrowded barracks a discouragement, and the isolation of different camps a complicating factor, but the shifting policies of Allied governments often discouraged cultural renaissance. Poles, for example, were pressured to go home, not to build a new existence in the camps. And the Allies had hoped that One World would emerge from the war, a world where victors and vanquished alike declared their solidarity in Humanity. But as occupation authorities tried to further these ends, they discovered that many of the DPs were stateless only according to diplomatic labels: these refugees revealed a tenacious attachment to their ethnic identity. The issue was faced by an American Quaker, working in Germany with DPs, who wrote that he was concerned over "the growth of nationalism among them at a time when the world at large is suffering from too much nationalism."[2]

More than Allied policies and occupation troops could thwart DPs, however. The immediate problem was often that of being identified only as a DP, submerged into a mass of refugees. Most

worked desperately for recognition of their group as a separate
people. This dominated Jewish thinking, as noted previously; it was
also part of the fear felt by Ukrainians and a variety of Yugoslav
groups. So touchy were Ukrainians about being classed as Russians
or Poles that the Ukrainian Free University broke off cooperation
with a Harvard research team because too many of the questions
were considered insulting—"Why did you declare yourself a
Ukrainian?" for example. As early as December 1945 the Association of Ukrainian Political Prisoners appealed to the American
military government to recognize Ukrainians as a "special national
group" and thereby prevent their "social decay" and "slow physical annihilation."[3]

While much of the focus of these efforts was against Allied
authorities or the surrounding Germans, the camps' rising nationalism often set DP group against DP group. In some camps
antagonism or resentment boiled up when German-speaking Balts
got many of the DP jobs that required contact with German officials, or when Ukrainians worked too hard for separate facilities.
Serbs and Croats could not be kept together, the UNRRA soon
learned; neither could Jews and Lithuanians.[4]

Emphasizing their uniqueness became a many-sided activity
among DPs. The cubicles in barracks, the tiny apartments amid
devastation, soon included corners where aspects of national
culture were on display. In a Ukrainian DP family's apartment
would be a shelf with a small sheaf of wheat, an icon, and some
folk-art embroidery. "The home became Ukraine," one DP scholar
recalled.[5]

Also common was the movement to make patriotic holidays the
occasions for new affirmations of ethnic loyalty. The outward appearance of these events varied, however, because different holidays had markedly different meanings. A Latvian thought back on
the ceremonies commemorating 18 November 1918, his country's
Independence Day: "In the camps it was a sorrowful day." The
event was marked in the Baltic camp at Hanau with "a very moving" church service attended by all Latvians, followed by speeches
and a parade. Other former DPs agreed that in the uncertain environment of these camps, traditional holidays, while punctuating
the boredom of refugee life, could sometimes become sad,
nostalgic, even painful. Since most groups marked several national
days during a year's passage, however, it was frequently the case
that some were sad and some joyful. Lithuanian DPs celebrated
"Nation's Day" on 8 September 1945 and marked Independence
Day on 16 February; the Estonians' celebration of independence

was 24 February. Many in the Baltic camps had themselves been participants in those exhilarating days of 1918; now they were in exile and their countries' hard-won independence was destroyed.[6]

The year the Balts remember, 1918, had also marked the start of Ukrainian independence, which lasted only until 1921. Former DPs described the Ukrainian camp celebrations on 22 January (east Ukraine) and 1 November (west Ukraine) as joyful and noisy, similar to Fourth of July observances in America. The sad day for Ukrainians was 30 January, the anniversary of the crushing defeat of a student battalion at the Battle of Kruty in 1918; young DPs led the ceremonies.

Croatian refugees celebrated a much more recent event: the proclamation of Croatian independence on 19 April 1941 at the outset of the tumultuous events associated with the outbreak of war in Yugoslavia. Serbians, however, reached far back into history for an event of national consecration in marking their defeat at the hands of the Ottoman Turks in the Battle of Kosovo on 28 June 1389. This day, known as *Vidov Dan,* had been commemorated over the centuries of foreign domination as the rallying point for Serbian patriotism and religion. It was carried in this form into the DP camps.

Polish DPs encountered problems staging their celebrations. Polish patriotism after the war ran into the wall of Communist domination—a domination symbolized by new Polish officials arriving from Warsaw. Allied support for these envoys complicated the observance of two national holidays in particular: 3 May 1791, the date of the adoption of the reformed Polish Constitution, and 11 November 1918, Independence Day.

There were difficulties with these celebrations now because slogans and songs that spoke of a free Poland either seemed inaccurate or—if emphasized—offended the West's wartime ally, the Soviet Union. "A lady taught Polish songs that had verses against the Russians," one DP leader recalled. A controversy erupted, until finally "she called me—'Would *you* direct the choir?' So I directed it." Others told of a camp crisis centering on which verse to use with the Polish national anthem. The pre-1918 verse was "O God return our freedom"; after 1918 and the creation of an independent Poland, it had been changed to "God Bless Poland." Now the people of the camps decided to revert to "O God return our freedom"—a direct affront to the Soviets.

Other events starting to appear on camp calendars were mournful, even bitter, for the survivors of war and exile. These new ceremonies honored those martyred in the struggles with Fascist or

Open-air orchestra. The DP orchestra at Oberammergau camp was typical of the burst of musical activity in the camps. Also typical was the fact that it was organized by an experienced leader, in this case the former head of the Budapest Symphony. *(UNRRA photo.)*

Communist forces. Balts commemorated 14 June each year, lowering flags to half-mast and holding church services to mark the night in 1941 when Soviet occupiers deported thousands of Estonians, Latvians, and Lithuanians to labor camps and/or death. Croats and Slovenes honored the martyrs of Tito at ceremonies in late May; Serbs commemorated the 17 July 1946 execution of their anti-Communist wartime leader General Draža Mihailovic. For Polish DPs, 1 August was a day of homage to those who died in the 1944 Warsaw uprising.

Honoring the past through national celebrations in the camps was one way to retain a culture; another was through artistic representations of that culture. DP camps soon became showcases for a wide variety of cultural activities—in literature, art, music, the theater—that stressed the underlying theme of national uniqueness. These efforts were helped by the fact that large numbers of creative persons had escaped to the West. (A Latvian scholar has estimated that 70 percent of his country's writers, artists, musicians, and actors made it to western zones in 1945.)[7]

The importance of cultural events in sustaining a people in exile was made forcefully, brutally, clear by the orders sent down by Allied and UNRRA officials who wanted the DPs to return home. The chief of staff of 30 Corps in the British Zone informed his detachments in December 1945 that Ukrainian books and other literature were not to be published, and "all Ukrainian organizations will be disbanded forthwith."[8] Nine months later the UNRRA at Stuttgart ordered that "all educational, recreational and other cultural activities are to be discontinued in all camps caring for one hundred or more Polish Displaced Persons." Such actions demonstrated that national culture and traditions *were* surviving beyond national boundaries. And since the authorities were seeking repatriation, anything that smacked of retaining that culture outside the homeland had to be discouraged.[9]

Folk dancing and choral presentations multiplied, and from these it was a short step to publishing the enduring classics of national literature, for use in the new camp schools and among the general camp population. When a new Latvian refugee press was launched in Stockholm, the first five volumes published were Latvian literary classics; from 1945 to 1950, 1,179 Latvian books were produced by DPs in Sweden, Denmark, and Germany. Lithuanians had sixteen publishing houses in Germany by 1950, reprinting folklore and national history as well as recollections and newly created works. A Lithuanian literary review, *Aidai* (Echoes), was launched by DPs, gained a wide following, and still survives.[10] Slovenians in the Spittal camp in Austria wasted little time in printing national literary classics on a creaking mimeograph machine scrounged by the UNRRA. Polish camps in Germany could boast 300 books published by their DPs within fourteen months of V-E day, including several volumes of masterpieces of Polish literature. And although Jewish DPs at the Belsen camp received thousands of books donated by the World Jewish Congress, they also turned out their own reprints of classics and religious works as well as a literary journal. "It was almost as if the men and women were trying to make up for lost time," a participant recalled.[11]

Make up for lost time they did, producing an enormous amount of reprints and original writing. These at first were geared to preserve national identity and point an accusing finger at the Nazi or Soviet defiler. In the realm of creative writing, lyric poetry provided an immediate response, typified by a 1945 work by the Lithuanian poet Kazys Bradūnas, *The Alien Bread*. In the poem, vignettes of home—a bend in the river, a flower—comfort the traveler until he realizes that this flower does not grow at home, and the river bears a strange German name. Estonian poet Kalju Lepik's "The Face in the Window" describes the return home of the poet, who presses his face against the window to see his mother welcoming him back. But Lepik finds instead the bloody face of a stranger, grinning, behind a broken windowpane.[12]

The DP camps themselves seldom figured as settings in early exile writing. As one Ukrainian poet later would explain, this was because creative writing requires an interval between the event and the time the emotions it aroused can be set down on paper. A rare exception was *Kāds Kura Nav* (Somebody who is not), by the Latvian writer Mārtiņš Zīverts, in which a DP woman realizes that the disfigured invalid who has entered the barracks is in reality her husband, long assumed dead in the war. Rather than fleeing the camp with her new lover as planned, she sacrifices that future to rescue the invalid from his plight. Sacrifice and love, against the backdrop of the war's human devastation—these were also themes amid the general nostalgia and pathos that characterized the literature produced in the camps.[13]

For many writers the end of the war marked an escape, a new freedom. As the Lithuanian critic Rimvydas Šilbajoris argued, home and prison are similar—"they both surround a person with four walls, encouraging the illusion that the world ends where they do. The holocaust of war blew down the walls of home, making us both naked and free." It was tragic, he argued, but it opened "new horizons, new countries, new civilizations, new ways of perceiving and understanding things." Many DP writers thrived in this setting and enlarged the vision of their literature. Later critics would find much outstanding writing produced in the period.[14]

But for many other writers, the trauma of the first months of exile became a fixation. Their new opportunity was like an icebreaker, which pushes through age-old barriers but leaves only a narrow route open to follow. Experimentation became difficult. Latvian critic Juris Silenieks argued that "if the political dimension of exile first enlarged the committed writer's vision, later it acted as a stranglehold." This was the two-edged sword of liberation.[15]

Books and music had their impact in the camps, but it seems probable that just as wide an audience was reached more consistently by the DP theater. An entire camp would turn out for a theatrical performance, and many attended the same play several times. This fact soon affected directors who had earlier been accustomed to putting on complex productions for dedicated, knowledgeable prewar audiences. Now directors tried for variety, alternating musical reviews and children's plays with more serious works. Early groups usually formed around a well-known director or actor, and large camps launched theater groups quickly. Samy Feder at Belsen encountered two veterans of the Jewish stage with whom he had worked in prewar Poland. New companies found enough actors—both experienced professionals and many inexperienced amateurs—but faced continual struggles with the lack of props, costumes, and makeup. Feder recalled the rehearsals for Belsen's first performance: "We had no book, no piano, no musical scores. But we could not wait for supplies from outside. There was a need to play, and an eager public. . . . Somebody remembered parts of a play; somebody remembered a song which we could write down—text and music. . . . We improvised scenery, too."[16]

In many ways this was nothing new. DP groups were only continuing a form of earlier resistance against foreign oppression. And just as the literature of exile, and underground literature, had existed earlier, the theater, too, had long helped groups maintain their identity in times of exile or foreign domination. One historian of Jewish life under the Nazis has written that "the chief forms of resistance in the Ghetto were in terms of creative expression through drama, satirical cabaret, poetry, and music." These activities lay in the immediate past for many DPs. Concentration camp theater, usually performed clandestinely but sometimes with the tacit permission of guards, had helped to keep the flame of opposition burning among many captive Europeans during the war.[17]

Now the Nazi oppressor was gone, and the theater flourished in exile as seldom—if ever—before. Estonians at the Geislingen camp created a large theater company early, and Croatians at the Fermo camp near Ancona, Italy, immediately launched a group to perform classic Croatian dramatic works. This choice of subject was perhaps the dominant one in the early months of DP theater, when feelings were most intense about retaining national culture. Professor Alfreds Straumanis, a former actor and director in Latvian DP theater, said that this desire was especially prominent in the extensive network of theatrical companies that spread through the Latvian camps. These had an immediate base to grow on, since most of the former Latvian National Theatre actors and actresses were in the Meerbeck DP camp; in fact, some fifteen of that organization's best professionals were joined by some twenty others who also had professional theater experience in Latvia. But it was more than actors: almost the entire Latvian Ballet escaped to the West and was re-established at Lübeck; a Latvian opera was launched in the camp at Oldenberg; and an active colony of artists, musicians, and theater and film directors was established at Blomberg, where the Riga film company (complete with equipment and technical personnel) started producing newsreels and movies. Lithuanian camp theater also emphasized folk plays in an attempt to sustain the national spirit. Most other groups reflected this trend, and folk festivals appeared in abundance.[18]

Polish camps were revisited by several Polish DP theater troups, which generally performed variety acts. These faced even greater obstacles than most groups—not only a lack of funds, but also Allied opposition, wide dispersal of Polish DPs, and a scarcity of experienced directors, actors, and actresses. The poet and writer Marek Gorden, who helped form a traveling Polish drama troupe, noted that many theater professionals had joined the wartime Resistance and were killed or imprisoned, while others stayed in Poland after the war to help build the new postwar government. The course of battle had predetermined the fate of Polish DP theater. Gordon added, "I had amateurs in my company. It was the same problem in different camps. We had ten or twelve groups, touring the camps, and we tried to get together to create a professional group—but it was impossible. We were too scattered." The sole Polish professional theater company in occupied Germany was in the Polish Second Panzer Division, part of the British forces based at the Maczkowo camp in the British Zone. Its director was Leon Schiller, a famous Warsaw professor of drama and director from pre-1939 days.[19]

One of the major examples of the DP cultural renaissance appeared among a group that had known several periods of independent nationhood interspersed with long years of foreign domination: the Ukrainians.

The phenomenon of living under foreign control was known to all DP groups, but the Ukrainians' situation included three important factors: their experience with outside control was both recent and lengthy; their numbers were large in the western zones; and a great many of their cultural elite had escaped during the Nazi retreat from the USSR and Poland in 1944–45. (Some of this was due purely to fate: the entire L'vov Opera House company was on vacation when the Soviets retreated in 1941, enabling members to fall under German control, from which they later escaped to the West.) A Quaker employee of the UNRRA noted the similarity between Ukrainians and Jews in their concern for national identity, writing that in the DP camps "the well-established Ukrainian political organizations began to circulate and to develop a consciousness of nationality, much as the Jewish organizations are doing." But unlike the Jews, this Ukrainian group showed "the great omnipresent fear," he added, "a fear so strong and terrible that it cast a cloud over every waking minute." That fear was real: forced repatriation to the USSR remained a constant threat to Ukrainian DPs, and their cultural life was strongly colored by it.[20]

Ukrainian culture drew heavily upon the long tradition of maintaining identity against foreign opposition, and Ukrainian DPs were in a strong position to resume their quest for identity in exile in 1945. A *New Yorker* writer found them "the most obstreperously nationalistic" group at the Aschaffenburg camp, scorning the Saturday night folk dancing of other groups and instead presenting scientific and anthropological lectures. "The DP Ukrainians snoozed through the lectures, and loved them," the reporter added.[21]

Newspapers, literature, journals, art, music, and theater proliferated in Ukrainian camps. Vitality was especially great in theatrical productions, so abundant that three distinct trends developed among the approximately thirty Ukrainian camp companies: national (more openly nationalistic, conservative in subjects and styles); a central type (willing to experiment); and performances by groups on the left such as the Theatrical Studio that were extremely modernistic. One of the more prominent companies of the central classification was the Ensemble of Ukrainian Actors at the Regensberg DP camp, led by the former artistic director of the L'vov Opera House. This company's productions ranged from serious modern works to nineteenth-century classics, from operetta to farce—all to satisfy the varied and eager camp audiences.

Dr. Valerian Revutsky, a Ukrainian-Canadian scholar, has maintained that DP camp productions marked "the highest accomplishment in Ukrainian theater." One of the reasons this was so, he contended, was because of the sudden exhilaration of performing without censorship. Allied authorities showed no inclination to scrutinize the DPs' theatrical material, and a brief attempt by some Ukrainian playwrights to provide "quality control" proved ineffective. As a result, such plays as *The People's Malakhii,* banned since 1929 in the Soviet Ukraine, were performed by the Ensemble Company, and an abundance of new interpretations of old works were staged by the Ensemble and the Theatrical Studio.[22]

Ukrainian literature also blossomed in this new freedom. Writers who had battled the frustrations of Polish controls in the western Ukraine, Soviet censorship in the eastern Ukraine, and Nazi threats throughout the war years now thrived in the heady atmosphere of the camps. This was a "golden era," another Ukrainian DP scholar has written, when "even an author with minor talent was able to publish a book," paying as little as "two or three cartons of American cigarettes from his regular rations."[23]

Responding to this opportunity, large numbers of Ukrainian writers met in Bavaria in 1945 to form the Artistic Ukrainian Movement (MUR), which issued a call through its journal *Arka:* "For a great nation, a great literature." MUR's parliaments of Ukrainian refugee writers repeated many of the Ukrainian literary debates of the 1920s, and, in fact, polemics based on political divisions dominated many of these discussions, as they did other aspects of Ukrainian DP life.[24]

But a wide-ranging literature was frightening to some, and not always welcome. At the first MUR conference at Aschaffenburg in December 1945, a young woman writer's short story dealing with prostitution in Paris upset many delegates and fueled a desire by some to install "quality control" of camp literature through MUR, similar to what some were attempting with camp theatrical productions. This effort resulted mainly in protests from writers who saw censorship behind it, and the controversy helped bring the demise of MUR. A "great literature" was not produced, after all, but a vigorous, varied, and exhilarating literature that enriched Ukrainian DP life. As noted by a later Ukrainian critic, Ukrainian literature in exile was "torn from its roots and twisted by homesickness," but it still was significant in helping preserve the refugees' identity, as well as in assisting them in "continuing a homogeneous cultural process."[25]

Others sensed this, too. And some came to realize that artistic endeavors were playing a much larger role in the camps than simply retaining cultures. This became apparent to a *New York Times* reporter who attended the Belsen camp theater for a performance of a realistic drama about the Jewish experience of the Holocaust. Flames reached onto the stage, children were crushed by German soldiers, and the reporter realized that this was not escapism, not fancy, not imagination: "It is the utilization of the theatre to project actual experience," and as such it was therapeutic for the DPs. The theater was healer, physician. The audience did not applaud at the end, but sat in painful silence. The *Times* reporter concluded:

> The theatre symbolizes their will to live. It represents a culture that survived a systematic attempted extermination. . . . They are anxious to demonstrate, despite the destruction of libraries, the banning of Jewish actors and musicians, that now amid the ashes and mass graveyards of Europe they are starting to rebuild their culture.

The Belsen theater, and other DP cultural activities, thus flowered behind camp walls.[26]

Outside the camps, however, the environments of Germany, Austria, and Italy were frequently hostile. DPs often returned the antagonism. As a result, the rise of nationalistic sentiments among refugees began colliding with the resurgent pride of their former enemies. For now the economies of the defeated nations were rebounding, self-government and pride were returning, and newly powerful local politicians were seeking control over the foreign groups in their midst.

Many DPs, however, would carry anti-German feelings the rest of their lives.

Among Jewish DPs the anti-German bitterness was visceral, unshakable. Even though Jewish DP camps were short of medical staff in the early months, they struggled to avoid bringing in German personnel. And when German doctors and nurses had to be used, the patients expressed shock; they remembered too well looking up into the faces of other German doctors in the concentration camps, short months earlier. At the Belsen camp, according to one resident, one principle "was that Germans must not enter the camp. . . . Belsen remained a kind of extra-territorial unit inside Germany to its last day." When a number of the camp's Jewish DPs had to travel to a conference at Bad Harzburg, 150 kilometers away, they demanded that the British remove all German police along the route, and went on their way flaunting a blue-and-white Israeli flag fifteen feet long. Many tried to avoid giving any aid to the German economy, which meant that Jewish DPs were notable by their absence from jobs outside the camps.[27]

Germans found many reasons to resent refugees, especially after 1945 as feelings of guilt began to diminish. They chafed at overcrowding, not only from the DPs—who numbered as high as 400 per square mile in the area bordering on Czechoslovakia—but also from the twelve million *Volksdeutschen* expelled into Germany under the Potsdam Agreement and cared for by German governmental units.[28]

Housing emerged as a special sore point in such circumstances, for not only had many habitations been destroyed in the war, but the DPs and the *Volksdeutschen* kept coming day after day, in an influx that seemed never to cease. Panic broke out in Augsburg in January 1946 when UNRRA officials were spotted measuring houses; the city was told that 4,000 Jewish DPs were being brought in, with 10,000 more expected. Eventually thousands of Germans were forced out of their homes—10,000 in Munich alone—and injured and ailing Wehrmacht veterans were transferred from hospitals to make way for DP patients. Residents of the Hochfeld workers' apartments were especially embittered by the Occupation's housing policy: They saw their homes taken for DP use and their household goods and clothing thrown into the street. When the apartments were returned to them in 1951 the fixtures, door frames, and windows had been stolen. It was evident also that hogs and cows had been kept in the cellars.[29]

Much bitterness also centered on disparities in food supplies. According to Allied policy the DPs were to eat better than the Germans—at one point the calorie level was officially set at 1,550 per day for the Germans, compared with the goal of 2,000 for regular DPs and 2,400 for persecuted persons. These levels varied by zone and were sometimes exceeded, or frequently not attained. To starving Germans, the food at Wildflecken camp looked "like a magic mountain made of sugar and Spam, of margarine and jam, bearing forests of cigarettes (four packs per week per worker) and carpeted with vitaminized chocolate bars," according to Kathryn Hulme.[30]

A German woman looked back on those years after the war and recalled feeling that "the DPs had everything they wanted." Germans trying to deal in the black market were sent to prison, she said, but not the DPs. The Germans got "hungrier and hungrier." Soon reports came of German workers collapsing from hunger in Hamburg, and food riots spread in the spring of 1946. (DPs charged that, after all, official caloric goals meant little; Germans had access to unofficial food supplies, from friendly farmers and others. The head of the Landsberg DP camp claimed that Bavarian farmers were sending 75 percent of their eggs and 40 percent of their pork to the black market.) German resentment also appeared over the decision by occupation authorities to guarantee DPs coverage under German social security and public relief systems, and to force local German governmental units to pay welfare costs for noncamp DPs.[31]

Confrontations developed frequently in such an environment— melees of shoving, yelling, killing. The most publicized DP-German clash occurred on 29 March 1946 and led to the angry resignation of the district's UNRRA chief and a reduction in the powers of German police. It erupted when a squad of German policemen, without giving notice to the UNRRA or military authorities, entered a Jewish DP camp at Stuttgart and set about with police dogs to search for black market goods. When the DPs angrily rushed at the police, shouting at them, one of the officers shot and killed a DP, a Jewish concentration camp survivor. Alexander Squadrilli, then UNRRA district director, recalled the incident: "I got word in less than an hour; I rushed down there. You can imagine the scene. . . . The policeman had not been menaced. This act turned my stomach so much—I decided to write a report on this incident, to serve as an admonishment."[32] But Squadrilli's "admonishment" angered his chief, Lt. Gen. Sir Frederick Morgan, UNRRA director for Germany; Squadrilli then resigned his position with the UNRRA and was promptly hired as the U.S. Army's DP executive for the zone. Morgan's attitude, however, was quickly contradicted by his own superior, the new UNRRA director general in Washington, Fiorello La Guardia. La Guardia denounced the Stuttgart shooting as "brutal, cruel, cowardly. It was unjustified. An armed German policeman, who had lived his adult life under the Nazi regime, cruelly and cowardly and in cold blood, murdered an unarmed, poor, unfortunate, defenseless Jew. There was no reason for it."[33]

This incident and other similar happenings led to a standard occupation policy banning German police from entering DP camps, except in the company of Allied military officers making investigations; German policemen were to enter without guns and only to identify persons or evidence. Further, any DPs arrested by German police had to be delivered immediately to military authorities, who were in charge of DP trials.[34]

But the issue festered, and by the spring of 1947 German authorities were again seeking some control over the large DP population. "The Bavarian government intends to demand that all DPs be placed under German jurisdiction," declared Bavarian minister-president Ludwig Erhard.[35]

Relations with Austrians and Italians were sometimes brutal for DPs, although most have recalled a more cogenial atmosphere in Italy. There, the natives rebelled mainly at thefts of olives and oranges, while envying the DPs for their superior food and housing. A Canadian visitor found that "many Italians married refugees simply to become a camp resident," until the Italian government forbade Italians from moving into the DP camps. After that order came down, the Canadian learned, "the marriage rate declined to zero."[36]

Fights between Polish DPs and Italian Communists erupted at times, however, and at one point UNRRA camp populations in extreme southern Italy were moved north due to local hostility. But these appear almost as aberrations in a generally peaceful scene.[37]

Austria was a much less pleasant DP environment. Austrians

derided the *verfluchte Ausländer* (lit. damned foreigners), and Ukrainian DPs in the French Zone complained that the Allies were "leaving far too much to the Austrians," who "treated the DPs more as prisoners than anything else." DPs were assigned "the worst and dirtiest jobs" in the zone, they charged; they complained that a Ukrainian colonel had been forced to sweep the streets. Austrian Communists unsuccessfully tried to stop Yugoslav DPs from enrolling at the University of Graz, although local Christian Democrats supported the refugee students there.[38]

Austrian mobs attacked one group of DPs in particular: the Jews, who came through the country in massive numbers as the Bricha from Poland, Czechoslovakia, and Hungary developed in 1946 and 1947. When a U.S. military court handed down severe sentences to ringleaders of an attack on Jews at Ischl, the Austrian government protested that "the sentence is not only contrary to the sentiment of justice of the Austrian population, but is likely to provoke extreme unrest." The prediction was accurate. Similar actions by other Allied officials led to renewed demonstrations against DPs. Soon Austrian authorities began to seek support from any occupation power, or from all, to oust the DPs. Only the Soviets showed interest, however. The chief Austrian political adviser to the Americans commented to a visiting UNRRA official, "Isn't it a pity that the Jews are now spoiling everything by making money out of Austria's misery? The DP camps are all black market centers, while our own people are starving."[39]

The Austrian Parliament protested vigorously in May 1946 when the Allied Council for Austria assessed the country's taxpayers fifty-six million shillings to aid the DPs. A year later the Austrian regime charged that Jewish DPs housed in eight leading Bad Gastein hotels were ruining the country's tourist trade. The Jews, they said, painted Zionist slogans on the walls and provoked minor incidents that discouraged visitors coming from Britain, then the single largest source of Austria's tourist trade. This spreading anti-DP campaign sent shudders through many UNRRA and voluntary agency leaders, who feared military occupation might end before other homes were found for the DPs. One U.S. Army officer said he "wouldn't give a plugged nickel" for the life of a Jewish DP in such a case. An official of the Jewish Joint Distribution Committee left no doubts on his feelings regarding the Austrians: without the presence of Allied military forces, he said, the 120,000 Jewish DPs passing through Austria would have lost their lives.[40]

Shifting policies complicated relations between the DPs, Allied forces, and conquered peoples. Initially the DPs and Allied soldiers shared an anti-German bitterness, and some top Allied officials sought vengeance on the Nazis through a scorched-earth policy. President Roosevelt turned down an early occupation plan in 1944 because it was too soft; it treated the Germans the same as the Dutch and Belgians. Every German, Roosevelt stressed, should recognize "this time" that his country was defeated. This attitude ran through a plan drawn up by U.S. secretary of the treasury Henry Morgenthau, which aimed for the permanent "pastoraliza-tion" of Germany by dismantling its industrial equipment, transfer-ring much of its territory to its neighbors, and making certain that German militarism would never rise again. France, especially, sought protection—through the transfer of the Saar to French con-trol and economic exploitation of Germany by its neighbors, to be carried out through firm international controls. All the Allies sought re-education of the German people.[41]

While the pastoralization plan was eventually rejected by Allied leaders, including Roosevelt, initial occupation policies were only slightly less harsh. Steel making and other industries were re-stricted or dismantled. General Eisenhower proclaimed in July 1945 that Germans were to obey orders "immediately and without ques-tion," and they faced restrictions on travel, mail, meetings, and telephone use. German parades, military songs, national anthems, even militaristic toys, were banned; no veterans' organizations could be formed. In this setting the bulk of aid went to the DPs; occupation officers said there was no chance, for example, that food would be brought in for starving Germans. Fraternization between occupation troops and Germans was forbidden.[42]

But cracks in these barriers began to appear quickly. When the harsh policy of Joint Chiefs of Staff Directive 1067 was announced in the spring of 1945, some American advisers with the Occupation reacted with shock. One said the plan was "assembled by economic idiots" who would "forbid the most skilled workers in Europe from producing as much as they can for a continent which is desperately short of everyting." From various Allied nations, economic experts questioned how Europe could fuel its furnaces, rebuild its industry, even feed itself, if Germany was destroyed economically. Ex-Presi-dent Herbert Hoover argued, following his inspection tour, "We can keep Germany in these economic chains, but it will also keep Europe in rags." To destroy Germany's coal and steel industries would not only strike a blow at Germany, a British Socialist warned; it would also "strike a blow at Europe."[43]

This growing awareness of Germany's economic importance to devastated Europe coincided with a rise in sympathy for the plight of the German people, a sympathy that had heretofore been restricted to the DPs and others of Hitler's victims. Even before the pitiful 1945 harvest came in, Allied military officers in Germany began warning higher-ups that they could not be held responsible for maintaining order among the German people unless food was brought in to satisfy minimum requirements. Mass starvation was imminent. Eventually 630,000 tons of military wheat were provided by the U.S. Army to head off German starvation that fall and winter.[44]

A new corollary to vengeance was developing. Perhaps the Germans *had* launched history's most tragic war, *had* been responsible for millions of deaths, *had* bombed Coventry, massacred Americans at Malmedy, and run cruel experiments on children. But they were also part of the Humanity that the Allies had preached must rise from the ashes of war. Policies such as Joint Chiefs of Staff Directive 1067 could not change that, nor could they overcome the growing vision for a better world blossoming with the birth of the United Nations.

Victor Gollancz, a noted Jewish humanitarian and British Socialist, leader of the "Save Europe Now" organization, toured Germany in the fall of 1946 and vividly described for British newspapers and journals the tragic, worsening condition of the German people. He found high rates of school absence because children lacked shoes and clothing: a frequent report was that a German child could not attend classes on a particular day because his father was to have the shoes then. Gollancz urged the vengeance crowd in Parliament to come visit German hospitals, where he found enormous numbers of hunger edema cases and emaciation. Soon two problems would be solved, he was told—the size of the German population and the supply of manure.[45]

Inevitably sympathizers with the Germans came under attack back home. Germans had been killing Europeans and Americans just months earlier, it was pointed out. Henry Morgenthau led the American campaign to severely punish Germany. He pressured the War Department, published a book urging a "hard" peace, and aided hard-line groups such as the "Society for the Prevention of World War III."[46]

Gollancz answered such critics by noting his own wartime leadership of the National Committee for Rescue from Nazi Terror and the China campaign committee, and he added:

> If we have had to concentrate the major part of our energy on Germany during the last eighteen months, that is not because we

believe that Germans are more important than anyone else: it is because we believe that they are not less important, and because they had few, and at first very few, to appeal in their name to the decency of the world. We further felt that as nationals of an occupying Power that had enforced unconditional surrender we had a very special responsibility before the bars of history and of our own consciences.

To make another war inevitable, Gollancz warned, the West needed only to "acquiesce in this godless destruction, and to drive a whole people, with whom somehow we have to live, into hatred and despair." Such thoughts appeared increasingly among Western leaders.[47]

Inexperienced American soldiers, soon arriving in numbers to replace the wartime GIs, also helped erode the hard line on Germany, but for other reasons. Many transferred their dislike of Germans to the DPs. A DP novelist from Poland, Tadeusz Borowski, referred to these troops as boys who had come like crusaders to teach the Germans baseball as well as profit taking on the black market. Borowski, who stayed a year in Germany before being repatriated, wrote scornfully of the American soldiers' lack of interest in politics and their contempt for those who had lost wealth and fallen to a lower status. His feelings were scarcely unique among the DPs.[48]

A German immigrant Jew who returned to Europe as a member of the U.S. Army had similar insights, even though he himself was now part of the occupation forces. The troops considered all Germans as "krauts," Gottfried Neuberger reported, but many soon discovered that the former Nazi officals at least knew how to address an officer and could help the Americans locate good houses, liquor, and women. And so the local U.S. Army colonel's secretary was a former SS girl, and an ex-SS trooper in the district got rich on illegal sales and purchases, made possible by helping Americans in black market deals. Similarly, Americans in charge of construction crews favored German POWs as workers over DPs or Italian POWs; the Germans were "generally industrious, obedient and well-behaved." More and more, incoming American soldiers from 1946 onward found it difficult to square the image of a bloodthirsty Nazi with the neat, clean, orderly world they found among Germans. DPs seemed less desirable.[49]

This preference for Germans over DPs, as well as the Allies' efforts to encourage a German economic renaissance, produced tensions between occupation soldiers and DPs that led to many confrontations. Some of these were violent. In August 1947 an angry crowd of Jewish DPs set upon soldiers in Ansbach, Germany, and kidnapped two before a flying squad of U.S. troops rescued the pair from the Bleidern DP camp. The abductions, according to one account, "were reported to be a retaliatory measure for an earlier alleged assault by American soldiers on two members of the camp's population."[50]

But much of the troops' dislike for the DPs was expressed verbally, on the numerous occasions when soldiers inspected, questioned, or merely walked on the same street with DPs.

A Polish Jew and veteran of Buchenwald recalled standing in a line of refugees to be queried by an Army Counter-Intelligence Corps officer. When told that this Polish Jew before him had been a tailor, the officer exploded: "Why are all Jews tailors? We ought to put them all on an island, and let them live off each other!" He continued berating the DPs as he went down the line, until one DP—a woman—picked up a chair and threw it at him. MPs quickly arrived, but the woman suffered no penalty.[51]

Such incidents pointed to a division, a gulf, in occupation policy: At the upper levels there was great concern for the DPs and their plight. But at lower, operational levels, American and British soldiers often shifted their preference to the Germans. A former occupation officer who worked in DP affairs recalled that the military appointed Germans to be mayors or to hold other local governmental positions, and close personal ties often developed. "The Germans gradually conditioned the military officers and military government to regard the DPs as inferior and undeserving people." One former military policeman admitted he looked on DPs as "troublemakers."

This was the dilemma: Punish the Germans or help them? Ferret out ex-Nazis or hire them? Block the fraternization of soldiers with Germans, or urge the troops to organize youth clubs so German young people could learn democratic ways?[52]

And a new element was soon added to the mix. The cold war grew rapidly in intensity, increasing the polarization that had never been entirely absent from wartime Europe. This nonshooting conflict began to emerge—now haltingly, now bluntly—as an everyday fact of life.

Memoirs of American and British military leaders during the occupation era described initial warm relations with their Soviet counterparts. But these did not last, for the memoirs also reported increasing danger signs: Russian agents kidnapped DPs; belligerent speeches were made by Stalin and other Communist leaders; the German Communist newspaper referred to the "illegal" General

Clay; there were unexplained disappearances of outspoken anti-Communist Germans.[53]

The public quickly felt the breakup of the wartime alliance. A British Socialist visited the British Zone in the spring of 1946 and reported a widespread feeling that a third world war between the West and the Communist bloc was inevitable. DPs frustrated with the Allies for abandoning their homelands to the Communists sometimes encouraged these war fears. The Memmingen DP camp newspaper argued that "it is precisely the present, strained international relations that give us more hope to believe that the freedom that Lithuania lost as a result of World War II can be regained as an outcome of World War III."[54]

All of this helped change priorities. When a UNRRA investigator in the summer of 1946 argued for better care for the DPs, General Clay responded that his orders were to reconstitute the German economy without delay. Soon after this came the 6 September 1946 speech by Secretary of State James Byrnes in Stuttgart, which blamed Germany's economic ills on the Soviet Union's refusal to go along with German unification. The Americans, Byrnes stressed, were now willing to join their zone with any other and wanted the government of Germany returned to the German people. Similar moves followed in 1947, after the Communists had been severely beaten in the Berlin city elections. The Marshall Plan to provide massive American aid to Europe was announced, the U.S. and British zones of Germany were merged, and all the while the Communists tightened their control over Eastern Europe. In 1948 came the Czechoslovak coup, followed by the Berlin blockade: the Soviets restricted Western traffic into Berlin and President Truman responded with a massive airlift of supplies into the city for almost ten months. The next step in Europe was the formation in August 1949 of the North Atlantic Treaty Organization, openly anti-Soviet. By then those working in European refugee programs were being instructed on escape routes and other preparations for an expected Soviet invasion.[55]

These changes placed Germany in a crucial position between East and West. They also turned Allied policies sharply away from anti-German vengeance. The situation of the DPs was also being transformed, and they found themselves given only a symbolic role as pillars in the growing anti-Communist struggle. That symbolic value was high: these people, after all, knew Communism firsthand. Their independence day rallies and their memorial services testified to that fact, over and over.

But the DPs were not on the front lines against the Communists;

West Germans were. And if these new allies disliked the DPs, then
the Americans and the British could not favor the DPs against the
Germans. Not any longer.

And so West Germany became a partner in the anti-Communist
crusade. The DP president of the Landsberg camp saw what the
transformation meant:

> Germany is no longer our foe in a war not yet concluded, but a
> potential ally in a war that has not yet begun. . . . Germany is to be
> transformed from a defeated enemy into the guardian of our Euro-
> pean front line. The Jewish survivors in the occupied zone of Western
> Germany are an obstacle to this development.[56]

He spoke for Jewish DPs, but his words covered the plight of all
DPs left in Europe.

Allied policies turned ever more sharply in favor of strengthening
Germany, and by early 1947 the U.S. Zone's UNRRA chief was
lamenting that new army orders cut down the supplies for DPs in
favor of providing more for Germans. Paralleling this was new
concern for giving Germans more control over their own territory.
Nonintervention in German life, once put forward reluctantly, now
became established policy. The numbers of U.S troops and occupation personnel declined sharply, more German civilians were hired
by the Americans (even as armed border patrolmen), and Germans
were gradually allowed to elect some of their own leaders—first in
local *Gemeinde* balloting in January 1946, then with elections for
Landkreis posts in April and *Stadkreis* officers in May 1946. Other
steps followed over the ensuing months and years, the final one
coming in the spring of 1949 when the West German Constitution
was approved by the occupation powers, leading to the first session
of the Federal Republic's Parliament on 7 September 1949. It was
the first freely elected parliament to meet in Germany since 1933.[57]

With the appearance of such German groups as the "Friends of
America" and the "Stuttgart American-German Young Women's
Progressive Club," with German cinemas showing *Young Tom Edi-
son* and *Abe Lincoln in Illinois,* and with 10,000 turning out in
Stuttgart to see two German teams play American-style football, it
was obvious that changes were in the air. And these portended a
new attitude toward the DP groups, whose increasing numbers of
theatrical productions, athletic competitions, and embroidery dis-

plays proclaimed their own uniqueness and their determination to remain separate, unassimilated.

The truth was that the DPs were becoming a collective anachronism. They were misfits in cold war Europe, and the Germans, Austrians, and Italians wanted them to leave.[58]

But where would they go?

8

THE GATES OPEN

It is unthinkable that they should be left indefinitely in camps in Europe.
—President Harry S Truman, 7 July 1947

THERE was desperation in the letter from DPs at the Salzburg camp.

Their anguished plea told of a fellow Ukrainian, a doctor, who had been taken away by the U.S. Army Counter-Intelligence Corps. He was seized, they said, after other refugees accused him of causing the arrest of several Jews when German troops occupied a Polish town during the war. No announcement of the charges had been made public, but the doctor's wife learned from some of the accusers that "the main charge against her husband is that he could have hidden some of the persecuted Jews in the hospital, but did not do it."

The twenty-three signers of the letter insisted that he *had* hidden Jews as patients, "for a long time," but had been unable to do it longer or "it would have caused the ruin of all of them" as well as of himself. They added that one of the accusers counseled the doctor's wife not to be afraid: "The Doctor will be free again, but it will be good for him to suffer a little too, they [the Jews] have suffered a great deal more."

This controversy in the Salzburg camp had thousands of parallels across liberated Europe. Accusations based on distant events, lack of formal charges, hidden accusers, allegations difficult to prove or disprove—all formed part of the chilling underside of DP life in those years. Denunciations, according to the Salzburg petitioners, were "general in war-torn Europe."[1]

But one aspect of the picture began to change, for the worse. Immediately after the war, when hatred of the Germans remained

178

high, a collaboration charge tossed about a DP camp could lead to beatings, scorn, jail. But two years later the mere whisper of such allegations could block emigration of the accused, or at least cause a lengthy delay in his emigration. And that could mean missing out on the chance for resettlement.

For emigration was suddenly in the wind. In late 1946 came startling news, exciting news, sometimes carried through the rumor-vines and at other times proclaimed in newspapers. Brazil said it would take 120,000 European refugees, and Venezuela was prepared to accept 50,000; even the tiny Dominican Republic, it was reported, was willing to take 100,000! That all of these totals proved enormously overoptimistic did not matter. (The Dominican Republic ended up taking only 413 DPs). What was important was that the gates were finally opening.

The possibility of actually leaving the camps brought a sudden transformation of the listlessness, the hopelessness, of many DPs. Cultural activities boomed. There was new concern for vocational training, for language classes, for any classes.[2]

There was a dark cloud over the bustle and hope in the camps, however. It hovered around the DPs as they read the resettlement notices on camp bulletin boards; it twisted through their conversations while they stood in lines winding around the emigration missions. It was the same fear known to the Ukrainian doctor in Salzburg camp—the fear of being charged with wartime collaboration with the Nazis.

Such charges had fertile soil in which to grow. Within the United States and Canada, left-wing groups published reports that many DPs had been, and still were, Nazi enthusiasts. Newspapers talked of "Ukrainian quislings" and "Nazi zealots," and wire service reports quoting military authorities bore such headlines as "U.S. Uncovers Baltic Nazis in DP Camps." A *New York Times* writer classified a third of the Baltic DPs as collaborators, and one of Eisenhower's aides condemned the Balts, Poles, and Ukrainians as "Nazis to the very core of their being." Ethnic solidarity was often absent on this issue, in Europe and overseas.[3] A pro-Soviet Ukrainian-Canadian group told the Canadian Parliament that the Ukrainian DPs in Europe consisted mainly of war criminals, collaborators, and people who were trying to avoid rebuilding their homeland.[4]

These charges, made so heatedly in the late 1940s, have never totally died out. Many concentration camp veterans today retain an understandable hatred of the non-Germans who helped the Nazis; many have transferred this hatred to all members of those na-

tionalities. "Ninety percent of them are here because they have
something to hide," a Polish Jew commented about other DPs in
America. "This is still hounding us. We see them here."

The issue is enormously complex. On one hand, the memories of
the concentration camp inmates and other Nazi victims are undoubtedly correct: the Germans had little trouble finding many
among the peoples of Europe who would help them round up Jews
and others, guard them, torture them, kill them.[5]

But it is also true that there were different types and levels of
collaboration. Philip J. Noel-Baker, British delegate to the United
Nations Policy Committee, admitted at one point that "no satisfac-
tory definition of a collaborator had yet been found." There was
what has been termed *collaboration d'etat,* in which people of
occupied countries gave calculated cooperation to keep civil administration functioning. Danes were urged to provide some help to
Germans as a way of continuing existing institutions or activities;
the bus system could keep operating if it was used to carry Germans, for example. Under this philosophy teachers continued
teaching, firemen kept fighting fires, farmers raised crops, shopkeepers served the invaders. Sometimes such persons were even
paid through the Third Reich.[6]

The realities of life under the Nazi occupation made judgment
difficult—then and now. A Slovenian begged for understanding of
the dilemma of his countrymen, caught in the Yugoslav civil war as
well as the world war during the early 1940s:

> Collaboration in Slovenia was a matter of biological survival. The pro-
> Tito Partisans began with extermination of "enemies of the revolu-
> tion" in the summer of 1941 and refugees escaping from villages
> found shelter in Ljubljana. There they were at the mercy of the
> Italians and later the Germans. They had a limited choice: (a) to join
> the Partisans. Many who were known anti-Communists were not
> acceptable. Some of these did—and vanished; (b) the other alter-
> native was to return "home" under Italian or German protection.
> Neutrality was simply not possible.[7]

Many who seemed to be cooperating with the invaders were secretly fighting them. Evidence from Yugoslavia has shown that the
Chetniks often fitted this category: they were both a resistance
movement and collaborationists, depending on their immediate
predicament. Even Tito's Partisans in the spring of 1943 quit battling the Axis forces so they could turn against the Chetniks. Was
Tito collaborating? And over all of occupied Europe the larger truth

was this: a helpless person confronting an armed enemy often saw no alternative but to cooperate—as the tales of Jewish collaborators in the concentration camps have made clear. But where is the line between forced cooperation, and willing, eager, enthusiastic collaboration? Both were present. Or between active aid to the invaders and an attempt to buy time while keeping the nation alive? Outsiders, one continent and perhaps two generations removed, will tread with care when condemning or excusing.[8]

No reluctance to make such allegations held back large numbers of refugees. Investigators were soon overwhelmed with these charges, although their efforts received significant aid at war's end with the capture of the entire contents of the Nazis' Berlin Document Center. The BDC kept twenty million names on record and a collection of data compiled "as only the Germans can do," according to an American who worked amid its files. (He encountered such minutia as travel vouchers for Hermann Göring.) These materials were useful in checking the denunciations that began pouring in as Allied armies appeared and neighbors ran out to accuse neighbors. One of the liberators of Dachau recalls that newly freed concentration camp inmates were soon pointing fingers of accusation at each other. And there was no honor among collaborators. A low-ranking Nazi turned in an Estonian who had been forcibly taken into the German forces in the closing months of the war. The Nazi knew he himself could not emigrate but wanted to make sure that neither could the Estonian.[9]

Ferreting out collaborators became a major activity in the initial refugee camps and assembly centers. A Polish DP leader in the French Zone of Germany was ordered to turn over a man who, it was charged, had helped the Nazis as they occupied a village. "The French authorities had the man's hair shaved, then paraded him around the blocks to show him to the people." According to another DP who worked in a Berlin transit camp for UNRRA, the typical collaborator had stolen or made a false identity card; camp policy was to arrange for someone from the suspect's supposed hometown to view him and decide if his story was accurate. The former UNRRA employee recalled such a case. "This one said he was from a town in central Poland. But one of our workers recognized him as an associate policeman, a quisling who would round up Jews for the Gestapo. I turned him loose without saying anything. But I let the word get out, and I waited four hours before I called the UNRRA. By that time he was beaten badly." And a veteran of a Baltic unit that had been thrown by the Germans against the advancing Russians admitted that his later reception in

the DP camps was quite cool—"similar to the return of the Vietnam
veterans" a generation later. This was so, he concluded, because
"the rest of the compatriot civilians thought that their status would
be compromised by accepting those who fought on the German
side."[10]

Complications on the issue were especially numerous among the
Ukrainians, who faced more charges of wartime collaboration than
any other group.

Roots of the Ukrainian controversy ran back to the First World
War, when the collapse of Czarist Russia and the Austro-Hungarian
Empire opened the way for proclamation of an independent
Ukrainian state in 1917. This state was recognized by Kaiser
Wilhelm's Germany in 1918, a fact that many Ukrainians would not
forget. But the Ukraine's demand for national rights and extensive
territory threw the new government into conflict with Russians,
Lithuanians, Poles, and others having competing claims. As a result, the Ukraine was forced during the Russian Revolution to take
on the Reds and Whites separately, and eventually to battle the
Polish army as well in a nine-month war. The Ukrainian independent state was defeated on all fronts by 1921, and Ukrainians faced
hatred and antagonism from their neighbors throughout central
Europe during the years between the wars. This meant that by 1939,
as one historian put it, "the Ukrainian national movement was left
with only one potential ally—the Nazis."[11]

Ukrainians' recollections today are remarkably similar regarding
the reception given Germans when the Wehrmacht invaded Ukrainian areas of Poland and the Soviet Union. In the words of a former
DP, "All Ukrainians accepted the Germans as liberators." German
policies sometimes played to this sentiment, building hopes that an
independent Ukraine—linked to the Third Reich—might emerge.[12]

This feeling blossomed again in 1943, when there was a sense that
both the German and Soviet war machines were being destroyed by
each other. In May of that year the Germans announced formation
of the Ukrainian "Halychyna" Division, slated to be the nucleus of
a Ukrainian National Army. One of its slogans was "Take advantage of your only opportunity to destroy communism and free your
native land." The Third Reich's aim was obvious: it was seeking
soldiers to stem the Soviet advance. The Ukrainians had other
aims, however, including a plan to restore their nation's independence during the expected breakup after the war, as had occurred at
the end of World War I. The Halychyna Division would be ready for
that.[13]

Recruiting was initally limited to the L'vov area, with the lion

Interrogation. Screening seemed almost constant in the DP era: Initially, as shown here at the refugee center in Vanviers, Belgium, the Allied investigators sought Nazi collaborators. Later the focus shifted to eligibility for receiving UNRRA or IRO aid. Then various nations' resettlement teams launched their own interrogations, seeking worthy immigrants. *(UNRRA photo.)*

emblem of Galicia chosen as the division's symbol. Ukrainian leaders aided these efforts, based on the firm German promise that Ukrainian troops would be used only on the eastern front, only against Soviet forces. Ukrainian refugee organizations would later contend that volunteering for service in the division was the best choice open to many young men. The Central Representation of Ukrainian Emigrants in Germany made this defense in 1949:

> The Ukrainian Division was formed at a time in the late war when young Ukrainians were forcibly incorporated in German Army formations. In order to avoid compulsory service in the German Army young Ukrainians joined the Ukrainian "Halychyna" Division, where they were commanded by Ukrainian commanders, were dressed in Ukrainian uniforms, where they had Ukrainian chaplains of their own Church and where the Ukrainian language was universally spoken. . . . The Ukrainian Division was also formed at a time when a determined drive to collect available young men for labor in Germany was in progress. . . . Formation of the Ukrainian Division thus also

provided, and was meant to provide, a legal means of escaping slave
labor in German industry and agriculture.[14]

Thrown into battle against Soviet troops for the first time in July
1944 at Brody, east of L'vov, the sixteen-thousand-man division was
mauled as German troops pulled back. The remnant, a few thousand, was placed in German concentration camps, then re-formed
with Ukrainians recruited principally from concentration camps
and other German military units. Moved to Austria by early 1945,
the division ultimately surrendered to the British at Klagenfurt and
was placed in a camp at Rimini, Italy, until it was shifted to England
in 1947.[15]

After repeated efforts to convince the Allies that their wartime
record was more anti-Soviet than pro-Nazi, and that many had
been forcibly recruited, the Ukrainians won sporadic concessions
from U.S. and British officials. But the pressure on them was
great—especially from the Soviet Union, whose spokesmen demanded their repatriation. From 1945 on, members of the division
lived in terror over the possibility of being forced out of U.S. and
British control, and they fought bitterly against collaboration
charges.[16]

The Baltic peoples presented another set of complications. Some
were of German ethnic background and had voluntarily migrated
into German-controlled Poland in 1939 and 1940, accepting German
citizenship and entering their names in the records of the *Einwan-
derer Zentralstelle* (Immigrants Central Bureau), which was later
captured by the Allies. Others voluntarily joined German military
forces after the German invasion and helped round up Jews.

Many Balts, however, had no choice but to collaborate during the
lengthy German occupation, and as the Soviet troops approached
in 1943 and 1944 large numbers were suddenly compelled to join
units of Germany's "Baltic Legions"—the Lithuanian, Latvian, and
Estonian Waffen SS. Some joined voluntarily at first, as did the
Lithuanians who enlisted in the *Lietuvos Vietine Rinktine* (Lithuanian Home Formation), then saw their leaders forcibly removed and
the units taken over by the Wehrmacht. Within the concentration
camps, meanwhile, Balts—notably Lithuanians—were frequently
employed by Nazis to control other prisoners as part of the German
policy of pitting nationalities against each other.[17]

The crucial issue with the Balts centered, then, on whether they
had voluntarily helped the Germans or had done so under compul-

sion. It was a question that could hinge on slight fragments of evidence. A finding of voluntary aid had ominous results.

One key question arose when the U.S. and British zones initially accepted Waffen SS troops as eligible for assistance, but the UNRRA did not. Some Waffen SS men spent months in prisoner-of-war compounds before being allowed into DP camps. They were finally cleared, although each case required lengthy interrogation as to whether the military service had been voluntary. The process left a bad taste in the mouths of many DPs, who today still criticize the Allies for failing to understand their lack of options at the time they entered the Third Reich's service.[18]

Americans who worked with the DPs have told of receiving unending denunciations, until they came to see that most were made in revenge, envy, or retaliation. Denunciation, after all, provided an easy way to settle old scores, particularly when the Army Counter-Intelligence Corps took the attitude (in the words of a former American official), "Why should we take a chance?" Congressmen and American editorial writers demanded that "Nazis" be rooted out. One Polish DP, who held leadership positions in several DP camps, has admitted that once he realized most charges of aiding the Nazis were made out of a desire for revenge, he began to hold the cases back. "I never gave those files to the U.S. authorities if I wasn't really sure," he said. At Wildflecken, denunciation became "the malevolent indoor sport" of those rejected for resettlement, permitting them to block the emigration of others.[19]

For one American the turning point came in a case that severely tried his credulity. Ben Kaplan, an executive in the American Displaced Persons operation, was so angered at the CIC's acquiescence in collaboration charges against ten DPs that he called a meeting with top CIC officials—and hid the accused DPs in an adjoining room. After discussing the charges with the CIC men and finding that they were based only on a denunciation, he called in the ten DPs. All were Orthodox Jews, with sidelocks and hats.

"Do they look like Nazis?" Kaplan asked the CIC chief. The denunciation, it was learned, had originated with a splinter Jewish sect over a doctrinal dispute. The charges were dropped.[20]

The desperation and bitterness with which such charges were fought was a measure, in turn, of the improved chances for leaving Europe.

Resettlement opportunities developed slowly, excruciatingly slowly. In the United States, where a 1946 poll found that a majority wished to see European immigration either reduced or eliminated,

ethnic and religious groups were silent on the issue for many
months. American Jewish groups favoring increased immigration
risked Zionist charges that this would retard the growth of Israel.
And although the American Friends Service Committee became
one of the major groups aiding refugee resettlement to the United
States, one of its leaders did not hold out much hope in August
1945:

> The fact is that we are no longer the "land of opportunity" of the usual
> European immigrant's dream, and this will be especially true if we
> have a serious unemployment problem following the war, as many
> people fear we will. Now that immigration to this country is not a
> matter of actual rescue from persecution or danger of persecution, we
> feel that plans for immigration should be given very careful considera-
> tion and should be weighed against all possible alternatives of return
> to the native country, remaining in the country of current residence,
> or possible migration to other countries.

As late as October 1946, the *New York Times* saw emigration
possibilities for DPs "constantly dwindling," leaving only repatriation or continued residence in the camps.[21]

But through these early postwar months the image of America as
a land of immigration was still alive, and many DPs who had
relatives across the Atlantic grasped at that possibility. President
Truman encouraged such actions in December 1945 by ordering
that DPs were to be given preference under existing U.S. immigration laws. Most quickly learned, however, that those laws included a
national origins quota system installed in the late 1920s. The quota
system heavily favored western and northern Europe. Great Britain
and Ireland qualified for 84,000 immigrant visas a year; Germany,
26,000. But quotas for the countries contributing the most DPs
totaled only 39,000 yearly, and many nations within this category
had miniscule annual quotas: Poland's was 6,524, the Soviet
Union's was 2,712, and Estonia's was 116. A Yugoslav DP learned
that his turn on the quota to the United States would come in the
year 2017. A Lithuanian had high hopes about traveling as a regular
emigrant to America: "I had an uncle in the U.S. He sent me
papers, and so I went to the consulate. They told me that the
Lithuanian quota was around three hundred a year. 'You can emigrate after thirty-five years,' they said. I just left my papers there
and walked away."[22]

Added to the reluctance of the outside world to accept DPs was
the continuing pressure for repatriation, encouraged by the

UNRRA as well as many Allied officials. Emigration ran counter to repatriation, and many East European officials argued against encouraging the former and thereby penalizing the latter. The Warsaw-based Polish Red Cross lashed out at anyone who talked to the DPs of resettlement, charging that they gave false information and were really "looking for cheap hands for industries."[23]

Caught amid this cross fire and seeking an escape, DPs clutched at any possibility. "Life in the camps turned on rumors, all the time," a Slovenian DP said. "You can't understand the camps until you see that." As an example he told of a report that refugees would be transported in large numbers to establish colonies along the southern Ecuadorian border. "There was nothing to it," he added, "but it attracted big attention for a while." A Polish DP recollected hearing a rumor in his camp that the refugees would simply be apportioned among various countries. And a Lithuanian group went further in October 1946 and proposed resettlement within Europe:

> . . . displaced Lithuanians (as well as Latvians and Estonians) would be settled in a compact mass in some area of Western Germany (e.g., the Rhineland), which would entail the transfer of the German population elsewhere.
>
> The area would be administered by the United Nations Organization . . .
>
> . . . [T]he sacrifice demanded of the Germans would be but a small redress for all material, moral, and political wrongs suffered by Lithuania at the hands of Nazi Germany.[24]

Rumors were fueled by the early dribbles of emigration—a thousand Baltic girls went to work in British hospitals; several dozen DPs left for Sweden and France; others managed to squeeze into U.S. immigration quotas or into Palestine. And these initial movements sparked varied responses in camps. Since a post-1945 criminal record could be easily uncovered by resettlement officials, camp authorities and parents alike had a new weapon to hold over the heads of their charges. One Ukrainian DP recalled that his father would say, "'Behave! Don't get in trouble—or nobody will take us anywhere!'"[25]

In addition, the increasing possibility of resettlement began to destroy a widely cherished but sometimes hidden hope among DPs: their fundamental belief that somehow they would be going home again. "Next Christmas in Croatia!" rang out the holiday toasts in the Croatian camps in Italy. And they believed it, for nearby, in

Naples, some Yugoslav DP leaders were working to weld together
a reborn Royal Yugoslav Army of Serbs, Croatians, and Slovenians
in order to overthrow Tito. "Our dream remained alive until we
were moved to Germany in 1947," a Serbian participant recalled.
Other groups held similar aspirations. A study of the Lithuanian DP
press concluded that "as late as 1948 the editorials still raised the
unrealistic issue of returning to the homeland, while the other parts
of the publications were increasingly filled with practical matters
relating to emigration." A reporter for the *New Statesman*
(London) found the dream of return still alive among many DPs
long after emigration had begun: "Politics to these people means no
more and no less than the fight for the 'liberation' of their countries.
In their political literature, page after page, is the assumption that
war is certain. . . . These are people, it seems, who indeed have a
vested interest in a Third World War." Many retain that dream
today. But many others jettisoned it with other unusable items
when resettlement became reality.[26]

The first large-scale emigration plan came from Belgium. That
country's call for thousands of men reverberated through the camps
of Germany in the fall of 1946. The Belgians sought 20,000 DPs to
work as coal miners, with family members expected to swell the
total to some 50,000. Poles, Ukrainians, and Balts were favored
initially, because they formed the major nonrepatriable groups in
the camps. UNRRA and IRO officials remained skeptical of some
aspects of the plan, eventually requiring that Belgium reunite families after only ninety days (instead of after two years), allow DPs to
shift to above-ground work if their health deteriorated in the mines,
and grant the refugees Belgian citizenship in five years. The UN-
RRA was aware that the plan was "not a humanitarian gesture on
the part of Belgium," as one official asserted, "but a means of
obtaining badly needed workers."[27]

References to economic motives could not dampen enthusiasm
for the project, for it was the first resettlement scheme calling for
thousands—not dozens or hundreds—of DPs. Kathryn Hulme
watched the reaction to it in the Aschaffenburg area:

> In our seven camps we saw in microcosm what was happening all
> through the DP world of Germany at that moment—the lifted faces as
> to a fresh breeze, the tense debating wherever men were gathered, the
> quiet wives standing aside waiting to see if decision for a risky
> separation was to be made (some praying for it, some planning to
> override it) and the stricken look of the men over forty years, sad

spectators of the first opening of a door to a new life for which they were already too old to qualify.[28]

Once final details were approved by occupation authorities and the new IRO, Belgium moved quickly to locate its 20,000 workers. The Belgians first invited a team of DPs to inspect the mines and the workers' homes, provided quick physical exams to DP applicants, and resettled some 16,000 in Belgium in the second half of 1947. Eventually 22,000 were brought in. "When the first trainloads went there was a tremendous celebration!" one American official recalled. Soon many became dissatisfied with labor underground, however, and began drifting back to the DP camps. This set off another controversy over whether they should be allowed to emigrate elsewhere, since they had already had one chance. Authorities finally ruled that since they had not been truly "resettled" in Belgium, they were eligible for other programs.[29]

Britain moved next into large-scale resettlement, putting together several programs that ultimately brought in 86,000 DPs, exclusive of large numbers of foreign war veterans. It was the earlier experience with foreign soldiers, however, as well as with refugees during the war, that prepared the way for welcoming DPs. The British found that the 115,000 Polish army veterans who elected to join the "Polish Resettlement Corps" and stay in Britain after 1945 were a benefit, not a problem. The Labour government was seeking industrial expansion, which required more workers due to wartime losses and changes in the birth and death rates. Under this policy, Britain also took in some 12,000 members of the controversial Ukrainian Halychyna Division.[30]

The eyes of Labour government planners soon turned to the regular DPs languishing in camps across Germany, Austria, and Italy. The early small-scale "Balt Cygnet" plan brought in some 2,500 Baltic women for hospital training and employment in Britain, and its success led to a second program for 6,000 Baltic women to work as domestics. Then, with "Operation Westward Ho" in 1947, Britain set a goal of up to 100,000 DPs and recruited 79,000 by mid-1948. They were officially known as European Voluntary Workers, or EVWs. Although these moves were widely hailed, a *New Statesman* writer noted that his country's motives "were not entirely altruistic. It was a few weeks after the great 'freeze-up'; we had a production crisis of the first magnitude, and we recognized an 'easy' labor market when we saw one."

Nevertheless, these programs made Britain—tiny, overcrowded Britain—the major recipient of European refugees by early 1948.[31]

Canada also began to look upon the DPs as potential immigrants in 1947. This marked a shift from previous policies, which had sought to limit immigration to groups already predominant in the Canadian population, that is, the British and French. In addition, government officials, like others to whom the 1930s were a very painful and very recent memory, were afraid that the postwar period would bring high unemployment as war industries converted to peacetime and war veterans flooded the labor market.

But, paradoxically, it was because of labor needs that the first group was allowed entry. Farmers on the Canadian prairies lost their German POW workers of wartime and cried out for government help in locating new harvest hands. At the same time, Britain was sounding out the Commonwealth for outlets for some of the thousands of Polish army veterans still camped on British soil. As a result, on 23 July 1946, the Canadian cabinet passed an Order-in-Council permitting 4,000 Polish army veterans to enter the country as "qualified agricultural workers."[32]

These were not DPs, however, and in the camps of Europe the possibility of emigrating to Canada still seemed remote in mid-1946. But changes were occurring in Canadian public opinion, as the long-feared depression turned instead into an economic boom and Canadian workers began moving by the thousands into better-paying industrial jobs. Now Canada had a labor shortage, and there were urgent calls to recruit workmen in Europe's DP camps.

Despite French Canada's opposition, Canadian leaders were turning toward the DPs by the fall of 1946 as the best solution for the nation's worsening labor shortages. Finally, on 7 November 1946, Prime Minister Mackenzie King issued emergency orders to bring DPs into Canada. In subsequent weeks two separate programs were approved: (1) a bulk-labor system, in which Canadian employers would specify types and numbers of workers to come in under contract; and (2) a close-relatives plan, soon broadened to permit Canadian residents to sponsor individuals who were not relatives if employment and housing were guaranteed for them.[33]

In January 1947 a Canadian immigration officer arrived in Germany, and by March 1947 two Canadian resettlement teams were operating in the camps. The first DPs sailed for Canada on 4 April 1947, beginning a stream that would reach flood tide at various times over the following five years. Lumbering operations, sugar beet farms, mines, railroads, and other major employers rushed to fill their labor needs with refugees.[34]

Complaints were heard that Canadian officials were arbitrary, and French Canadian spokesmen denounced turning the nation into a "dumping ground for the countries of Europe." Others objected to the lack of public debate on the issue; the federal cabinet made all major decisions on which nationalities and ethnic groups could be admitted. "To avoid embarrassment all around," one critic charged, "the Cabinet and its loyal parliamentary majority have decided to let these touchy questions be settled in private."

The totals kept growing, however, until Canada was one of the major countries receiving DPs: some 14,000 came as domestic workers; 56,609 entered under the bulk-labor schemes; and others arrived under individual sponsorship to put the Canadian total at 157,687 DPs by the end of 1951.[35]

Australia embarked on an immigration program immediately after the end of the war, seeking 70,000 newcomers a year. But these were to be of British stock only, people who could be assimilated easily into life in Australia. Accordingly, the Australian minister for immigration went to London soon after the war's close to start a flow of Britons.

But the British were not interested. Concerned over an inadequate population to support economic growth, the British detoured the Australian minister across the Channel and urged that he seek his immigrants among the DP camps of the Continent. Fearing that any influx of non-Britons would provoke hostility at home, the minister and his entourage moved cautiously among the camp inhabitants, picking blue-eyed, blond DPs less likely to offend native-born Australians. The first boatload of DPs arrived in Australia on 27 November 1947.[36]

These newcomers met no significant hostility. DPs soon began flocking to the Australian resettlement program, which became known for conducting operations that accepted or rejected applicants quickly. An Australian writer summarized the criteria as the need to be "healthy, free of fascist sympathies and ready to live anywhere and work at anything in Australia." Family members were less happy about the enforced separation, which sometimes ran for the entire two years of the initial contract.[37]

Eventually 182,159 DPs emigrated to Australia, led by 60,000 Poles and 36,000 Balts. Enough of an East European mixture was admitted through Australian gates to constitute a small revolution in the nation's much-publicized homogeneity. The long tradition of allowing only British stock down under was broken. By 1966 almost one in five Australians was a postwar immigrant or the child of one, and 60 percent of this group had non-British ethnic backgrounds. The DPs' entry had become a precedent of far-reaching importance. As one scholar has concluded, "Their generally trouble-free integration encouraged the Australian Government to seek other sources of Continental migrants."[38]

Representatives of many countries now moved into the camps, and ships loaded with DPs began to move away from European ports in large numbers. This was in addition to the continuing exodus overland and through the Mediterranean to British-controlled Palestine. Up to mid-May of 1948, Palestine had received some 50,000 immigrants, but with the creation of the state of Israel the total exploded to 650,000 over the following three years. In addition to the DPs, Israel also received heavy immigration directly from Eastern Europe, North Africa, and the Middle East.[39]

Other recruitment programs launched in 1947 ranged from Iraq's appeal for ten unmarried doctors (which one journalist called "merely the smallest and most candid national project") to requests for more substantial numbers from French Morocco (1,500), Venezuela (17,000), Brazil (29,000), Argentina (33,000), and France (38,000). Some fifty national missions sought immigrants from the camps at the peak of operations between 1948 and 1951; many shopped for specific skills, others acted out of gratitude (the Netherlands admitted 2,000 Poles in appreciation for the Polish Corps' role in its liberation), and some felt a sense of duty to the destitute.[40]

Venezuela sought agricultural and industrial workers, French North Africa wanted building tradesmen, and the first 861 DPs to arrive in Brazil included 69 percent farmers, 26 percent industrial workers, and 5 percent with miscellaneous skills. Some countries favored specific national groups. The preference for Balts has been noted, and Slovenians still tell of a Slovenian Catholic missionary, a Reverend Hladnik, who appealed directly to Argentine president Juan Perón. Perón yielded and promised to admit Slovenian DPs. (IRO records show that half of the 10,000 Yugoslavs admitted to Argentina were Slovenians.) One Slovenian remembered when the first group left his camp for Argentina: "We were crying and happy. We held a mass for them first, then they left in trucks, to transfer to a train for Italy" and the port.

This opening of South America's gates was especially welcome to those DPs concerned about losing status as they crossed the ocean. As one of them put it, "Every European was considered something better there, not like in America where immigrants are at the bottom."[41]

But despite the hopes it kindled, resettlement began to draw criticism. Many of the complaints came from the very officials who had long been campaigning for opened gates. Their opposition centered on the fact that most of the early nations recruiting DPs were taking mainly the young, single, and strong. As the *Times* (London) put it, "There is a whiff of the slave market in the invitations to DPs to enter most countries." IRO leaders attacked this "skimming the cream" as ruinous, a denial of the organization's humanitarian aims.[42]

Critics pointed especially to the emphasis on physical strength. Many DPs were rejected as too old or too weak; others were unacceptable because of health problems or dependents or both. "It is a pity to state that free countries select workers by their muscles," an Estonian pastor complained. Several DPs told of being forced to show Canadian authorities the callouses on their hands; a Ukrainian noted that Canadian railroad representatives examined his father's arms and shoulders to see if he was fit for railway labor. The aim was to recruit workers, not to prove their humanitarianism.[43]

This emphasis on muscle had another bad effect, the critics charged: it encouraged DPs to lie.

After a worker with the United Ukrainian American Relief Committee met with IRO leaders in Austria, he hurriedly wrote home: "It is plainly stressed that: INTELLECTUALS ARE TO BE TOLD TO FORGET THAT THEY ARE INTELLECTUALS. THAT THEY WERE TO TAKE ADVANTAGE OF EMIGRATION, ON A GOING SCHEME, AND THEN UPON ARRIVAL TO THAT PARTICULAR COUNTRY, INQUIRE OF POSSIBILITIES TO CONTINUE WITH THEIR PROFESSION." No country in the world, he added, "is interested in an intellectual who has been educated outside of that particular country's boundary, unless that intellectual has passed the rigid examinations of that country." Canadian Labour Department officials in Europe received a memo in early 1948 warning that many of the DP girls being interviewed for employment as domestics "fail to disclose the fact that they have higher education." The officials were instructed that when this was suspected, "please reject."[44]

Stretching the truth followed naturally. "If they needed five beekeepers in Brazil, they got five hundred signatures right away of people wanting to go there," a DP recalled. DP nurses with diplomas from Leningrad or Warsaw learned of resettlement openings for tailors and immediately testified to having worked as tailors. When a request for 160 pocket-basters came to the U.S. Zone of Germany, the majority of the 7,000 DPs in the Aschaffenburg area camps suddenly became master tailors. A Lithuanian eager to go to Canada later told interviewer Milda Danys of her preparations for the interview with the Canadian Commission:

> We had already learned from the men [selected for forestry work].
> They had made themselves into specialists who had worked for years
> and years in the woods and knew how to do this and how to do that.
> Well, we were just as smart as them. In our transport, [a dentist] used
> to say, "Girls, there's only one truth—and that's what's written
> down."

Others discovered various ways to get around the strict medical
requirements—sending a healthy look-alike to substitute at a TB
screening, obtaining injections to keep blood pressure down, even
bribing German doctors to fill out a good health record.[45]

One country was yet to be heard from: the United States.

There was initially little hope that America would take in many
DPs. President Truman's early moves brought in 40,000 DPs in less
than three years, as regular immigrants, but it is noteworthy that
Truman did not propose to go beyond existing immigration laws in
1945 and 1946.

Wheels were starting to turn, however, slowly and painfully. More
and more Americans began to realize that Europe's refugee problem could not end without massive immigration into the United
States. The other possible solutions—large-scale repatriation or
assimilation into overcrowded Germany—were finally seen to be
impossible. A Citizens Commitee on Displaced Persons (CCDP)
was created in the fall of 1946 and led by Earl G. Harrison, who had
made the controversial report on the DPs' plight to President
Truman a year earlier. The long list of prominent sponsors ranged
from labor leader David Dubinsky to business executive Marshall
Field, from Eleanor Roosevelt to black spokesman A. Philip Ran-
dolph. Eventually some 250 national groups supported the CCDP
campaign; organized opposition came mainly from the American
Legion (which eventually reversed its stand), the Veterans of Foreign Wars, and the Daughters of the American Revolution. President Truman responded in his State of the Union message in
January 1947 with a call for Congress to authorize a massive influx
of DPs.[46]

As detailed by Leonard Dinnerstein in *America and the Survivors of the Holocaust,* the legislative drive began on 1 April 1947,
when Rep. William C. Stratton of Illinois, a Republican, introduced
a bill backed by the CCDP to allow 400,000 DPs into the United
States over a four-year span. Paralleling the push in Congress, the
CCDP launched a nationwide campaign to convice the public that
DPs would not take jobs or homes from Americans, that they were

neither collaborators nor Communists, and that only a small proportion were Jews, contrary to widespread belief.

The fight in Congress was bitter, and opponents delayed the DP bill's passage until the spring of 1948 using "all the parliamentary tactics of stall, evasion, confusion and deception," according to one scholar. At the same time that President Truman signed the compromise measure on 25 June 1948, he attacked it for combining the worst features of the Senate and House bills, resulting in "a pattern of discrimination and intolerance wholly inconsistent with the American sense of justice." Truman said he was signing it, despite its negative features, to allow resettlement to proceed for the 200,000 DPs authorized to enter over the next two years.[47]

One feature attacked by Truman and the CCDP specified that 40 percent of those allowed to enter were to be DPs "whose place of origin or country of nationality has been *de facto* annexed by a foreign power," which favored the Balts, who comprised barely 20 percent of the DP population. Another part of the law required that 30 percent of those to be admitted had to have been "previously engaged in agricultural pursuits," which worked against the east European Jews, most of whom had urban backgrounds. The requirement that DPs had to have entered one of the western zones on or before 22 December 1945 discriminated against Jews of the *Bricha* as well as many Poles and Yugoslavs who fled in 1946 and 1947.[48]

These negative features came under attack immediately, and a new drive was launched to amend the 1948 act. The second DP act, signed by Truman on 16 June 1950, moved the cutoff date for entry into the western zones to 1 January 1949; raised the admission total to 400,000 (which included 55,000 *Volksdeutschen* expelled from areas outside Germany, as well as 18,000 Polish army veterans in Britain, 10,000 Greek refugees, and 2,000 refugees from the Venezia Giulia area of Italy, which had been ceded to Yugoslavia); and dropped both the 40 percent "Baltic preference" and the 30 percent agricultural preference. Later the final deadline for issuing visas under the act was extended six months to 31 December 1951.[49]

It was soon apparent that U.S. recruiters stood at the end of the line. Many of the most physically fit, the young single men and women, had gone elsewhere. Still, an elaborate system of recruitment was worked out quickly, known in the U.S. Displaced Persons Commission as "the pipeline." It carried DP applicants through twenty-two steps, ranging from medical and skills checks to an FBI investigation and a search among records of the Nazis' Berlin Document Center.[50]

The crucial feature of the American program was the "assurance," a promise from an American sponsor that a specific DP would be provided housing for his family and employment. (This was a moral, not a legal, obligation.) Assurances were mainly collected by voluntary agencies, then approved by the DP Commission in Washington before being sent on to the field staff in Europe. Some assurances arrived bearing names of specific DPs, gathered earlier by agency workers in Europe and mailed back to the United States; but many were "anonymous"—simply promises to assist anyone who could fit the sponsor's criteria. This arrangement has remained a solid fixture of later U.S. refugee programs. Alexander Squadrilli, the commission's European coordinator, described operation of "the pipeline" this way:

Washington would validate the assurances, and send them on to me. Many anonymous assurances came; sometimes a letter arrived with five hundred anonymous assurances, for five hundred family units. I would break this into five hundred European numbers, with five hundred file folders set up. Then representatives of the voluntary agencies in Europe would nominate persons for those.

We had flow-chart control. Each day Ben Kaplan, my Executive Assistant, would be in touch with all the centers. He knew the number of Army Counter-Intelligence Corps reports, the number of assurances, the number of people visaed by a consul, and so on. This gave us a picture of how the flow was going, each day.

We maintained this flow chart for several purposes but mainly so that we could tell the IRO six weeks in advance the rate at which ships would be required at the port of embarkation. With a capacity of five thousand accommodations at the embarkation point—Camp Grone at Bremen—and a shipload generally of twelve hundred persons, the flow of visaed DPs to the port had to be controlled according to the availability of ships. At one stage sailings were averaging around one ship every two or three days. Occasionally a ship would depart from Naples with DPs processed in Italy.

Squadrilli recalled that when a thousand visas were issued in a single day, the staff celebrated with champagne. By the spring of 1949 assurances were being cleared for processing at up to four thousand per week.[51]

The DPs, their hopes raised by earlier resettlement possibilities, rushed to the American program as perhaps their last chance to emigrate. Many had declined other opportunities against the hope that the United States would change its closed-door policies. Camp

Matching "assurances." Once the U.S. DP Act went into effect, the voluntary agencies launched massive campaigns to locate sponsors in the United States, then to match them to DPs in Europe. These Lutheran World Federation workers in Frankfurt sought to match family DP registration cards with "assurances," or guarantees to aid DPs, received from the National Lutheran Council in New York. *(Lutheran World Federation photo.)*

populations declined by the hundreds overnight as DPs moved into the "pipeline." Schooling suffered. Squadrilli admitted later that the U.S. program "was idealistic—but the most complex and costly of all the resettlement programs" because of the required provision for jobs and housing. The DPs soon found the American requirements and paperwork to be a frightening quagmire, and many still recall their frustration. Some could find a grim humor in the situation:

> One DP was asked whether he would be willing to join the U.S. Army. He said he would. Then the Immigration officer asked, "If, while in the Army, you had a chance to capture Stalin, what would be the worst punishment you could give him?" The DP shot back: "I'd bring him here to Funk Kaserne and make him go through processing for emigration to the States!"

Another anecdote focused on the paperwork:

> Two DPs met and one asked where the other planned to emigrate.
> "Canada or Australia."
> "Why not the U.S.?"
> "Because the Americans put you on a scale, and start adding papers to the other side. When the paper equals your weight, you're ready to go."

There was truth behind this humor. A resettlement officer once laid out the documents in a single case file for entry to the United States: they stretched seventeen yards.[52]

Time spent in the "pipeline" ran from three months to more than twelve months, depending on the nature of medical problems (such as old TB scars) or collaboration charges. That many persisted despite the red tape is obvious. Why they persisted is perhaps less obvious, and must be looked at in the context of beliefs, traditions, and hopes. An Estonian DP called America "the land of a thousand possibilities," and this view of America as representing opportunity drew many. So did the image of America as a wealthy country—the world's richest nation—and this had enormous importance to those who had lived for years amid war's devastation. The United States already held large communities of all DP nationalities, many possessing a thorough ethnic life, and this also served as a magnet for DPs.[53]

Another reason for putting up with the endless questioning and delays in the U.S. program can be seen in the case of a Polish Jew. All set to emigrate in 1950, he wrote a nervous letter to his American cousin, admitting that he suddenly had doubts now that the United States was embroiled in another war, in Korea. After all, he had just come out of a war. But the cousin wrote back to assure him: "Don't you know? *The Americans always win!*" That settled it for the DP, and before long he was en route to Chicago.[54]

The first ship crossing with refugees under the DP act was the *General Black,* which left Bremerhaven on 21 October 1948 with 338 Poles, 168 Lithuanians, 53 Czechoslovaks, 32 Latvians, 17 Ukrainians, 6 Hungarians, and 83 listed only as "stateless." When they landed on 30 October in New York Harbor they were hailed by the U.S. attorney general as "the Pilgrims of 1948." The arriving DPs chose a spokesman who responded, "Today we are liberated from every misery of existence in Europe and we thank you very much. We are born today the second time in our lives."[55]

The chance to move thousands of refugees to America shifted voluntary agencies' operations into high gear, and they competed in friendly fashion to locate sponsors in the United States and match these with DPs in Europe. The staffers in the camps also helped DPs write to relatives in America, even to remote shirttail relatives, as potential sponsors. In addition to agencies linked to national groups, such as the Polish National Alliance and the Serbian National Defense Council, organizations from Roman Catholic, Jewish, Lutheran, and other religious bodies blanketed the DP camps with representatives. The Lutheran World Federation was finally spurred into action by the realization that one out of ten Lutherans in the world in 1947 was a refugee, and one out of three DPs was a Lutheran.[56]

Faced with an enormous task, the organizations pleaded, scrounged, and advertised to locate sponsors in the United States. Churches were especially active, and American Protestants designated June 1949 as "DP month." Catholics had a DP resettlement committee in each diocese, usually working with ethnic organizations. It became a unifying activity for congregations to find a job for a DP, raise funds through church suppers, then fix up or even construct a house for their DP family. Jews ran a massive program, only occasionally plagued by divisions between Zionists and non-Zionists.[57]

A typical assurance was this one received by Lutheran World Federation workers in a German camp, as described by Kathryn Hulme:

> Everything was written into it except the name of the DP it would eventually cover. The sponsor was a Scandinavian farmer in the

Midwest who had five hundred acres with no mortgage, a guesthouse
(with running water) that could accommodate a family of four, preference Balts, for farm work with all modern equipment.[58]

Inevitably corners were cut. Some DPs arrived in the United
States, asked for their sponsors, and found that they did not exist.
An ethnic organization had brought the DP in, and it would find him
housing and a job, but the alleged sponsor was fictitious, dreamed
up to satisfy the authorities. Such activities were scarcely unique to
the United States. A Ukrainian who entered Canada under the
close-relatives plan later remarked, "You can't pick your parents—
but we learned after the war that you *can* pick your uncles and
aunts. And when we arrived here we were often surprised to see
how little they looked like us."[59]

The same voluntary agencies that had pushed for new laws now
fought most vigorously against rigid interpretations that would
block emigration. They were usually supported by DP Commission
employees and opposed by workers for other U.S. government
agencies. "I was very much impressed with the DP Commission
workers there," recalled Gertrude Sovik, a Lutheran World Federation employee. "They were completely honest and dedicated, and
were willing to fight for their cases. When the Baltic Legion was
approved for American resettlement, a call came. I ran up to the
office, and the DP Commission man picked me up and whirled me
around in his excitement!"

And it was a DP Commission man who instructed Miss Sovik:
"When you write up your appeals, make them human interest—
don't try to make them sound legal." He referred especially to
cases in which DPs had been rejected on grounds of "moral tur-
pitude," on orders of the Immigration and Naturalization Service
through U.S. consular officials. One such case involved an eighteen-
year-old who had been caught picking grapes and was fined the
equivalent of twenty cents; another concerned a woman who had
grabbed a dress when seeking temporary refuge in a bombed-out
dwelling; a third arose when a DP threw a stick that accidentally
killed a neighbor's chicken foraging in the DP's garden. All three of
these cases initially meant no emigration for the DPs involved. And
all the rulings were overturned through appeals brought by voluntary agency workers.[60]

The spirit behind the organizations' efforts, as well as the pitfalls
and hurdles facing DPs trying to emigrate, can be seen in Gertrude
Sovik's description of a case that came up as time ran out for the DP

The final day. An Estonian couple, Heino and Lia Heinlo, and their children, were among the final DPs to qualify to emigrate under the U.S. DP Act, which expired on 31 December 1951. They are sworn in here by a U.S. vice-consul. The act's final day brought massive crowds to U.S. offices in the DP camps. (*UNRRA photo.*)

act in late 1951. The family's papers had been lost three times, the last time just two days before the deadline:

> We thought that we had everything in order by then, only to find that the Berlin Document Center check was missing in both the husband and wife, and that Mrs. A's medical papers were missing. With little more than twenty-four hours to go, I made arrangements for a new medical examination, with new X-rays and all. While she was at the doctor's office, I spent several hours in the DPC file room, looking through everything that had the appearance of a medical report. Mrs. S., head of the DP Commission at Funk Kaserne, aided me in my search, and finally I said to a German secretary: "Go and find the papers for me. They *must* be found." She told me that she was new and did not know where to look, but she was off, and in a few minutes she returned with the missing medical papers which she found in the *Dead File*.
>
> I took the report in my own hands and put it with the other papers. Then I happened to be at a desk where a woman was phoning to Berlin about Berlin Document Center checks, and I hurriedly pulled

A's file from the drawer, put it right under her nose until I heard her spell out the name as one of the urgent cases. At noon on December 31st the Berlin Document Center check came back, and I left the DP Commission office after a solemn promise that the case would be hand-carried to the consul at once.

In the evening, about 8:30, I found out that the case was still not at the consulate. In desperation I rushed to the consulate, where I forced my way through a mob of several hundred people.

With the file under my arm, I ran back to the office, grabbed Mrs. A by the arm, and with her husband trailing after us, we ran to get the papers to the consulate before it was too late. I think this must have been the last case that reached the consulate on the 31st."[61]

And so it was over, in a final rush that saw long lines winding through the camps. Some DPs were carried on stretchers. All clung to precious documents as they desperately tried to get papers approved before the end of 1951 and the U.S. DP act. Just as refugee-clogged European roadways ushered in the immediate postwar era, so the closing of that era was marked by crowds of DPs moving through lines to have papers validated or to board the ships and airplanes carrying them away to a new life elsewhere. Nearly 400,000 made it into America under the DP act, part of the more than 1 million of the war's refugees resettled in 113 countries over a four-and-one-half-year period. After that it was a trickle for several months, with special legislation permitting a few thousand others to enter various countries. In 1953 the United States allowed 185,139 more to come in over a four-year period. The Intergovernmental Committee for European Migration was established in 1951 to help resettle additional European refugees, and the United Nations that year created the Office of the High Commissioner for Refugees to watch over refugees and seek new homes for them.[62]

But many could not leave. When the International Refugee Organization took its final census on 1 January 1952, it found 177,000 DPs still on the rolls, less than half of whom were employed in the German or Austrian economy. These were overwhelmingly the middle aged, the elderly, and the disabled. A Canadian investigation three years later estimated that there were 253,000 refugees still in Europe, the great majority with paralysis, missing limbs, or a history of TB. Although recommending that Canada resettle some of these on a compassionate basis, the report nevertheless summed up reasons why many would never be accepted anywhere:

The age of the majority of adult males, 40 to 50, would be a handicap in seeking employment. Their children are young, considering the age of the parents, and would prevent the mother from working to help the family become established. Their occupation, usually unskilled general laborer, is not one for which there is widespead continuing demand. They are, in most cases, not in good health, by our present medical standards. Many of them have criminal records. Moreover, those in camps are low in both morale, and, it is said, morals.[63]

The elderly and disabled proved a major problem, heart-rending to the voluntary agency workers who had lived among them. Norway took in 50 totally blind DPs; Belgium opened its doors to 237 aged refugees; 480 handicapped DPs went to the United States; and Sweden set up a program to receive several hundred tubercular cases and their families. "It's cheaper to heal a TB case than to raise a Swede," one Swedish resettlement official quipped to his American counterpart. Only Israel drew no lines on age or physical condition. The IRO director general observed that "no Jewish refugee ever has been found to be too sick, too poor, too helpless for admission and warm welcome by Israel."[64]

To the hard core remaining in Europe, the closing months of the resettlement programs were psychologically devastating. Life was passing them by. Two daughters refused to leave their aged, blind father in the Augsburg resettlement center, after they were accepted for admission into the United States but he was not; the assurance was for two young women, not including a blind old man. The next morning his body was found hanging in the attic of the barracks; a letter in his pocket begged the Almighty and his daughters to forgive him. Now they could emigrate. At Aschaffenburg, a Ukrainian chose the same path when he was called back for a second lung X-ray. Although assured it was only because the first picture was unclear, he suspected otherwise and fell to pieces emotionally. His body was discovered hanging from a steam pipe in the basement of the blockhouse where he had lived. Suicides often occurred shortly after one of the massive farewell parties, as the train carried the ebullient, successful applicants away to the port and the waiting ship.[65]

Others underwent the agony of separation, as assurances came in requiring one or two young people but no other family members. A son would go to England, a daughter to Australia, and the parents would remain behind. A cartoon on a DP camp bulletin board showed a couple standing with three young children before the resettlement notices, then looking sadly down on their offspring and commenting, "If they were kittens, we could drown them." When the Canadian investigators returned to Europe in 1955 they encountered almost two hundred cases in which wives and children had been unable to join the husband and father in Canada, usually because of TB scars. "In some cases," the investigators reported, "the separation has lasted five years or more, and in some instances the husband in Canada has stopped communicating with his wife."[66]

The elderly found some special homes in Europe, often maintained by donations sent back by their countrymen who had been able to emigrate. Such was the case with a group of elderly Serbian military officers, cared for through aid from the Serbian Brothers Help organization overseas, as well as by the West German government. The Lutheran World Federation established several homes for the DP aged in Germany.[67]

West Germany provided some care for hard-core DPs when it took over operation of the remaining DP camps in 1951, finally closing the last one at Foehrenwald in 1957. Refugees in Austria were placed in care of the Austrian government in 1950. Those remaining in West Germany were guaranteed legal equality with Germans, except for voting rights, and citizenship could be granted after five years. Soon the Bonn administration was transferring refugees and others from areas of high unemployment to the emerging West German industrial centers. But there were problems: every fifth inhabitant of West Germany was a refugee—usually an ethnic German rather than a DP—and these people constituted a political force that could not be ignored. Groups outside Germany exerted claims also. In 1953, bowing to international pressure, the Federal Indemnification Law provided a system for compensation to Nazi victims, paid by West Germany.[68]

But by then most DPs were far from Europe, facing new problems and challenges as they sought, once again, to rebuild their lives.

9

LEGACIES

Why, for heaven's sake, does one revive the tragedy of the past?
Let it be but a bad dream and leave it behind, beyond those cool
red walls, behind that iron gate of a DP camp. No, you can't! It
lies too deep in the heart and is so clear in mind that you can
never forget it.
—Ernst Vähi, Estonian DP, upon leaving DP camp in 1949

SHUFFLING forward slowly, the Ukrainian group prepared to
board the plane for Canada, which would whisk them away from
Europe and their lives as refugees. But as they stood waiting for
final clearance, another group of emigrating DPs, Latvians, suddenly began a folk dance, cheerfully singing and clapping as they
circled about the passenger waiting room.

One of the Ukrainians, a young girl, turned away in tears. It was
not joyful, this moment, but sad—the end of her happy life in the
DP camp. Years later, in Toronto, she would still look back on her
departure as a sorrowful moment.[1]

The contrast between the feelings of the young Ukrainian girl and
those of the Latvian dancers pointed to a basic division in the
displaced persons experience from 1945 to 1951: although DPs felt
relief at having survived the war, they also longed for their homeland; contented with living in a camp brimming with activities and
friends, they had to deal at the same time with the overriding fear of
repatriation, coupled with despair over an uncertain future.

Displaced Persons shared all these feelings. Interviews with them
today bring out these contrasts quickly and point to a division
between age groups: those who were young in the camps usually
hold on to happier memories than their parents and grandparents,
who shouldered the burdens of caring for a family while worrying
what would happen next.

For the DP story is one of mixed results and mixed endings, and the contrasts did not stop when some refugees boarded ships and planes for distant lands. Within his own memory, each DP can search and find great joy and great pain as images of those years come into view.

To their new communities, whether Cleveland, Buenos Aires, or Winnipeg, the DPs brought a new impulse for ethnic identity. A Canadian investigator found that while Baltic girls were crossing the ocean to Canada, presumably to become Canadians, they did not attempt to mix with other immigrant groups but filled their shipboard life with close identification with members of their own ethnic group—through folk dancing, ship newspapers, talking, even flirting. The teachers who in 1945 launched elementary schools when a camp was formed, upon emigration created "Saturday schools" in their new communities, to retain the children's national identification. Although young DP men rushed to join the military in their adopted homelands, and most adult DPs sought citizenship as soon as possible, they held tenaciously to their original nationality. A poll of Latvian DPs in Australia found that 77 percent did not feel that Australian naturalization meant dropping their loyalty to Latvia.[2]

Many of their predecessors—immigrants from the pre-1940 years—resented this. Divisions appeared between the "Americans," who had immigrated earlier for economic reasons and lost much of their cultural apparatus, and the DPs, who started newspapers and Saturday schools quickly and strove to develop a cultural renaissance as they had done in the camps. And the newcomers found many of the older immigrants colossally ignorant about conditions in the old homeland, a homeland that perhaps had lacked electric lights and indoor plumbing when the earlier group departed. Feelings between the two groups occasionally flared into open feuding, leaving psychological wounds that have not healed. In a Ukrainian cemetery in Lachine, Quebec, deceased DP graves are divided from those of other Ukrainian immigrants by an eight-foot steel fence, symbolizing the rifts that have plagued immigrant communities.[3]

Not surprisingly, many of the postwar refugees have tried to forget the letters DP, seeking identity instead as Polish-Americans, Croatian-Americans, or even "New Americans."

Shunning the name DP may seem unwarranted in view of the struggles of the postwar years. After the battles came the victory. Why should anyone be ashamed of a condition from which he or she emerged with some glory and some good memories? Why not take pride in the fact that programs worked out for DPs set precedents still in use in a world that since 1945 has never been without refugees?

This reluctance to identify themselves as DPs seems inconsistent in view of the fact that the European refugees of 1945–51 show no similar reluctance in linking up with groups tied to World War II experiences. They rush into such organizations as the Polish Concentration Camp Association, complete with buttons displaying the concentration camp "P" motif; the *Bund Jüdischer Verfolgter des Naziregimes* (Federation of Jewish victims of the Nazi regime); the Association of Ukrainian Former Combatants; *Daugavas Vanagi A.S.V.* (Hawks of the River Faugava in the United States, a Latvian war veterans' group); the *Irgun Sheerit Hapleita* (The society of the survivors, an Israeli group for former concentration camp inmates); the Polish Political Ex-Prisoners Association; and many others connected with wartime military, resistance, or concentration camp experiences. Suffering did not block these survivors from later joining together to share memories of their years of peril. Even the children of refugees have formed groups based on their parents' *wartime* experiences, such as "Second Generation" in several U.S. and Canadian cities, established by sons and daughters of Holocaust survivors.[4]

But this author has learned of only one continuing organization dedicated to renewing friendships of the DP years, a group of ex-DPs who knew each other as students at the University of Graz. There appear to be few—if any—beyond this: no "Ex-Displaced Persons Association," no "Veterans of Wildflecken DP Camp." Occasional reunions have been held of small groups of people who knew each other in a DP camp, but when DPs get together they almost always do so within a national ethnic festival or gathering. There seems no organizational equivalent of the multitude of war veterans' and concentration camp veterans' groups.

Why not? Why should not the DP experience have produced loyalties as profound as those of wartime? Why not celebrate the DP experience, too?

Former DPs give various answers.

In Europe the letters *DP* themselves seemed pejorative, an epithet. Applied to Polish refugees, "dipisi" was equated with the German word *Untermensch,* or subhuman, and they felt they were at the bottom of postwar European society. An Estonian wrote with relief as he left his camp that he was "no more marked with these two branded letters which I could not shake in recent years." Those letters, a Slovenian wrote, "seemed to mean so very little to the outside world, but pressed with an enormous weight on every aspect of our lives."[5]

In addition, refugee life was transitory, and its conditions were sometimes degrading. DPs moved, or were moved, repeatedly. The experience left a bad taste in the mouths of many who went through it. And the previously wealthy, the highly trained, were now on a level with the peasant. Women who once had maids now had to cook, clean, sew. "I was ashamed to dig through donated clothing piles and to receive food without earning it," a Latvian doctor admitted. Moreover, if there was a Girl Scout group and a camp theater, and peasant children went to school with the offspring of gentry, there was also the "green horror" dished out in UNRRA camps as split-pea soup, and guards who ran dragnets through the cubicles, and Germans who yelled at DPs to "go home." But the refugees could not go home and the DP camp came to symbolize their impotence. An Estonian admitted that he had enjoyed some happy times in his camp, but as he prepared to leave for the last time he wrote, "I feel happy. Happy to get rid of you and never to see you again."[6]

One unremovable thread worked into the fabric of those years, and remains still: anticommunism. It persists like bedrock, an unyielding antagonism toward the Communist regimes of the Soviet Union, its satellites,and Yugoslavia. Many DPs have admitted to continuing nightmares over Soviet capture. The USSR's efforts to lure the DPs back have never totally ceased, and several have told of receiving pro-repatriation newspapers for years at their American homes; the papers keep coming every time they move, delivered directly to the new address without having been forwarded. Similar cases have been reported in Australia. Some originate with the "Committee for Return to the Fatherland," a Communist group formed in 1955 in East Berlin and aimed at DPs who came from areas now under Soviet control. (So strong was their fear of the Soviets that an elderly Lithuanian couple in Australia, former DPs, lived in almost total isolation in a cave near Sydney for twenty-eight years. They feared they would be caught by the KGB.)[7]

This anticommunism, so widespread among ex-DPs, perhaps reinforces the feeling of gratitude toward their new countries. The American flag and a rendition of "The Star-Spangled Banner" have top billing at ethnic gatherings in the United States, and pledges of loyalty to America are prominent. When questioned on the subject, former DPs agree that the DP act represented the best of America, that it set a worthy precedent for dealing with later groups of refugees.

Dual loyalty is still difficult to handle for some, however. To these, pledging allegiance to a new country and planning a future there implies accepting the defeat of the homeland. The flag of the new country is seen through eyes dimmed with tears for the old. And so when the Lithuanians hold their Canadian–United States song festival they sing "O River Nemunas, how our eyes and sad hearts long for you," and they chorus "Farewell my beloved Lithuania, with an aching heart I must leave you." DPs still search out friends from home, and they still run into them, unexpectedly, decades after they parted in Łódź, Zagreb, Riga. Reunions rekindle their love of the homeland.[8]

Some DP writers still find it difficult to change the settings of their stories to Toronto or New York. As literary critic Rimvydas Šilbajoris put it (in words that could apply to other DP groups as well as the Lithuanian exile authors he was discussing):

> There are many novels, short stories, and poems being written now, amid the noise and bustle of the great American cities, in which the quiet brooks of the homeland keep on flowing, and the trees rustle, and old neighbors from a village, not knowing that they have become mere ghosts, come over and shake your hand.[9]

And while some ex-DPs return for short visits to the Ukraine or Croatia on charter flights, where they are allowed to visit restricted areas and talk with approved relatives, many others may not, or will not, return. The homeland lives for them in the newspapers of their political splinter, where the old controversies are endlessly fought and refought, and in those pages the hopes that seemed real in 1945 are still proclaimed as articles of faith.

They are still exiles, and they still try to catch a glimpse of their old homes. "We went to the Austrian border with Hungary," a Hungarian former DP recounted. "We could see the lights of our town, only a few kilometers away. But we didn't go. We were afraid to enter." One group of Estonians, drawn from Canada and the United States, went to the control tower at the Helsinki Airport and tried to peer across the Gulf of Finland to Tallinn, but clouds blocked their view. And an Estonian-Canadian recounted: "When we went to Sweden last year, I went along the coast and I tried to see our little island. But I couldn't. I wanted so badly to see it," he said, choking back tears.[10]

Their experiences as displaced persons, like their identities with their homelands, will live on in memory and in the stories they tell their children. And other refugees will come to suffer on the pages of history—Palestinians, Laotians, Salvadorans—and tales of those displaced by Hitler's war and Stalin's peace will gradually merge with the outlines of those years of conflict, and of Europe at midcentury, and ultimately of the twentieth century and its wars. The letters *DP* will sound distant and far away, and grandchildren will ask, "What is a DP?" And, finally, Neustadt, Lienz, Reggio, Landsberg and the others will again be only cities on a map, not the sites of camps that once took in refugees from a war, and protected them until the outside world could awaken to their plight and welcome them to new lives across the seas.

NOTES

NOTE: More than eighty interviews were conducted for this study. A large number were with persons who still have relatives in Communist countries, or who for other reasons did not want their names published. These have been indicated as (anonymous).

Chapter 1. A Continent in Ruins

1. *Times* (London), 15 May 1945, 5. Yugoslav (anonymous), interview with author.

2. On British celebrations, see *New Statesman,* 12 May 1945, 300–301. On Continental celebrations see *New York Times,* 5 May 1945, 1; 6 May 1945, 4; 8 May 1945, 3. John R. Deane, *The Strange Alliance: The Story of Our Efforts at Wartime Co-operation with Russia* (New York: Viking, 1947), 180–81.

3. *New York Times,* 6 May 1945, 5. *Commentary* 2, no. 3 (September 1946): 230.

4. *New Statesman,* 14 July 1945, 22–23. Eisenhower to Merrill Mueller, 22 May 1945, *The Papers of Dwight David Eisenhower,* (Baltimore: Johns Hopkins University Press, 1978), 6:88.

5. *UNRRA Review,* September 1945, 15–16; January 1946, 5; June 1946, 15. Norman Davies, *God's Playground: A History of Poland* (New York: Columbia University Press, 1982), 2:463. George Woodbridge, *UNRRA: The History of the United Nations Relief and Rehabilitation Administration* (New York: Columbia University Press, 1950), 2:200, 231–33.

6. Delbert Barley, "Refugees in Germany: Relationships between Refugees and the Indigenous Population of a Rural Black Forest Community" (Ph.D. diss., University of Pennsylvania, 1957), 169.

7. Malcolm J. Proudfoot, *European Refugees: 1939–1952—A Study in Forced Population Movement* (Evanston, Ill.: Northwestern University Press, 1956), 115, 120–21, 377, 380. *Times* (London), 5 May 1945, 3. Lucius D. Clay, *Decision in Germany* (Garden City, N.Y.: Doubleday, 1950), 231–32.

8. Proudfoot, *European Refugees,* 158–61.

9. Eugene M. Kulischer, *Europe on the Move: War and Population Changes, 1917–1947* (New York: Columbia University Press, 1948), 278n. *Times* (London), 12 May 1945, 4; 15 May 1945, 4–5; 19 May 1945, 4.

10. Hannah Arendt, "The Stateless People," *Contemporary Jewish Record* 8, no. 2 (April 1945): 144. *Times* (London), 15 May 1945, 5.

11. John Prcela and Stanko Guldescu, eds., *Operation Slaughterhouse: Eyewitness Accounts of Postwar Massacres in Yugoslavia* (Philadelphia, Pa. Dorrance, 1970), 65–66. *Times* (London), 28 May 1945, 5.

211

12. *New York Times,* 7 May 1945, 3. *Stars and Stripes,* 8 April 1945, 4.

13. *Times* (London), 6 July 1945, 3.

14. Kulischer, *Europe,* 302. Davies, *God's Playground* 2:563–64.

15. *Times* (London), 8 August 1945, 4; 10 August 1945, 3.

16. *Times* (London), 28 May 1945, 5.

17. Proudfoot, *European Refugees,* 59, 72, 303–307.

18. John Toland, *The Last 100 Days* (New York: Random House, 1965), 10. *Times* (London), 5 May 1945, 4. Belsen visitor was Col. H. W. Bird, commander 102 Control Sec., 2d Army; quote is from his "Notes on Belsen Camp," 18 May 1945, American Friends Service Committee Archives (AFSC), Foreign Service 1945.

19. *Belsen* (Israel: Irgun Sheerit Hapleita Me'haezor Habriti, 1957), 106.

20. Ira A. Hirschmann, *The Embers Still Burn* (New York: Simon and Schuster, 1949), 88–89. *Times* (London), 2 May 1945, 8.

21. Edward L. Homze, *Foreign Labor in Nazi Germany* (Princeton: Princeton University Press, 1967), 23–25, 37, 81–83, 156–66, 231, 235, 291, 297–99.

22. Proudfoot, *European Refugees,* 89–90. David P. Boder, *I Did Not Interview the Dead* (Urbana: University of Illinois Press, 1949), 139–40. Ukrainian (anonymous), interview with author. Homze, *Foreign Labor,* 237–38, 267, 297.

23. Joseph Albert Hearst, "The Government of a Displaced Persons' Camp" (Master's thesis, University of Washington, 1948), 52–53. Kulischer, *Europe,* 263–64.

24. Władysław Anders, *An Army in Exile: The Story of the Second Polish Corps* (London: Macmillan, 1949), esp. 65–69, 151–54, Chap. 17. Davies, *God's Playground* 2:271–72, 455, 484. Woodbridge, *UNRRA* 2:83.

25. *Ivan Franko Poems and Stories,* trans. John Weir (Toronto: Ukrainska Knyha, 1956), 19–20.

26. Władysław Anders, *Hitler's Defeat in Russia* (Chicago: Regnery, 1953), 205. George Fischer, *Soviet Opposition to Stalin: A Case Study in World War II* (Cambridge, Mass.: Harvard University Press, 1952), 21.

27. Vladimir Dedijer et al., *History of Yugoslavia* (New York: McGraw-Hill, 1974), chap. 43 passim. Serbian Eastern Orthodox Diocese for the United States and Canada, *Martyrdom of the Serbs* (Chicago: Palandech's Press, n.d.), 47, 55.

28. Matteo J. Milazzo, *The Chetnik Movement & the Yugoslav Resistance* (Baltimore: Johns Hopkins University Press, 1975), 11, 181.

29. Edgars Andersons, ed., *Cross Road Country—Latvia* (Waverly, Iowa: Latvju Gramata, 1953), 306–12. Albertas Gerutis, ed., *Lithuania 700 Years* (New York: Manyland Books, 1969), 151–64, 185–86, 260–86.

30. Gerutis, *Lithuania,* 260–77. Andersons, *Cross Road,* 319–23. J. Hampden Jackson, *Estonia* (London: George Allen & Unwin, 1948), 21–23.

31. Boder, *I Did Not,* 175–81. Jackson, *Estonia,* 239–41, 242ff. Gerutis, *Lithuania,* 277–86. Andersons, *Cross Road,* 321, 323.

32. Andersons, *Cross Road,* 323–40. Gerutis, *Lithuania,* 286–97. Jackson, *Estonia,* 247, 249, 251–54. Fischer, *Soviet Opposition,* 10–11.

33. Andersons, *Cross Road,* 325–27. Jackson, *Estonia,* 254–57. Kulischer, *Europe,* 269.

34. Davies, *God's Playground* 2:464–65.

35. Fischer, *Soviet Opposition,* 19, 26–36, 42–48, 52–53. Anders, *Hitler's Defeat,* 184–86, 189–90. Elena Skrjabina, *The Allies on the Rhine—1945–1950* (Carbondale: Southern Illinois University Press, 1980), 18–19.

36. Arendt, "Stateless People," 137–53 passim.

37. Barley, "Refugees," 149–52.
38. David Bernstein, "Europe's Jews: Summer 1947," *Commentary* 4, no. 2 (August 1947): 103.
39. Paul Friedman, "The Road Back for the DP's," *Commentary* 6, no. 6 (December 1948): 505, 507.

Chapter 2. Into the Camps

1. Material on Team I at Neustadt is from Bernard Warach interview, and Bernard Warach, "The Care of United Nations Displaced Persons in the U.S. Zone of Germany 1 April 1945–30 June 1947," report submitted to UNRRA U.S. Zone headquarters, 15 September 1947, and from UNRRA Center Neustadt, Field Reports, no. 2 (2 May 1945), no. 3 (24 May 1945), no. 4 (8 June 1945), no. 5 (2 June 1945), in possession of author.
2. U.S. Army, *Displaced Persons,* Occupation Forces in Europe Series, 1945–46, Training Packet 53 (Frankfurt am Main, Germany: U.S. Army, n.d.), 9–10. Malcolm J. Proudfoot, *European Refugees: 1939–1952—A Study in Forced Population Movement* (Evanston, Ill.: Northwestern University Press, 1956), 107–10. 116–17.
3. Joseph Albert Hearst, "The Government of a Displaced Persons' Camp" (Master's thesis, University of Washington, 1948), 7–9. Proudfoot, *European Refugees,* 94–97, 162–63.
4. Edward N. Peterson, *The American Occupation of Germany: Retreat to Victory* (Detroit: Wayne State University Press, 1977), 156–57. Kathryn Hulme, *The Wild Place* (Boston: Little, Brown, 1953), 109–12. Proudfoot, *European Refugees,* 117, 128–30, 170, 333. Nicholas Bethell, *The Last Secret: Forcible Repatriation to Russia 1944–7* (London: Andre Deutsch, 1974), 64–65.
5. W. J. Jones, "Report re Euskirchen Camp," UNRRA Team 8, to G-5 HQ 15th Army Group, 15 June 1945, UNRRA Archives, Germany Mission, British Zone (Lemgo) Central Registry, Narrative and Special Reports.
6. Peterson, *American Occupation,* 295–97. Ira A. Hirschmann, *The Embers Still Burn* (New York: Simon and Schuster, 1949), 160. Gen. Dwight D. Eisenhower memorandum, 20 September 1945, *The Papers of Dwight David Eisenhower* (Baltimore: Johns Hopkins University Press, 1978), 6 : 358–59, 363–64.
7. *UNRRA Review,* December 1945, 23. David Henley to Cornelius Kruse, 24 June 1946, AFSC Archives, Foreign Service 1946, Displaced Persons Service (Expellees). George Woodbridge, *UNRRA: The History of the United Nations Relief and Rehabilitation Administration* (New York: Columbia University Press, 1950), 2 : 500–502. Hulme, *Wild Place,* 9–10.
8. Genêt, "Letter From Aschaffenburg," *New Yorker,* 30 October 1948, 98.
9. Woodbridge, *UNRRA* 2 : 500–502.
10. Yugoslav (anonymous), interview with author.
11. *Lithuanian Bulletin,* January–February 1947, 14–15.
12. Hulme, *Wild Place,* 23–24, 27–28.
13. Woodbridge, *UNRRA* 1 : xxv–xxix. Jacques Vernant, *The Refugee in the Post-War World* (New Haven: Yale University Press, 1953), chap. 3 passim. Edward A. Raymond, "The Juridical Status of Persons Displaced from Soviet and Soviet-Dominated Territory" (Ph.D. diss., American University, 1952), 292–93. Proudfoot, *European Refugees,* 406, 409.
14. Proudfoot, *European Refugees,* 144–45. Woodbridge, *UNRRA* 2 : 482–84. *UNRRA Review,* May 1945, 8.

15. UNRRA, *Displaced Persons Operations: Report of Central Headquarters for Germany* (Washington: UNRRA, 1946), 97–99. *Social Service Review,* March 1948, 34–39. *UNRRA Review,* June 1945, 10.

16. Proudfoot, *European Refugees,* 260.

17. *UNRRA Review,* September 1944, 9; February 1945, 5–6; May 1946, 27. Proudfoot, *European Refugees,* 139–41, 143–44, 147–48, 234–35, 262–63. Woodbridge, *UNRRA* 1:251–52; 2:485. Inter-Governmental Committee on Refugees (IGCR) *Memorandum: From the American Resident Representative,* no. 21, 23 June 1947, 5.

18. Woodbridge, *UNRRA* 2:521–22, 529–30. Proudfoot, *European Refugees,* 172.

19. U.S. Army, *Displaced Persons,* 50. Preparatory Commission for the International Refugee Organization, *PCIRO News Bulletin,* 19 November 1948, 1. *Lithuanian Bulletin,* October 1946, 20, MEJ (*sic*) to AFSC, 4 March 1946, AFSC Archives, Foreign Service 1946, Switzerland Refugees file. *UNRRA Review,* October 1946, 6. Woodbridge, *UNRRA* 2:491–92, 502. Proudfoot, *European Refugees,* 257.

20. *Times* (London), 17 November 1945, 3. Arnold W. Nelson, British Zone director, Report, Lutheran World Federation Service to Refugees (LWFSR) Collection 2:39.

21. Yugoslav (anonymous), interview with author. Hearst, "Government," 60, 73–74.

22. *UNRRA Review,* July 1945, 1–2; November 1945, 6; December 1945, 23. Hulme, *Wild Place,* 43. *Social Service Review,* December 1946, 560–61. Hearst, "Government," 38. Jones, "Report re Euskirchen Camp." Lt.-Gen. Sir Frederick Morgan, *Peace and War: A Soldier's Life* (London: Hodder and Stoughton, 1961), 221.

23. *Epidemiological Information Bulletin,* vol. 2, no. 17, quoted in *UNRRA Review,* October 1946, 7–8.

24. Earl F. Ziemke, *The U.S. Army in the Occupation of Germany, 1944–1946* (Washington: U.S. Army Center of Military History, 1975), 53. Camp doctor to director Team 158, Nammen, Germany, 30 June 1945, UNRRA Archives, Germany Mission, British Zone (Lemgo) Central Registry. Hearst, "Government," 38–39.

25. Camp doctor to director Team 158, Nammen, 30 June 1945, UNRRA Archives. Hulme, *Wild Place,* 53–54.

26. *Epidemiological Information Bulletin,* vol. 2, no. 17, quoted in *UNRRA Review,* December 1945, 23; October 1946, 7–8. Woodbridge, *UNRRA* 2:528. Hearst, "Government," 78.

27. Warach, "The Care," 4. Proudfoot, *European Refugees,* 147–48, 172–73, 451.

28. *UNRRA Review,* June 1946, 1. Woodbridge, *UNRRA* 1:328–29, 409; 2:306, 503. Proudfoot, *European Refugees,* 172–73, 252ff., 413–14. Peterson, *American Occupation,* 118–19.

29. U.S. Forces European Theater, "Care and Feeding of United Nations Displaced Persons, Persecutees, and Those Assimilated to Them in Status," 27 May 1946, Directive AG 383.7, GEC-AGO, APO 757. Hulme, *Wild Place,* 55ff.

30. Hearst, "Government," 41.

31. Latvians and Yugoslavs (anonymous), interviews with author. Edna and Howard Hong, "Report," 1 July 1948, LWF Service to Refugees Collection 1:188. Leo Srole, "Why the DPs Can't Wait," *Commentary* 3, no. 1 January 1947:16.

32. *UNRRA Review,* April 1945, 5–6. Hearst, "Government," 40. Woodbridge, *UNRRA* 1:139–43, 2:503. Proudfoot, *European Refugees,* 253n. *Stars and Stripes,* 28 August 1945, 4.

33. I. F. Stone, *Underground to Palestine* (New York: Boni and Gaer, 1946), 87–88. I. A. R. Wylie, "Returning Europe's Kidnapped Children," *Ladies' Home Journal,* October 1946, 255. Rt. Rev. Edward E. Swanstrom, *Pilgrims of the Night: A Study of Expelled Peoples* (New York: Sheed and Ward, 1950), 24–26.

34. *Belsen* (Israel, 1957), 179. Srole, "Why the DP's Can't Wait," 19. Elena Skrjabina, *The Allies on the Rhine—1945–1950* (Carbondale: Southern Illinois University Press, 1980), 96–97. Swanstrom, *Pilgrims,* 48–49.

35. *UNRRA Review,* November 1944, 10. Yugoslav (anonymous), interview with author.

36. Etta Deutsch, Report to Board of Directors of Central Location Index, 4 April 1946, AFSC Archives, Foreign Service 1946, Displaced Persons Services; also Deutsch report covering April 1946-April 1947, in AFSC Archives, Foreign Service 1947, Displaced Persons Services.

37. *PCIRO News Bulletin,* 12 November 1947, 1–2. Woodbridge, *UNRRA* 2:530–31. Proudfoot, *European Refugees,* 414–15. *IRO Digest,* May 1949, 8. *UNRRA Review,* December 1945, 22; January 1946, 19; October 1946, 10. Deutsch reports, AFSC Archives.

38. Proudfoot, *European Refugees,* 240–42. *Lithuanian Bulletin,* October 1946, 22.

39. Woodbridge, *UNRRA* 2:510, 512. Vernant, *Refugee,* 32. U.S. Displaced Persons Commission, *Memo to America* (Washington: GPO, 1952), 25. Hulme, *Wild Place,* 161. *Lithuanian Bulletin,* January–February 1947, 13.

40. Morgan, *Peace and War,* 234. Many DPs recalled rumors of expulsions.

41. On the Hochfeld incident, see *Lithuanian Bulletin,* January–February 1947, 31–32. This issue includes reprints of U.S. and other newspaper accounts, as well as petitions and letters from DP leaders.

42. B. Panchuk, telegram (n.d.) to United Ukrainian American Relief Committee (UUARC), Philadelphia, Pa., UUARC Papers, Box 192.

43. Proudfoot, *European Refugees,* 340–42. Leonard Dinnerstein, *America and the Survivors of the Holocaust* (New York: Columbia University Press, 1982), 112. Yehuda Bauer, *Flight and Rescue: BRICHAH* (New York: Random House, 1970), chap. 7 passim.

44. Eisenhower to President Truman, 18 September 1945, *Papers of Dwight David Eisenhower* 6:358. Proudfoot, *European Refugees,* 256, 259. Woodbridge, *UNRRA* 2:496. Sir Herbert Emerson, Inter-Governmental Committee on Refugees (IGCR) director, speech, 20 November 1944, cited in "The Problem of Refugees of Ukrainian Origin," 16 August 1945, AFSC Archives, Foreign Service 1945, Conditions of DPs.

45. Warach, interview with author.

Chapter 3. Repatriation

1. Information on the Soviet officer's visit is taken from "Visit of Russian Liaison Officer to Schleswig," 11 October 1946, UNRRA Field Hq., 506/712 (R) Det. Mil. Gov., BAOR, in UNRRA Archives, Germany Mission, British Zone (Lemgo) Central Registry, Repatriation.

2. A convenient source for the Yalta Pact is Henry Steele Commager, ed.,

Documents of American History (New York: Appleton-Century-Crofts, 1968), 2:487–93.

3. Herbert Feis, *From Trust to Terror: The Onset of the Cold War, 1945–1950* (New York: Norton, 1970), 20–22. Władysław Anders, *An Army in Exile: The Story of the Second Polish Corps* (London: Macmillan, 1949), 248–54. Julius Epstein, *Operation Keelhaul: The Story of Forced Repatriation from 1944 to the Present* (Old Greenwich, Conn.: Devin-Adair, 1973), chap. 3 passim. Julius Epstein, "American Forced Repatriation," *Ukrainian Quarterly* 10, no. 4 (Autumn 1954): 356–57. George Fischer, *Soviet Opposition to Stalin: A Case Study in World War II* (Cambridge, Mass.: Harvard University Press, 1952), 112–13. Mark R. Elliott, *Pawns of Yalta: Soviet Refugees and America's Role in Their Repatriation* (Urbana: University of Illinois Press, 1982), 40.

4. U.S. Army, *Displaced Persons,* Occupation Forces in Europe Series, 1945–46, Training Packet 53 (Frankfurt am Main, Germany: U.S. Army, n.d.), 67–68. Elliott, *Pawns,* 81–82, 102–104. Malcolm J. Proudfoot, *European Refugees: 1939–1952—A Study in Forced Population Movement* (Evanston, Ill.: Northwestern University Press, 1956), 214.

5. Nicholas Bethell, *The Last Secret: Forcible Repatriation to Russia, 1944–7* (London: Andre Deutsch, 1974), 9, 33–35. Fischer, *Soviet Opposition,* 112–13. Dwight D. Eisenhower, *Crusade in Europe* (New York: Doubleday, 1948), 438. Nikolai Tolstoy, *Victims of Yalta* (London: Hodder and Stoughton, 1977), 95. Elliott, *Pawns,* chap. 2 passim, esp. 41.

6. Epstein, "American Forced Repatriation," 360. Władysław Anders, *Hitler's Defeat in Russia* (Chicago: Henry Regnery, 1953), 203. *Times* (London), 19 May 1945, 5. Elliott, *Pawns,* 43–44.

7. Proudfoot, *European Refugees,* 207–20, 224–25, 228–29. Elliott, *Pawns,* 82–83.

8. Dorothy E. Curtis, "What They are Doing in Germany," *Public Health Nursing,* October 1945, 503–504.

9. Raymond G. Krisciunas, "The Emigrant Experience: The Decision of Lithuanian Refugees to Emigrate, 1945–1950," *Lituanus* 29, no. 2 (Summer 1983):33. Tolstoy, *Victims,* 382–88. *New York Times,* 20 November 1945, 6; 1 December 1945, 7; 2 December 1945, 31; 4 December 1945, 8.

10. *New York Times,* 7 March 1946, 2. Tolstoy, *Victims,* 378. Proudfoot, *European Refugees,* 215. U.S. Army, *Displaced Persons,* 64, 70.

11. Bethell, *Last Secret,* 54–57.

12. Tolstoy, *Victims,* chap. 9 passim, 218–19. Epstein, *Operation Keelhaul,* 75–81. Bethell, *Last Secret,* 166–68. *Times* (London), 2 July 1945, 4.

13. Tolstoy, *Victims,* 337–39, 342–43. Elliott, *Pawns,* 90–91.

14. This material is based on interviews with two former U.S. government officials and an Estonian former DP, all of whom asked to remain anonymous.

15. Slovenian (anonymous), interview with author.

16. Croatian (anonymous), interview with author.

17. Serbian (anonymous), interview with author.

18. Fischer, *Soviet Opposition,* 116–17. William Sloane Coffin, *Once to Every Man: A Memoir* (New York: Atheneum, 1977), 72–78. Tolstoy, *Victims,* 360–70.

19. Anders, *Army in Exile,* 194–97. Proudfoot, *European Refugees,* 221. *New York Times,* 15 February 1947, 8.

20. Tolstoy, *Victims,* chap. 18 passim; 22, 340–41, 344–47, 352–58. Proudfoot, *European Refugees,* 238–39. Eisenhower to Truman, 18 September 1945, *The Papers of Dwight David Eisenhower* (Baltimore: Johns Hopkins University Press,

1978), 6:358. *Times* (London), 5 October 1945, 3. Bethell, *Last Secret,* 182, 188–89. Eliott, *Pawns,* 121–22. Coffin *Once to Every,* 77.

21. Field Report No. 5, DP Center, Neustadt, 1–30 June 1945, 2 June 1945, to UNRRA Headquarters, Germany, 5 (in possession of author).

22. George Woodbridge, *UNRRA: The History of the United Nations Relief and Rehabilitation Administration* (New York: Columbia University Press, 1950), 1:xxix. *Times* (London), 20 August 1945, 2. David Martin, "Not 'Displaced Persons'—But Refugees," *Ukrainian Quarterly* 4, no. 2 (Spring 1948): 110. A. Edmund Birch to Capt. A. Duncan-Johnstone, UNRRA div. liaison officer, Hq. 52 L Div., 23 February 1946, and Sir Raphael Cilento, BAOR UNRRA dir., Report to District Directors, 14 January 1946, UNRRA Archives, Germany Mission, British Zone (Lemgo) Central Registry, Repatriation.

23. Myer Cohen, acting chief, UNRRA DP Operations, Statement of 24 March 1947, copy in John Panchuk Papers, B.2, F. 9, Immigration History Research Center (IHRC).

24. IRO Constitution quoted in Anthony T. Bouscaren, *International Migrations Since 1945* (New York: Praeger, 1963), 12–13. Proudfoot, *European Refugees,* 403–404. IRO staff member (anonymous), interview with author.

25. *UNRRA Review,* September 1945, 10–11. Order 199 reprinted in *Lithuanian Bulletin,* January–February, 1947, 25–27. Eugene Lyons, *Our Secret Allies—The Peoples of Russia* (New York: Duell, Sloan and Pearce, 1953), 260–61.

26. Edward A. Shils, "Social and Psychological Aspects of Displacement and Repatriation," *Journal of Social Issues* 2, no. 3 (August 1946): 15. *New York Times,* 23 July 1946, 8; 5 October 1947, 15. Tolstoy, *Victims,* 311–12. Dorothy E. Curtis, "Turnover Troubles," *Public Health Nursing,* December 1945, 616–18. Proudfoot, *European Refugees,* 281–84. Kathryn Hulme, *The Wild Place* (Boston: Little, Brown, 1953), 151–52.

27. Proudfoot, *European Refugees,* 281–85. Woodbridge, *UNRRA* 2:515–16. *New York Times,* 15 April 1947, 8. Preparatory Commission for the IRO, *PCIRO News Bulletin,* 7 October 1948, 2.

28. *New York Times,* 16 March 1946, 8; 23 March 1946, 4; 1 July 1946, 10; 2 July 1946, 15; 27 July 1946, 1; 15 February 1947, 4.

29. Eileen Egan, "When a Voluntary Agency Saved Displaced Persons," *Worldview,* September 1979, 28–30. Norman MacLeod, UNRRA Arnsberg, BAOR, to regional UNRRA director, Iserlohn, Germany, 8 August 1946, UNRRA Archives, Germany Mission, British Zone (Lemgo) Central Registry, Narrative and Special Reports . . . Lippstadt.

30. Elliott, *Pawns,* 156–57. Joseph Melaher, interview with author.

31. Tolstoy, *Victims,* 338–39. *New York Times,* 1 April 1947, 7. New York *Herald-Tribune,* 25 January 1947, 1, quoted in *Lithuanian Bulletin,* January–February, 1947, 32–33.

32. E. H. Wheatman, UNRRA field supervisor, North Rhine region, report, undated 1946, UNRRA Archives, Germany Mission, British Zone (Lemgo), Central Registry, Repatriation.

33. Woodbridge, *UNRRA* 2:518. Proudfoot, *European Refugees,* 415–18. *PCIRO News Bulletin,* 14 September 1948, 4.

34. Information on reasons for return is drawn heavily from interviews with Ukrainian and Estonian former refugees and former voluntary agency staff members. Harold Smith, *Refugees Defense Committee Report,* 1947, 6, John Panchuk Papers, B.2, F. 11.

35. *Stars and Stripes,* 29 August 1945, 8.

36. "Roman," Vienna, Austria, to John Panchuk, 27 December 1947, John Panchuk Papers, B. 2, F. 11. *Lithuanian Bulletin,* October–November 1945, 15. Tolstoy, *Victims,* 376–78.

37. Yugoslav invitation is in AFSC Archives, Foreign Service 1945; Jugoslavia file. *New York Times,* 30 March 1947, 47; 8 June 1947, 29. Proudfoot, *European Refugees,* 224–25, 288–91. Serbian (anonymous), interview with author.

38. Elliott, *Pawns,* 154. *New Times* article is reprinted in Edward A. Raymond, "The Juridical Status of Persons Displaced From Soviet and Soviet-Dominated Territory" (Ph.D. diss., American University, 1952), app. C, 369–72; also see 83–84.

39. Information on repatriation visits is drawn from interviews with Latvian and Slovenian former DPs. Grensstrasse incident described in director, UNRRA Team 130, 220 (R) Mil. Gov. Det., to Mr. Craig, protective officer, UNRRA Regional HQ, HQ Mil. Gov., Schleswig-Holstein region, BAOR, 24 October 1946, UNRRA Archives,Germany Mission, British Zone (Lemgo) Central Registry, Repatriation.

40. F. K. C. Adams, dir. Team 807, to E. R. Heath, chief Repat. Off., 400 UNRRA HQ, BAOR, 18 March 1946, UNRRA Archives, Germany Mission, British Zone (Lemgo) Central Registry, Repatriation. *Lithuanian Bulletin,* January–February 1947, 30.

41. Joseph Albert Hearst, "The Government of a Displaced Persons' Camp," (Master's thesis, University of Washington, 1948), 53. Hungarian (anonymous), interview with author. Voluntary agency worker (anonymous), interview with author. Norman Davies, *God's Playground: A History of Poland* (New York: Columbia University Press, 1982), 2:451–52.

42. On Soviet moves in Poland, see *Times* (London), 3 May 1945, 8; 11 May 1945, 3; 12 May 1945, 3; 25 May 1945, 5. Davies, *God's Playground,* 2:472–73. UNRRA, *Displaced Persons Operations: Report of Central Headquarters for Germany* (Washington: UNRRA, 1946), 10.

43. English translation of Polish broadside, "What Every Returning Citizen Should Know," is in UNRRA Archives, Germany Mission, British Zone (Lemgo) Central Registry, Repatriation.

44. Channing Richardson to "Norman," undated 1946, AFSC Archives, Foreign Service 1946, Displaced Persons Service (Expellees), DP Svcs (Possible).

45. J. Hampden Jackson, *Estonia* (London: George Allen & Unwin, 1948), 239–41. Edgars Andersons, *Cross Road Country—Latvia* (Waverly, Iowa: Latvju Gramata 1953), 321–24. Albertas Gerutis, ed., *Lithuania 700 Years* (New York: Manyland Books, 1969), 277–86.

46. Dr. Guiseppe Massucci, quoted in John Prcela and Stanko Guldescu, eds., *Operation Slaughterhouse: Eyewitness Accounts of Postwar Massacres in Yugoslavia* (Philadelphia, Pa.: Dorrance, 1970), 41–42. Wm. H. Taylor, UNRRA Jugoslav Mission, to AFSC, Philadelphia, Pa., 8 February 1946, AFSC Archives, Foreign Service 1946, Yugoslavia: Reports 1946.

47. Fischer, *Soviet Opposition,* 108–109. Ukrainian (anonymous), interview with author.

48. T. J. King, UNRRA regional director, 460 UNRRA Hq., BAOR, to Zone Hq. for Repat., 15 November 1946, UNRRA Archives, BZ/ZO: RR/Repatriation Report files. David J. Dallin and Boris I. Nicolaevsky, *Forced Labor in Soviet Russia* (New Haven: Yale University Press, 1947), 284–89, 291–95.

49. Tolstoy, *Victims,* 310–11. Slovenian (anonymous), interview with author.

50. Aleksandr I. Solzhenitsyn, *The Gulag Archipelago—1918–1956: An Experi-*

ment in Literary Investigation (New York: Harper and Row, 1973), 1:85. Ukrainian-Canadian (anonymous), interview with author.

51. Statement of H. Brining, acting dir., UNRRA Team No. 16/72, Eller, nr. Dusseldorf, Germany, 17 November 1945, UNRRA Archives, Germany Mission, British Zone (Lemgo) Central Registry, Repatriation.

52. Edward N. Wright, Köln-Marienburg, Germany, to George E. Rundquist, AFSC, Philadelphia, Pa., 23 March 1946, AFSC Archives, Foreign Service 1946, Country Germany, AFSC/UNRRA Team 1946, letters from GS Series. Serbian, Ukrainian, and Lithuanian former DPs (anonymous), interviews with author.

53. Monsignor Andrew P. Landi, interview with author.

54. Ukrainian-Canadians, Poles, and IRO staff members (anonymous), interviews with author. The issue of Mrs. Roosevelt's enthusiastic support for the DPs was raised several times at the conference on "The D.P. Experience: Ukrainian Refugees After World War II" at St. Michael's College, University of Toronto, 3–6 November 1983.

55. President Truman to Secretary of State Byrnes, 17 April 1946, quoted in Leonard Dinnerstein, "The U.S. Army and the Jews: Policies Toward the Displaced Persons After World War II," *American Jewish History* 68, no. 3 (March 1979): 361. Egan, "When a Voluntary Agency," 28–30. *New York Times,* 16 March 1946, 8; 23 March 1946, 4.

56. Fischer, *Soviet Opposition,* 108–109. Elliott, *Pawns,* 173. Ukrainians, Poles, and IRO staff members (anonymous), interviews with author.

57. *New York Times,* 25 May 1946, 8; 7 February 1947, 9.

58. *New York Times,* 27 January 1947, 4; 28 January 1947, 9. Proudfoot, *European Refugees,* 289–90. Serbians and Slovenians (anonymous), interviews with author.

59. These issues are examined in Elliott, *Pawns,* 136; Tolstoy, *Victims,* 196–97, chap. 17 passim; Clarence A. Manning, "The Significance of the Soviet Refugees," *Ukrainian Quarterly* 2 no. 1 (Autumn 1945): 23.

60. Dallin and Nicolaevsky, *Forced Labor,* 296–98.

61. Tolstoy, *Victims,* 48–49, 398; chap. 17 passim.

62. Walter Bedell Smith, *My Three Years in Moscow* (Philadelphia, Pa. Lippincott, 1950), 26. Rene Ristelhueber, "The International Refugee Organization," *International Conciliation* 470 (April 1951): 167–228, quoted in Raymond, "Juridical Status," 304–305.

Chapter 4. Displaced Children

1. Joseph A. Hearst, "The Government of a Displaced Persons' Camp" (Master's thesis, University of Washington, 1948), 76.

2. Dorothy Macardle, *Children of Europe—A Study of the Children of Liberated Countries: Their War-Time Experiences, Their Reactions, and Their Needs, with a Note on Germany* (Boston: Beacon Press, 1951), 79, 244.

3. Macardle, *Children of Europe,* 155–56. Zelda Popkin, "Europe's Children," *Ladies' Home Journal,* August 1946, 168.

4. Zlatko Balokovic, "A Nation Cares for Its Own," *The Child,* July 1946, 29–30.

5. *IRO Digest,* March 1949, 5.

6. Cornelia Goodhue, "We Gain New Candidates for Citizenship," *The Child,* July 1946, 4. Macardle, *Children of Europe,* 47–48.

7. Macardle, *Children of Europe,* 231, 292, 305.

8. Macardle, *Children of Europe*, 264n, chap. 23 passim. Ernst Papanek, "They Are Not Expendable: The Homeless and Refugee Children of Germany," *Social Service Review* 20, no. 3 (September 1946): 313.

9. Papanek, "They Are Not Expendable," 313.

10. Balokovic, "A Nation Cares," 28.

11. *New York Times*, 10 March 1946, 16; 24 October 1948, 63. Macardle, *Children of Europe*, 55–56, 59–60.

12. Macardle, *Children of Europe*, 11.

13. Ruth Crawford, "The United States Has Helped Before," *The Child*, July 1946, 8–9.

14. Becky Althoff, "Observations on the Psychology of Children in a D.P. Camp," *Journal of Social Casework* 29 (January 1948): 17–18. Preparatory Commission for the International Refugee Organization, *PCIRO News Bulletin*, 12 February 1948, 1–2, 5.

15. Macardle, *Children of Europe*, 45–46, 67–69. Ukrainian (anonymous), interview with author. Kathryn Hulme, *The Wild Place* (Boston: Little, Brown, 1953), 65–66.

16. Estonian (anonymous), interview with author. Macardle, *Children of Europe*, 99.

17. Pole (anonymous), interview with author. Balokovic, "A Nation Cares," 31.

18. *New York Times*, 9 March 1947, 12. I. A. R. Wylie, "Returning Europe's Kidnapped Children," *Ladies' Home Journal*, October 1946, 256–57. Marion E. Hutton, "UNRRA Shelters Unattended Children," *The Child*, July 1946, 24–26.

19. Hutton, "UNRRA Shelters," 24–25. Macardle, *Children of Europe*, 241.

20. Ira A. Hirschmann, *The Embers Still Burn* (New York: Simon and Schuster, 1949), 17. *New York Times*, 9 March 1947, 12. Wylie, "Returning Europe's Kidnapped Children," 23. Polish Red Cross Report, January 1949, 1–2, John Panchuk Papers, B.2, F. 14 (IHRC).

21. Macardle, *Children of Europe*, 53–54, 75–76, 235–36.

22. Macardle, *Children of Europe*, 235–36.

23. *UNRRA Review*, July 1946, 7–8.

24. Macardle, *Children of Europe*, 235–38. *UNRRA Review*, July, 1946, 8.

25. *New York Times*, 1 December 1946, 14.

26. The search for lost children is discussed in the following: *UNRRA Review*, July 1946, 7–8; Macardle, *Children of Europe*, 233–40; *New York Times*, 2 June 1946, 22; Hirschmann, *Embers Still Burn*, 244–61.

27. The postwar search for children from Lidice and other areas is discussed in Macardle, *Children of Europe*, 50–53, 235–40.

28. Vera Jakesová, letter to *Central European Observer* (London), 5 July 1946, quoted in Macardle, *Children of Europe*, 63–64.

29. Althoff, "Observations," 21–22. Paul Friedman, "Can Freedom Be Taught?" *Journal of Social Casework* 29, no. 7 (July 1948): 251. Paul Friedman, "The Road Back for the DP's," *Commentary* 6, no. 6 (December 1948): 504–505.

30. Friedman, "The Road Back," 508. Popkin, "Europe's Children," 168.

31. P. Warszawski, "Pupils and Teachers in Belsen," in *Belsen* (Israel: Irgun Sheerit Hapleita Me'haezor Habriti, 1957), 162–63. Balokovic, "A Nation Cares," 30. Goodhue, "We Gain," 4–5. Macardle, *Children of Europe*, 62–64, 241–42. Hirschmann, *Embers Still Burn*, 244–45. Bertha L. Bracey, "Practical Problems of Repatriation and Relocation," *International Affairs* 21, no. 3 (July 1945): 301.

32. Frances Balgley, "Rebuilding Life for Homeless Children," *The Child*, July 1946, 19–20. Macardle, *Children of Europe*, 219. Martha Branscombe, "UNRRA

Works for Children," *The Child,* September 1945, 38. Balokovic, "A Nation Cares," 29–30.

33. Balgley, "Rebuilding Life," 22–23. *New York Times,* 24 October 1948, 63. Macardle, *Children of Europe,* 141.

34. Curt Bondy, "Helping Children to a New Start," *The Child,* July 1946, 15. Macardle, *Children of Europe,* 306–12. S. Adler-Rudel, "The Surviving Children," *Belsen,* 127–28. Balgley, "Rebuilding Life," 23.

35. Much of the information on DP camp schools is drawn from interviews with former DPs and voluntary agency workers, most of whom asked to remain anonymous. Juozas Masilionis, interview with author. Jan Giello, "I Saw Polish D/P Camps in Germany," *Polish Review,* 7 March 1946, 4.

36. Former DP educators (anonymous), interviews with author. Hearst, "Government," 39–40.

37. Leo Srole, "Why the DPs Can't Wait," *Commentary* 3, no. 1 (January 1947): 18. Bishop J. Kopp, "The Estonian Church," LWF Service to Refugees Collection 1:82. *Lithuanian Bulletin,* January–June 1950, 26.

38. UNRRA, *Displaced Persons Operations—Report of Central Headquarters for Germany* (Washington: UNRRA, 1946), 37. Malinauskas, et-al., *14,000 Displaced Lithuanian School Children and Students Calling for Help* (Augsburg, Germany: P. Haas, 1947), 7.

39. Former DPs of various nationalities, interviews with author. Hearst, "Government," 42n. Macardle, *Children of Europe,* 208–209.

40. Balgley, "Rebuilding Life," 19–23. U.S. Army, *Displaced Persons,* Occupation Forces in Europe Series, 1945–46, Training Packet 53 (Frankfurt am Main, Germany: U.S. Army, n.d.), 95, UNRRA, *Displaced Persons Operations,* 131.

41. Giello, "I Saw Polish D/P Camps," 4–5. *New York Times,* 9 June 1946, 34. *DP Baltic Camp at Seedorf* (Seedorf, Germany: UNRRA Team 295, 1946), 70.

42. Ukrainian (anonymous), interview with author. *The Refugee* (London), January 1947, 1–2.

43. Hirschmann, *Embers Still Burn,* 257. UNRRA, *Displaced Persons Operations,* 34–35. *New York Times,* 9 June 1946, 34.

44. "My Children Live in a D.P. Camp," 1–2, Lutheran World Federation Service to Refugees Collection.

45. Lithuanian (anonymous), interview with author.

Chapter 5. Camps Become Communities

1. F. Treus, "The Birds of God," LWF Service to Refugees Collection 1:57–58.

2. Lithuanian (anonymous), interview with author.

3. Earl G. Harrison, "The Last Hundred Thousand," *Survey Graphic,* December 1945, 470.

4. Tadeusz Grygier, *Oppression: A Study in Social and Criminal Psychology* (Westport, Conn.: Greenwood Press, 1954, 1973), 128. David Bernstein, "Europe's Jews: Summer, 1947," *Commentary* 4, no. 2 (August 1947): 102.

5. Joseph Albert Hearst, "The Government of a Displaced Persons' Camp" (Master's thesis, University of Washington, 1948), 77. UNRRA, "Displaced Persons Property," orders TWE/E (EC4) 14 and TDP/E (44) 19, 1945, nos. 2, 1.

6. Hearst, "Government," 73. Giles E. Gobetz, "Adjustment and Assimilation of Slovenian Refugees" (Ph.D. diss., Ohio State University, 1962), 120. Grygier,

Oppression, 86–87, 111–12. Polish and Slovenian former DPs and former agency workers (anonymous), interviews with author.

7. Polish and Slovenian former DPs (anonymous), interviews with author.

8. Slovenian (anonymous), interview with author.

9. Pole (anonymous), interview with author. "My Children Live in a D.P. Camp," anonymous report in LWF Service to Refugees Collection.

10. Kathryn Hulme, *The Wild Place* (Boston: Little, Brown, 1953), 99. Pole (anonymous), interview with author.

11. James Anderson, "Show Us What They've Built," 1949, in LWF Service to Refugees Collection 2:201–20. Rev. Vytautas Bagdanavičius, interview with author.

12. Bishop J. Kopp, "The Estonian Church," LWF Service to Refugees Collection 1:87. Alexander Baran, "The Catholic Church," paper delivered at conference on "The D.P. Experience: Ukrainian Refugees After World War II," 6 November 1983, St. Michael's College, University of Toronto, Toronto, Canada.

13. Mark R. Elliott, *Pawns of Yalta: Soviet Refugees and America's Role in Their Repatriation* (Urbana: University of Illinois Press, 1982), 166. Otto Bremer, "Your Man in the Camps," LWF Service to Refugees Collection 2:23.

14. Jan Giello, "I Saw Polish D/P Camps in Germany," *Polish Review,* 7 March 1946, 4–5. Samuel Weintraub, "Daily Life in Belsen," 129–30, and Vida Kaufman, "An American in Belsen," 155, in *Belsen* (Israel: Irgun Sheerit Hapleita Me'haezor Habriti, 1957). Polish Jew (anonymous), interview with author.

15. Ben Kaplan, interview with author. Giello, "I Saw Polish D/P Camps," 4–5.

16. Wasyll Gina, United Ukrainian American Relief Committee report for Salzburg, Austria, 1–15 April 1948, UUARC Collection (IHRC).

17. Ukrainian (anonymous), interview with author.

18. Gobetz, "Adjustment and Assimilation," 118. Monthly Report of UNRRA Team 81, 23 May 1946, UNRRA Archives, Germany Mission, British Zone (Lemgo) Central Registry, Narrative and Special Report. *IRO Digest,* March 1950, 1–3.

19. George Woodbridge, *UNRRA: The History of the United Nations Relief and Rehabilitation Administration* (New York: Columbia University Press, 1950), 2:519–20. Hearst, "Government," 70. Lt. Col. Jerry M. Sage, "The Future of the Displaced Persons in Europe," in U.S. Department of State, *The Displaced-Persons Problem: A Collection of Recent Official Statements,* U.S. Dept. of State Pub. 2899, (Washington: GPO, 1947), 91. Preparatory Commission for the IRO, *PCIRO News Bulletin,* nos. 6, 8 December 1947, 5.

20. Author's interviews with a variety of former DPs and voluntary agency workers provided information on the use of cigarettes as currency. Julian Bach, Jr., *America's Germany: An Account of the Occupation* (New York: Random House, 1946), 15, 61–62, 68–70.

21. *Frankenpost* editor quoted in Office of U.S. Military Government for Germany, *Weekly Information Bulletin,* no. 110, 15 September 1947, 11–12.

22. Bohdan Panchuk, *Heroes of Their Day: The Reminiscences of Bohdan Panchuk* (Toronto: Multicultural History Society, 1983), 88. Information from author's interviews with a variety of DPs.

23. Hungarian (anonymous), interview with author.

24. Ukrainian (anonymous), interview with author. *New York Times,* 27 January 1946, 1, 27; 17 November 1946, 29; 4 December 1946, 18. U.S. Military Government, *Weekly Information Bulletin,* no. 84, 17 March 1947, 19. Bach, *America's Germany,* 61.

25. *New York Times,* 3 January 1947, 11; 17 November 1946, 29; 4 December 1946, 18. Ukrainian (anonymous), interview with author. Edward N. Peterson, *The American Occupation of Germany: Retreat to Victory* (Detroit: Wayne Sate University Press, 1977), 91. Harold Zink, *The United States in Germany, 1944–1955* (Princeton: Van Nostrand, 1957), 138–39.

26. Hearst, "Government," 77.

27. Woodbridge, *UNRRA* 2:522–23. UNRRA, "Employment, Recreation, and Occupation of Leisure Time for Displaced Persons in Assembly Areas," orders TWE/E (EC4) 12 and TDP/E(44)47, 1945, nos. 8, 3.

28. Woodbridge, *UNRRA* 2:523. Polish and Ukrainian former DPs and former agency worker (anonymous), interviews with author.

29. Arnold F. Pikre, interview with author.

30. Ukrainian (anonymous), interview with author.

31. Hearst, "Government," 80.

32. Leo Srole, "Why the DPs Can't Wait," *Commentary* 3, no. 1 (January 1947): 20. Woodbridge, *UNRRA* 2:529–30. *Lithuanian Bulletin,* December 1946, 11. James Anderson, interview with Eduard Kirchner of IRO, Munich, Germany, transcript in LWF Service to Refugees Collection 1:332–37. 81 District UNRRA Team Monthly Report, 21 May 1946, 2, UNRRA Archives, Germany Mission: British Zone (Lemgo) Central Registry, Narrative and Special Reports.

33. *Lithuanian Bulletin,* July–August, 1945, 16–17; December 1946, 11. Channing Richardson, UNRRA Team 47, Pfarrkirchen/Eggenfelden, Germany, to "Norman," undated 1946, American Friends Service Committee Archives, Foreign Service 1946, Displaced Persons Service (Expellees), Disp. Pers. Svcs.-Svcs. (Possible) for Expellees, 1946.

34. Information from author's interviews with various DPs.

35. Lithuanian Bulletin, December 1946, 11. *DP Baltic Camp at Seedorf* (Seedorf, Germany: UNRRA Team 295, 1946), 91. S. Adler-Rudel, "Jewish Literature in the DP Camps," *Jewish Spectator,* September 1947, 9. Srole, "Why the DPs Can't Wait," 19.

36. Alfons Hering, interview with author.

37. Former agency worker (anonymous), interview with author. Srole, "Why the DPs Can't Wait," 19. Alexander E. Squadrilli, interview with author.

38. *New York Herald-Tribune,* 1 January 1947, reprinted in *Lithuanian Bulletin,* January–February 1947, 14–15.

39. Dr. B. I. Balinsky memoir, 15 April 1982, in possession of the author.

40. Slovenian (anonymous), interview with author.

41. Slovenian former DPs and former agency workers, interviews with author. Inter-Governmental Committee on Refugees (IGCR), *Memorandum: From the American Resident Representative,* no. 15, 17 February 1947, 2.

42. *Lithuanian Bulletin,* October–November, 1945, 15. Woodbridge, *UNRRA* 2:526. *New York Times,* 3 April 1946, 12. UNRRA, *Displaced Persons Operations: Report of Central Headquarters for Germany* (Washington: UNRRA, 1946), 37–38. Dr. Visvaldis Janavs memoir, 9 December 1983, in possession of the author.

43. Balinsky memoir. Ukrainian (anonymous), interview with author. *Ukrainian Review* (London), no. 3, 1956, 92–93. *Ukrainian Weekly,* 21 April 1947, 4. *Ukraine: A Concise Encyclopedia* (Toronto: University of Toronto Press, 1971), 2:284–85, 386–88.

44. Yngve Frykholm, "The UNRRA University at Munich," report to World Student Relief for UNRRA Central Headquarters, 1–3, UNRRA Archives, Ger-

many Mission, Displaced Persons Newspapers. I. A. R. Wylie, "Returning Europe's Kidnapped Children," *Ladies' Home Journal,* October 1946, 254.

45. Balinsky memoir.

46. Frykholm, "UNRRA University," 1–5. Balinsky memoir.

47. Balinsky memoir. *UNRRA Team News,* 8 February 1947, 1.

48. *Lithuanian Bulletin,* December 1946, 11. R. C. Riggle, UNRRA Team 289, copy of radio speech, 7 February 1947, 1–6, UNRRA Archives, Germany Mission, British Zone (Lemgo) Central Registry, Hamburg Study Center.

49. Riggle speech, 1–6.

50. Minutes of meeting, 31 July 1946, at Bunde, BAOR, Education Branch, with UNRRA and Hamburg DP University representatives, 1–3, UNRRA Archives, Germany Mission, British Zone (Lemgo) Central Registry, Hamburg Study Center.

51. Riggles speech, 1–6. *Lithuanian Bulletin,* November 1946, 1, 4; September–October 1947, 32; January–June, 1950, 26. C. V. Aylin, regional commissioner, Hq. Mil. Govt. Land., Schleswig-Holstein, Kiel, Germany, to PWDP Division, Zonal Exec. Offices, Hq. CCG (BE), Lemgo, BAOR, 27 February 1947, UNRRA Archives, Germany Mission, British Zone (Lemgo) Central Registry, Hamburg Study Center.

52. Former Catholic War Relief worker (anonymous), interview with author. Władysław Anders, *An Army in Exile: The Story of the Second Polish Corps* (London: Macmillan, 1949), 65–66. Hearst, "Government," 39.

53. Channing Richardson to "Norman," 1946, AFSC Archives. Srole, "Why the DPs Can't Wait," 19. Croatians and Ukrainians (anonymous), interviews with author.

54. Koppel S. Pinson, "Jewish Life in Liberated Germany: A Study of the Jewish DP's," *Jewish Social Studies* 9 (April 1947): 119. Hearst, "Government," 61. Ukrainian (anonymous), interview with author.

55. Panchuk, *Heroes,* 85, 109.

56. Hal Lehrman, "The 'Joint' Takes a Human Inventory—The End of the DP Problem is in Sight," *Commentary* 2, no. 6 (January 1949): 19–20.

57. Former LWF worker (anonymous), interview with author. Malcolm J. Proudfoot, *European Refugees: 1939–1952—A Study in Forced Population Movement* (Evanston, Ill.: Northwestern University Press, 1956), 275–76, 415. Leonard Dinnerstein, *America and the Survivors of the Holocaust* (New York: Columbia University Press, 1982), 200–203.

58. *New York Times,* 15 August 1946, 2. *UNRRA Team News,* 8 February 1947, 1, 8.

59. Proudfoot, *European Refugees,* 275–76. Woodbridge, *UNRRA* 2:70. *IRO Digest,* February 1950, 3. Panchuk, *Heroes,* 72ff. *UNRRA Team News,* 8 February 1947, 8.

60. Channing Richardson, Eggenfelden/Pfarrkirchen, Germany, to Jack Hollister, 5 October 1946, AFSC Archives, Foreign Service 1946, Displaced Persons Service (Expellees), Disp. Pers. Svcs-Services (Possible) for Expellees 1946. Oscar Ratti, interview with author. Howard Hong, former LWF worker, interview with author.

61. Slovenian (anonymous), interview with author. Elena Skrjabina, *The Allies on the Rhine—1945–1950* (Carbondale: Southern Illinois University Press, 1980), 16–17.

Chapter 6. Jews of the Surviving Remnant

1. I. F. Stone, *Underground to Palestine* (New York: Boni and Gaer, 1946), 43, 60–62.

2. Leo Srole, autobiographical article in *Harvard Class of 1933: Fiftieth Anniversary Report* (Cambridge, Mass.: Harvard Class of 1933, 1983), 523.

3. Nora Levin, *The Holocaust: The Destruction of European Jewry, 1933–1945* (New York: Schocken Books, 1973), 5–6, 315–16.

4. Levin, *Holocaust,* 20, 254–55. Malcolm J. Proudfoot, *European Refugees: 1939–1952—A Study in Forced Population Movement* (Evanston, Ill.: Northwestern University Press, 1956), 334–42. Henry L. Feingold, "Who Shall Bear Guilt for the Holocaust: The Human Dilemma," *American Jewish History* 68, no. 3 (March 1979): 278.

5. Stone, *Underground,* 46. Josef Rosensaft, "Our Belsen," in *Belsen* (Israel: Irgun Sheerit Hapleita Me'haezor Habriti, 1957), 29. Helen Epstein, *Children of the Holocaust: Conversations with Sons and Daughters of Survivors* (New York: Putnam's, 1979), 105–107, 115. Samuel Gringauz, "Jewish Destiny as the DP's See It," *Commentary* 4, no. 6 (December 1947): 504.

6. Koppel S. Pinson, "Jewish Life in Liberated Germany—A Study of the Jewish DP's," *Jewish Social Studies* 9 (April 1947): 110. Hal Lehrman, "Austria: Way-Station of Exodus—Pages from a Correspondent's Notebook," *Commentary* 2, no. 6 (December 1946): 571.

7. Pinson, "Jewish Life," 110. Epstein, *Children,* 105–107, 213. Tadeusz Grygier, *Oppression: A Study in Social and Criminal Psychology* (Westport, Conn.: Greenwood Press, 1954, 1973), 200–201. Cornelia Goodhue, "We Gain New Candidates for Citizenship," *The Child,* July 1946, 6–7.

8. Grygier, *Oppression,* 41–44. Yehuda Bauer, *Flight and Rescue: BRICHAH* (New York: Random House, 1970), 266, 272.

9. British official quoted in Bauer, *Flight and Rescue,* 51–52. Leonard Dinnerstein, "The U.S. Army and the Jews: Policies toward the Displaced Persons After World War II," *American Jewish History* 68, no. 3 (March 1979): 355–56; Dinnerstein, *America and the Survivors of the Holocaust* (New York: Columbia University Press, 1982), 13, 28.

10. Norbert Wollheim, "Belsen's Place in the Process of 'Death-and-Rebirth' of the Jewish People," in *Belsen,* 55. Bauer, *Flight and Rescue,* 35–36. Gringauz, "Jewish Destiny," 503.

11. *Times* (London), 21 July 1945, 4. *Jewish Chronicle,* quoted in Dinnerstein, *America,* 17.

12. Bauer, *Flight and Rescue,* 76. Paul Trepman, "On Being Reborn," *Belsen,* 134.

13. "Report of Earl G. Harrison," *Department of State Bulletin,* 30 September 1945, no. 13, 456–63 (reprinted in Dinnerstein, *America,* app. B, 291–305). Earl G. Harrison, "The Last Hundred Thousand," *Survey Graphic,* December 1945, 469–73.

14. Joseph B. Schechtman, *The United States and the Jewish State Movement—The Crucial Decade: 1939–1949* (New York: Herzl, 1966), 137–38, 142.

15. Gen. Dwight D. Eisenhower to President Harry S Truman, 8 October 1945, in *The Papers of Dwight David Eisenhower* (Baltimore: Johns Hopkins University Press, 1978), 6:414–17. Dinnerstein, *America,* chap. 2, passim. Order from R. B. Longe, lt. col., for brigadier, chief, PW & DP Div. Hq., PW & DP Div. Main Hq., Control Commission for G (BE), Bunde, BAOR, 19 November 1945, UNRRA Archives, Germany Mission, British Zone (Lemgo) Central Registry, Repatriation.

16. Proudfoot, *European Refugees,* 342n. Bauer, *Flight and Rescue,* 69, 73. Levin, *Holocaust,* 710–11.

17. Bauer, *Flight and Rescue,* 84–87. Samuel Gringauz, "Our New German

Policy and the DP's," *Commentary* 5, no. 6 (June 1948): 510–11. Ephraim Londner, "Religious Life in Belsen," in *Belsen,* 184.

18. Pinson, "Jewish Life," 117.

19. Yehuda Bauer, *The Jewish Emergence From Powerlessness* (Toronto: University of Toronto Press, 1979), 63. Gringauz quote from *Landsberger Lager Cajtung,* reprinted in Pinson, "Jewish Life," 114n. Stone, *Underground,* 52.

20. Marion E. Hutton, "UNRRA Shelters Unattended Children," *The Child,* July 1946, 29.

21. S. Adler-Rudel, "The Surviving Children," in *Belsen,* 125. Pinson, "Jewish Life," 116–17. *New York Times,* 27 November 1945, 5. Gringauz, "Jewish Destiny," 501–509. Bauer, *Flight and Rescue,* 59–60. Gerold Frank, "The Tragedy of the DP's," *New Republic* 114, no. 13 (1 April 1946): 437–38.

22. Bauer, *Jewish Emergence,* 47, 52–53. M. Lubliner, "Jewish Education in Belsen," 160–61; Josef Fraenkel, "The Cultural Liberation of Belsen," 166; and Z. Zamarion (Halpern), "A Shaliach in Belsen," 179, in *Belsen.* Levin, *Holocaust,* 19–20, 61–62, chap. 17. Bauer, *Flight and Rescue,* 29–30, 36. Jon Kimche and David Kimche, *The Secret Roads: The 'Illegal' Migration of a People—1938–1948* (New York: Farrar, Straus and Cudahy, 1955), 171–72.

23. Polish Jew (anonymous), interview with author.

24. Levin, *Holocaust,* 279. "The Infiltrees," *Commentary* 1, no. 2 (February 1946): 43.

25. Levin, *Holocaust,* 165–68. Tatiana Berenstein and Adam Rutkowski, *Assistance to the Jews in Poland—1939–1945* (Warsaw: Polonia, 1963), 18–19. Bauer, *Jewish Emergence,* 62–64. Polish Jew (anonymous), interview with author.

26. Stone, *Underground,* 51.

27. Inter-Governmental Committee on Refugees, *Memorandum: From the American Resident Representative,* no. 4, 30 April 1946, 3–4. Bauer, *Jewish Emergence,* 64. Yitzhak Arad, *The Partisan: From the Valley of Death to Mount Zion* (New York: Holocaust Library, 1979), 176–77.

28. Władysław Anders, *An Army in Exile: The Story of the Second Polish Corps* (London: Macmillan, 1949), 19. *The Dark Side of the Moon* (London: Faber and Faber, 1946), 210. Arad, *Partisan,* 27, 160–61, 186. Pole (anonymous), interview with author.

29. Bauer, *Flight and Rescue,* 115. Bauer, *Jewish Emergence,* 65. *Commentary,* November 1945, 33–34. Arad, *Partisan,* 186.

30. Dinnerstein, *America,* 107–109. *New York Times,* 13 July 1946, 1, 5. *Commentary,* 2, no. 2 (August 1946): 140. Bauer, *Jewish Emergence,* 65.

31. *Commentary,* 1, no. 1 (November 1945): 33; 2, no. 4 (October 1946): 327–35.

32. Proudfoot, *European Refugees, 340–42.* Dinnerstein, *America,* 112. Bauer, *Flight and Rescue,* chap. 7 passim. Ira A. Hirschmann, *The Embers Still Burn* (New York: Simon and Schuster, 1949), 75–76.

33. Lt.-Gen. Sir Frederick Morgan, *Peace and War—A Soldier's Life* (London: Hodder and Stoughton, 1961), 236–37, 246–51, 256. *Commentary* 1, no. 4 (February 1946): 44–46; March 1946, 66.

34. Frank, "The Tragedy," 437. Genêt, "Letter From Wurzburg," *New Yorker,* 6 November 1948, 116–17. Jay B. Krane, "Observations on the Problem of Jewish Infiltrees" (confidential) 18 January 1946, UNRRA Archives, Germany Mission, Infiltrees. David Bernstein, "Europe's Jews: Summer, 1947," *Commentary* 4, no. 2 (August 1947): 104.

35. *New York Times,* 27 January 1946, 1, 27. Jay B. Krane, "Report on Infiltrees

in the U.S. Zone" (confidential) 10 July 1946; "Observations," 18 January 1946, UNRRA Archives, Germany Mission, Infiltrees.

36. Bauer, *Jewish Emergence,* 66–67. Krane, "Observations," 18 January 1946.

37. Polish Jew (anonymous), interview with author.

38. Bauer, *Flight and Rescue,* pp. vii–viii, 118–19. Bauer, *Jewish Emergence,* 62–63, 65–67. Kimche and Kimche, *Secret Roads,* 83–84.

39. Kimche and Kimche, *Secret Roads,* 85–86. Bauer, *Flight and Rescue,* 28–29.

40. Bauer, *Flight and Rescue,* 45, 66–67, 118–19, 121. Bauer, *Jewish Emergence,* 63, 67.

41. Kimche and Kimche, *Secret Roads,* 87–89.

42. Ibid., 87–92. Stone, *Underground,* 43. Krane, "Observations," 18 January 1946, 6.

43. Alexander E. Squadrilli, interview with author.

44. Bauer, *Flight and Rescue,* 81–82, 87–89, 190–91, 248–49. Dinnerstein, *America,* 105. Krane, "Observations," 18 January 1946, 4. Lehrman, "Austria: Way-Station," 565–72.

45. *New York Times,* 17 April 1947, 6. Lucius D. Clay, *Decision in Germany* (Garden City, N.J.: Doubleday, 1950), 232.

46. U.S. Office of Military Government for Germany, *Weekly Information Bulletin,* no. 78, 3 February 1947, 24.

47. Proudfoot, *European Refugees,* 238–39. Preparatory Commission for the IRO, *PCIRO News Bulletin,* no. 6, 8 December 1947, 1–3; no. 11, 24 March 1948, 1–2. *New York Times,* 26 October 1946, 7.

48. Stone, *Underground,* 112–13. Hirschmann, *Embers Still Burn,* 74ff. Bernstein, "Europe's Jews," 107.

49. Leo Srole, interview with author. See accounts of Srole's acts in *New York Times,* 6 December 1945, 7; 7 December 1945, 5. U.S. Army, *Displaced Persons,* Occupation Forces in Europe Series, 1945–46, Training Packet 53 (Frankfurt am Main, Germany: U.S. Army, n.d.), 105.

50. H. Hrachovska, dist. welfare officer, Hq. 8 Corps District, to Col. C. J. Wood, UNRRA dist. dir. Hq. 8 Corps Dist. British Zone, 29 March 1946, UNRRA Archives, Germany Mission, British Zone (Lemgo) Central Registry, Repatriation. This is another Neustadt than the camp discussed at the beginning of chap. 2.

51. Krane, "Report on Infiltrees," 10 July 1946, 2.

52. *New York Times,* 6 February 1947, 3. Polish Jew and former Jewish agency worker (anonymous), interviews with author.

53. Information on the Landsberg carnival is from Toby Blum-Dobkin, "The Landsberg Carnival: Purim in a Displaced Persons Center," Yeshiva University Museum, 1979 Catalogue, *Purim: The Face and the Mask* (New York: Yeshiva University, 1979), 52–58. For information on the Landsberg DP camp, see Leo Srole, "Why the DPs Can't Wait," *Commentary* 3, no. 1 (January 1947): 13–21.

54. Kimche and Kimche, *Secret Roads,* 84, 98, 100–106. *New York Times,* 8 September 1947, 6.

55. Carl Friedman oral history interview, William E. Wiener Oral History Library of the American Jewish Committee, 1 December 1974, 20–23.

56. Schechtman, *United States,* 153. Bauer, *Jewish Emergence,* 74–75. Bauer, *Flight and Rescue,* 320–21. Arad, *Partisan,* 207. *New York Times,* 1 December 1947, 5.

57. Proudfoot, *European Refugees,* 358–61. Bauer, *Flight and Rescue,* 319–21. Bauer, *Jewish Emergence,* 73.

58. Proudfoot, *European Refugees,* 361.

Chapter 7. Cultures in Exile

1. Croatian (anonymous), interview with author.

2. Channing Richardson, UNRRA Team 47, Pfarrkirchen/Eggenfelden, Germany, to "Norman," n.d., AFSC Archives, Foreign Service 1946, Displaced Pers. Svcs.-Svcs. (Possible) for Expellees, 1946.

3. "The Ukrainian Free University in Munich and the Harvard University Refugee Project," *Ukrainian Quarterly* 7, no. 3 (Summer 1951): 267–68. Memorandum of the General Headquarters of the Association of Ukrainian Political Prisoners, Munich, Germany, 12 December, 1945, 1–3, IHRC.

4. *Lithuanian Bulletin,* January–February 1947, 11, contains typical reports showing antagonisms between DP groups.

5. Themes on the DP home as representative of national culture were presented during the conference, "The D.P. Experience: Ukrainian Refugees After World War II," 4 November 1983, St. Michael's College, University of Toronto, Toronto, Canada. Ukrainians (anonymous), interviews with author.

6. Reminiscences of former DPs provided much of the information on the celebration of national days in the camps, in this and following paragraphs; also see Dymtro Doroshenko, *A Survey of Ukrainian History* (Winnipeg, Canada: Humeniuk Foundation, 1975), 616. Vladimir Dedijer, Ivan Bozic, Sima Cirkovic, and Milorad Ekmecic, *History of Yugoslavia* (New York: McGraw-Hill, 1974), 572–73.

7. Andrejs Johansons, "Latvian Literature in Exile," *Slavonic Review* 30, no. 75 (June 1952): 472.

8. Brigadier, chief of staff, 30 Corps Dist., BAOR, to Mil. Gov. Detachments, 29 December 1945, reprinted in Bohdan Panchuk, *Heroes of Their Day: The Reminiscences of Bohdan Panchuk* (Toronto: Multicultural History Society, 1983) 133–34.

9. *Polish Review,* 28 November 1946, 7.

10. *Lithuanian Bulletin,* December 1946, 11; January–June, 1950, 26. Johansons, "Latvian Literature," 472.

11. *Polish Review,* 28 November 1946, 7. Josef Fraenkel, "The Cultural Liberation of Belsen," in *Belsen* (Israel: Irgun Sheerit Hapleita Me'haezor Habriti, 1957), 164–67. Interviews with former DPs of all major DP groups provided information on the cultural renaissance in the camps.

12. Rimvydas Šilbajoris, "The Experience of Exile in Lithuanian Literature," 44, 51, and Ilse Lehiste, "Three Estonian Writers and the Experience of Exile," 16–17, 28, in *Lituanus* 18, no. 1 (Spring 1972).

13. Juris Silenieks, "Latvian Literature in Exile: The Recycling of Signs," *Lituanus* 18, no. 1 (Spring 1972): 34.

14. Rimvydas Šibajoris, *Perfection of Exile: Fourteen Contemporary Lithuanian Writers* (Norman: University of Oklahoma Press, 1970), 22–23.

15. Silenieks, "Latvian Literature in Exile," 32–34.

16. Samy Feder, "The Yiddish Theatre of Belsen," in *Belsen,* 135–38.

17. Nora Levin, *The Holocaust: The Destruction of European Jewry, 1933–1945* (New York: Schocken Books, 1973), 484–85.

18. Prof. Alfreds Straumanis, interview with author. Johansons, "Latvian Literature," 473. Croatian (anonymous), interview with author.

19. Marek Gordon, interview with author.

20. Channing Richardson, Eggenfelden/Pfarrkirchen, Germany, to Clarence Pickett, AFSC, Philadelphia, Pa., 1 September 1946, AFSC Archives, Foreign Service 1946, Disp. Pers. Svcs.-Svcs.(Possible) for Expellees, 1946. Doroshenko, *A Survey*, 720–24, 730–31, 736–37, 749–50, 754–55.

21. Genêt, "Letter From Aschaffenburg," *New Yorker*, 30 October 1948, 99.

22. Prof. Valerian Revutsky, interview with author. *Ukraine—A Concise Encyclopedia* (Toronto: University of Toronto Press, 1971), 2:471–72, 658–59. Luke Myshuha, "An Appraisal of the New Ukrainian Immigrants," *Ukrainian Weekly*, 21 April 1947, 3, copy in United Ukrainian American Relief Committee (UUARC) Papers, Box 192 (IHRC).

23. S.H., "Ukrainian Writers in Exile, 1945–1949," *Ukrainian Quarterly* 6, no. 1 (Winter 1950): 73.

24. Ibid., 74.

25. Roman V. Kuchar, "Ukrainian Emigre Literature After 1945," *Ukrainian Quarterly* 33, no. 3 (Summer 1974): 269–70.

26. John Wolhandler, *New York Times*, 30 June 1946, sec. 2, p. 1.

27. Hadassa Bimko-Rosensaft, "The Children of Belsen," 107; Josef Rosensaft, "Our Belsen," 47; and Noah Barou, "Remembering Belsen," 83–84, in *Belsen*. Koppel S. Pinson, "Jewish Life in Liberated Germany—A Study of the Jewish DP's," *Jewish Social Studies* 9 (April 1947): 113.

28. Genêt, "Letter From Wurzburg," *New Yorker*, 6 November 1948, 116. Malcolm J. Proudfoot, *European Refugees: 1939–1952—A Study in Forced Population Movement* (Evanston, Ill,: Northwestern University Press, 1956), 375–77.

29. Edward N. Peterson, *The American Occupation of Germany—Retreat to Victory* (Detroit: Wayne State University Press, 1977), 295–97. Earl F. Ziemke, *The U.S. Army in the Occupation of Germany, 1944–1946* (Washington: U.S. Army Center of Military History, 1975), 285.

30. Kathryn Hulme, *The Wild Place* (Boston: Little, Brown, 1953), 125–26. Harold Zink, *The United States in Germany, 1944–1955* (Princeton: Van Nostrand, 1957), 296–98.

31. German (anonymous), interview with author. *New York Times*, 23 March 1946, 4. Samuel Gringauz, "Our New German Policy and the DP's," *Commentary* 5, no. 6 (June 1948): 513. Proudfoot, *European Refugees*, 413–14. Edward A. Raymond, "The Juridical Status of Persons Displaced from Soviet and Soviet-Dominated Territory" (Ph.D. diss., American University, 1952), 140. Oliver J. Frederiksen, *The American Military Occupation of Germany, 1945–1953* (Frankfurt am Main, Germany: U.S. Army, 1953), 74.

32. U.S. Army, *Displaced Persons*, Occupation Forces in Europe Series, 1945–46, Training Packet 53 (Frankfurt am Main, Germany: U.S. Army, n.d.), 109–10. Alexander Squadrilli, interview with author.

33. Fiorello H. La Guardia to Gen. McNarney, 4 August 1946, reprinted in Ira A. Hirschmann, *The Embers Still Burn* (New York: Simon and Schuster, 1949), 97–98. Leonard Dinnerstein, *America and the Survivors of the Holocaust* (New York: Columbia University Press, 1982), 49–50. Squadrilli interview.

34. Frederiksen, *American Military Occupation*, 61.

35. Gringauz, "Our New German Policy," 512.

36. G. D. A. Reid, "Report (respecting the suitability and desireability as immigrants of refugees of Polish, Ukrainian, and Baltic origin and refugees recently come from Yugoslavia)," 5 January 1956, 31, Dr. V. J. Kaye Collection, Public Archives of Canada.

37. *New York Times,* 12 November 1946, 8. Slovenian (anonymous), interview with author.

38. Slovenian (anonymous), interview with author. Memorandum of interview with Mgr. Perridon in Paris, 26 September 1945, UUARC Papers, Box 192 (IHRC).

39. Gringauz, "Our New German Policy," 512. Hal Lehrman, "Austria: Way-Station of Exodus—Pages from a Correspondent's Notebook," *Commentary* 2, no. 6. (December 1946): 569–70. *New York Times,* 25 May 1946, 8; 5 October 1947, 15.

40. *New York Times,* 11 January 1947, 5; 8 February 1947, 4; 17 May 1947, 4.

41. F. Roy Willis, *The French in Germany—1945–1949* (Stanford, Calif.: Stanford University Press, 1962), 23, 27–32, 45–46. Ziemke, *U.S. Army,* 86, 104–6. Bradley F. Smith, *Reaching Judgment at Nuremberg* (New York: Basic Books, 1977), 22ff.

42. Peterson, *American Occupation,* 90, 138, 156–57. Zink, *United States,* 295–96. Frederiksen, *American Military Occupation,* 9. Ziemke, *U.S. Army,* 97.

43. John Gimbel, *The American Occupation of Germany: Politics and the Military, 1945–1949* (Stanford, Calif.: Stanford University Press, 1968), 1. Peterson, *American Occupation,* 121. Fenner Brockway, *German Diary* (London: Gollancz, 1946), 140. Lt.-Gen. Sir Frederick Morgan, *Peace and War—A Soldier's Life* (London: Hodder and Stoughton, 1961), 214–15. Ziemke, *U.S. Army,* 275.

44. Zink, *United States,* 295–96.

45. Eugene M. Kulischer, *Europe on the Move: War and Population Changes, 1917–47* (New York: Columbia University Press, 1948), 279–81. Victor Gollancz, *In Darkest Germany* (Hinsdale, Ill.: Henry Regnery, 1947), 30–31, 54, 74, 178, 184. Brockway, *German Diary,* 4–5, 10, 70.

46. Gimbel, *American Occupation,* 3–5, 45–46.

47. Gollancz, *In Darkest Germany,* 19–20, 178, 184. Gimbel, *American Occupation,* 45–46.

48. Tadeusz Borowski, "The January Offensive," in *This Way for the Gas, Ladies and Gentlemen* (New York: Penguin 1959; 1976), 164–65.

49. Gottfried Neuburger, "An Orthodox G.I. Fights a War," *Commentary* 8, no. 3 (March 1949): 271. Frederiksen, *American Military Occupation,* 52–53. David Bernstein, "Europe's Jews: Summer, 1947," *Commentary* 4, no. 2 (August 1947): 105.

50. *New York Times,* 5 August 1947, 19.

51. Polish Jew (anonymous), interview with author.

52. Peterson, *American Occupation,* 3, 221ff; 244ff. Frederiksen, *American Military Occupation,* 129–31. Former UNRRA official (anonymous), interview with author.

53. Lucius D. Clay, *Decision in Germany* (Garden City, N.Y.: Doubleday, 1950), 133–35. Peterson, *American Occupation,* 29. Typical memoirs that detail the increasing cold war tensions are Morgan, *Peace and War,* and Gen. Mark Clark, *Calculated Risk* (New York: Harper, 1950).

54. Brockway, *German Diary,* 138. *Laisvoji Lietuva* (Memmingen, Germany), 30 April 1947, quoted in Raymond G. Krisciunas, "The Emigrant Experience: The Decision of Lithuanian Refugees to Emigrate, 1945–1950," *Lituanus* 29, no. 2 (Summer 1983): 35–36.

55. Hirschmann, *Embers Still Burn,* chap. 8 and 9 passim. Frederiksen, *American Military Occupation,* 131, 140, 147–48, 186. Gimbel, *American Occupation,*

3–5. Clay, *Decision in Germany,* 133–35, 139, 156–59. Former Lutheran World Federation worker (anonymous), interview with author.

56. Gringauz, "Our New German Policy," 508.

57. *New York Times,* 8 February 1947, 4. Frederiksen, *American Military Occupation,* 50–53, 131–32, 197. U.S. Department of State, *American Policy in Occupied Areas,* Pub. no. 2794 (Washington: GPO, 1947), 16, 27. Peterson, *American Occupation,* 10, 93, 351–52. Willis, *French in Germany,* 47–48.. U.S. Office of Military Government for Germany, *Weekly Information Bulletin,* no. 74, 6 January 1947, 16, 35.

58. U.S. Office of Military Government for Germany, *Weekly Information Bulletin,* no. 74, 6 January 1947, 35, 40, 42; no. 100, 7 July 1947, 6. Frederiksen, *American Military Occupation,* 131–36.

Chapter 8. The Gates Open

1. Letter from Salzburg DP camp, n.d., in John Panchuk Papers, B. 2, F. 11, IHRC.

2. Reg. Dir., 460 UNRRA Hq., to BAOR Zone Hq. for Repatriation, 15 November 1946, UNRRA Archives, BZ/ZO/Repatriation Report, Germany Mission, British Zone (Lemgo) Central Registry. Jacques Vernant, *The Refugee in the Post-War World* (New Haven: Yale University Press, 1953), 595.

3. *Lithuanian Bulletin,* Spring 1946, 6–7. *New York Times,* 15 October 1945, 8. Leonard Dinnerstein, *America and the Survivors of the Holocaust* (New York: Columbia University Press, 1982), 22–24. Leonard Dinnerstein, "The U.S. Army and the Jews: Policies toward the Displaced Persons After World War II," *American Jewish History* 68, no. 3 (March 1979): 354.

4. Myron Momryk, "Ukrainian Displaced Persons and the Canadian Government—1946–1952," paper given at conference on "The D.P. Experience: Ukrainian Refugees After World War II," 5 November 1983, St. Michael's College, University of Toronto. Former DPs (anonymous), interviews with author.

5. Material on collaboration charges is from interviews with former DPs and agency workers. Dinnerstein, *America,* 177, 207–209.

6. *UNRRA Monthly Review,* April 1946, 10. Danes and Lithuanians (anonymous), interviews with author.

7. Slovenian (anonymous), interview with author.

8. Matteo J. Milazzo, *The Chetnik Movement & the Yugoslav Resistance* (Baltimore: Johns Hopkins University Press, 1975), 133–34, 182–83. Yugoslav and U.S. agency worker (anonymous), interviews with author.

9. U.S. Displaced Persons Commission, *Memo to America: The DP Story* (Washington: GPO, 1952), 144–45. Former DPs and government workers, interviews with author.

10. Polish and Latvian former DPs and former UNRRA employee (anonymous), interviews with author.

11. Norman Davies, *God's Playground: A History of Poland* (New York: Columbia University Press, 1982), 2: 521–23. *Shevchenko Library & Museum* (magazine), 2 June 1963, 12–13. Walter Dushnyck, review of *The Other Holocaust, Many Circles of Hell,* by Bohdan Wytwycky, *Ukrainian Quarterly* (Spring 1981): 74–76.

12. Ukrainian (anonymous), interview with author.

13. Bohdan Panchuk, *Heroes of Their Day: The Reminiscences of Bohdan Panchuk* (Toronto: Multicultural History Society, 1983), 152–53.

14. Panchuk, *Heroes of Their Day,* 153. Statement by Dr. O. Fundak, president,

Central Representation of Ukrainian Emigrants in Germany (CRUEG), to IRO Review Board, Geneva, Switzerland, 8 December 1949, CRUEG Collection (IHRC).

15. Panchuk, *Heroes of Their Day,* 74–77, 146–47, 154–56.

16. Zenon Pelenskyj, liaison officer to U.S. Zone IRO Hqs., Frankfurt/Main, Germany, to IRO Review Board, Geneva, Switzerland, 29 June 1950, CRUEG Collection (IHRC).

17. Malcolm J. Proudfoot, *European Refugees: 1939–1952—A Study in Forced Population Movement* (Evanston, Ill.: Northwestern University Press, 1956), 242, 242n. *Lithuanian Bulletin,* October 1946, 12–13. Albertas Gerutis, ed., *Lithuania 700 Years* (New York: Manyland Books, 1969), 294–96.

18. Proudfoot, *European Refugees,* 242, 242n. Vernant, *The Refugee,* 32, 68. Estonian (anonymous), interview with author.

19. Kathryn Hulme, *The Wild Place* (Boston: Little, Brown, 1953), 188–89. George Woodbridge, *UNRRA: The History of the United Nations Relief and Rehabilitation Administration* (New York: Columbia University Press, 1950), 2:517n. Pole (anonymous), interview with author.

20. Ben Kaplan, interview with author.

21. Amy Zahl Gottlieb, "Refugee Immigration: The Truman Directive," *Prologue* 13, no. 1 (Spring 1981): 6–7. Anthony T. Bouscaren, *International Migrations Since 1945* (New York: Praeger, 1963), 7. Kathleen H. Hanstein, AFSC, Philadelphia, Pa., to Jack Waddington, AFSC, UNRRA, AFHQ, APO 512, AFSC Archives, Foreign Service 1945; DP Svcs.-Corr. w/Overseas Offices, 1945. *New York Times,* 6 October 1946, 35.

22. Vernant, *The Refugee,* 473–74. Gottlieb, "Refugee Immigration," 6. Yugoslav and Lithuanian (anonymous), interviews with author.

23. Polish Red Cross, "Memorandum regarding the problem of refugees and Displaced Persons," January 1949, John Panchuk Papers, B. 2, F. 14 (IHRC).

24. Former DPs of various nationalities, interviews with author. *Lithuanian Bulletin,* October 1946, 15.

25. Proudfoot, *European Refugees,* 294. Ukrainian (anonymous), interview with author.

26. Yugoslavs (anonymous), interviews with author. Raymond G. Krisciunas, "The Emigrant Experience: The Decision of Lithuanian Refugees to Emigrate, 1945–1950," *Lituanus* 29, no. 2 (Summer 1983): 39. George Leather, " 'Westward Ho' and After," *New Statesman,* 8 December 1951, 659–60.

27. *UNRRA Team News,* 8 February 1947, 3. *Ukraine—A Concise Encyclopedia* (Toronto: University of Toronto Press, 1963), 1:916. USFET confidential cable to AGWAR, 28 September 1946, UNRRA Archives, BZ/ZO: RR/Repatriation Report, Germany Mission, British Zone (Lemgo) Central Registry.

28. Hulme, *Wild Place,* 178–79.

29. International Labour Office, *International Migration: 1945–1957* (Geneva: ILO, 1957), 144. Former U.S. official (anonymous), interview with author. Hulme, *Wild Place,* 232.

30. Proudfoot, *European Refugees,* 425. Vernant, *The Refugee,* 342–44. *Ukraine—A Concise Encyclopedia,* 1:916.

31. *UNRRA Team News,* 8 February 1947, 8. Vernant, *The Refugee,* 342. Leather, " 'Westward Ho,' " 659–60. *Refugees Defense Committee Report,* 1947, 10–11, John Panchuk Papers, B. 2, F. 11 (IHRC). Edward A. Raymond, "The Juridical Status of Persons Displaced From Soviet and Soviet-Dominated Ter-

ritory" (Ph.D. diss., American University, 1952), 212–13. Bouscaren, *International Migrations,* 69. ILO, *International Migration,* 139–40.

32. Momryk, "Ukrainian Displaced Persons," 6.

33. Ibid., 3. Vernant, *The Refugee,* 548–49.

34. Inter-Governmental Committee on Refugees, *Memorandum: From the American Resident Representative,* no. 21, 23 June 1947, 2–3. Vernant, *The Refugee,* 558–60. Preparatory Commission for the IRO, *PCIRO News Bulletin,* no. 2, 3 October 1947, 4. *New York Times,* 2 June 1947, 17. *Refugees Defense Committee Report,* 1947, 14. Wasyll Gira, United Ukrainian American Relief Commmittee Report, 1–15 May 1947, UUARC Papers, B. 189 (IHRC).

35. David C. Corbett, *Canada's Immigration Policy: A Critique* (Toronto: University of Toronto Press, 1957), 20–21, 70–72. Vernant, *The Refugee,* 560.

36. Hew Roberts, ed., *Australia's Immigration Policy* (Nedlands: University of Western Australia Press, 1972), 16–18. Aldis L. Putniņš, *Latvians in Australia: Alienation and Assimilation* (Canberra: Australian National University Press, 1981), 15–16.

37. Putniņš, *Latvians in Australia,* 16.

38. Egon F. Kunz, "European Migration Absorption in Australia," *International Migration* 9, no. 1/2 (1971): 71. Roberts, *Australia's Immigration,* 16–18, 42. Putniņš, *Latvians in Australia,* 15–16. Vernant, *The Refugee,* 705–706.

39. Bouscaren, *International Migrations,* 89–90.

40. Genêt, "Letter From Aschaffenburg," *New Yorker,* 30 October 1948, 100–101. Proudfoot, *European Refugees,* 422, 425. IGCR memorandum, no. 17, 1 April 1947, 4.

41. IGCR Memorandum, no. 20, 2 June 1947, 1. *Refugees Defense Committee Report,* 1947, 12–15. Vernant, *The Refugee,* 602–603. Milda Danys, "The Emigrant Experience: Contract Hiring of Displaced Persons in Canadian Domestic Employment, 1947–1950," *Lituanus* 29, no. 2 (Summer 1983): 43. Slovenians (anonymous), interviews with author.

42. Genêt, "Letter From Aschaffenburg," 100–101. Proudfoot, *European Refugees,* 429.

43. V. Viks, dean, report, BAOR, 1948, LWF Service to Refugees Collection, 1 : 66. Slovenians and Ukrainians (anonymous), interviews with author.

44. "Wasyll," report on conference of PCIRO and voluntary agency representatives in Austria, 11–13 August 1948, UUARC Papers, B. 189 (IHRC). Danys, "Emigrant Experience," 45.

45. Hulme, *Wild Place,* 199–200, 243–44. Danys, "Emigrant Experience," 44. DPs of various nationalities commented on the struggle to become an expert in different occupations and on how to pass a medical exam.

46. Gottleib, "Refugee Immigration," 6–7. William S. Bernard, "Refugee Asylum in the United States: How the Law Was Changed to Admit Displaced Persons," *International Migration* 13, no. 1/2 (1975); 6–7, 14. Dinnerstein, *America,* 5–6. U.S. DP Commission, *Memo to America,* 9–27.

47. Dinnerstein, *America,* 131ff. Bernard, "Refugee Asylum," 15–16. U.S. DP Commission, *Memo to America,* 27.

48. Hulme, *Wild Place,* 225. *Social Service Review* 22, no. 3 (September 1948): 365–66. U.S. Displaced Persons Commission, *Second Semi-Annual Report,* 1 August 1949, 12.

49. U.S. DP Commission, *Memo to America,* 28, 38–39. U.S. DP Commission, *Fourth Semi-Annual Report,* 1 August 1950, 15–17; *Fifth Semi-Annual Report,* 1 February 1951, 15; *Sixth Semi-Annual Report,* 1 August 1951, 24.

50. U.S. DP Commission, *Memo to America,* 100, 102.

51. Ibid., 189. Dinnerstein, *America,* 189–91, describes the steps involved in obtaining an assurance. Alexander Squadrilli, interview with author; also see Squadrilli speech to National Resettlement Conference for Displaced Persons, Chicago, Ill., 5–7 April 1949, reprinted in U.S. 81st Congress, 1st sess., House Document 220.

52. Squadrilli, interview with author. U.S. DP Commission, *Memo to America,* 73–76. Hulme, *Wild Place,* 231. Former voluntary agency workers, interviews with author.

53. U.S. DP Commission, *Memo to America,* 76. Ernst Vähi, report, 1949, Lutheran World Federation Service to Refugees Collection 2 : 192.

54. Polish Jew (anonymous), interview with author.

55. U.S. DP Commission, *Memo to America,* 63–65.

56. *Encyclopedia of the Lutheran Church* (Minneapolis, Minn.: Augsburg, 1965), 1 : 711–12. Howard Hong, report to Lutheran World Federation Service to Refugees, 1 July 1948, Lutheran World Federation Service to Refugees Collection 1 : 189.

57. U.S. DP Commission, *Memo to America,* 78–79. Dinnerstein, *America,* chap. 5, discusses the Jewish resettlement program. Former Catholic worker (anonymous), interviews with author.

58. Hulme, *Wild Place,* 228–29.

59. Ukrainian (anonymous), interview with author.

60. Gertrude Sovik, interview with author.

61. Sovik interview. See Sovik description of final days of the DP act in *Lutheran Herald,* 15 April 1952, 359–60.

62. Sovik interview. Raymond, "Juridical Status," 329. Bouscaren, *International Migrations,* 17, 27, 33.

63. Raymond, "Juridical Status," 311. G. D. A. Reid, "Report (respecting the suitability and desireability as immigrants of refugees of Polish, Ukrainian and Baltic origin)," 5 January 1956, 2, 4, Dr. V. J. Kaye Collection, Public Archives of Canada.

64. U.S. DP Commission, *Memo to America,* 198. Sovik interview. *IRO Digest,* no. 15, November 1949, 3, 5; no. 18, Feburary 1950, 4; no. 19, March 1950, 5.

65. Karlis Kalnins, "Those Who Remain," n.d., Lutheran World Federation report in possession of the author. Hulme, *Wild Place,* 240–41.

66. Howard Hong, report (1948?), LWF Service to Refugees Collection 2 : 170–74. *IRO Digest,* no. 15, November 1949, 5. Reid, "Report," 5–6.

67. Gertrude Sovik, Monthly Report, December 1951, 11, LWF Service to Refugees Collection.

68. Dinnerstein, *America,* 256. H. G. Van Dam, "Legal Protection in Belsen," in *Belsen* (Israel: Irgun Sheerit Hapleita Me'haezor Habriti, 1957), 151. Walter Laquer, *The Terrible Secret: Suppression of the Truth About Hitler's "Final Solution"* (Boston: Little, Brown, 1982), 89. Office of the U.S. High Commissioner for Germany, *4th Quarterly Report on Germany—July 1–September 30, 1950,* 30–31, and *5th Quarterly Report on Germany—October 1–December 31, 1950* (n.p., 1950), 56–63. International Labour Office, *International Migration,* 18. Proudfoot, *European Refugees,* 431–32.

Chapter 9. Legacies

1. Ukrainian (anonymous), interview with author.

2. Milda Danys, "The Emigrant Experience: Contract Hiring of Displaced Persons in Canadian Domestic Employment, 1947–1950," *Lituanus* 29, no. 2 (Summer 1983): 45. I. Jaunzems and L. B. Brown, "A Social-Psychological Study of Latvian Immigrants in Canberra," *International Migration* 10, no. 1/2 (1972): 60.

3. Lithuanian (anonymous), interview with author. Bohdan Panchuk, *Heroes of Their Day: The Reminiscences of Bohdan Panchuk* (Toronto: Multicultural History Society, 1983), 124.

4. Names of these organizations were located through Ukrainian and Latvian records in the Immigration History Research Center; in *Belsen* (Israel: Irgun Sheerit Hapleita Me'haezor Habriti, 1957); and through interviews. On "Second Generation," see Helen Epstein, *Children of the Holocaust: Conversations with Sons and Daughters of Survivors* (New York: Putnam's, 1979), 337–38.

5. Ernst Vähi, "Thoughts of Departure," LWF Service to Refugees Collection 1:373–76. Giles E. Gobetz, "Adjustment and Assimilation of Slovenian Refugees" (Ph.D. diss., Ohio State University, 1962), p. ii.

6. Latvian (anonymous), interview with author. Vähi, "Thoughts of Departure," 373–76.

7. Aldis L. Putniņš, *Latvians in Australia: Alienation and Assimilation* (Canberra: Australian National University Press, 1981), 32. Dmytro Andriewsky, "Soviets and the Emigration," *Ukrainian Quarterly* 11, no. 2 (Spring 1955): 127ff. DPs of various nationalities told of Soviet efforts to lure them back.

8. See program of Sixth Lithuanian Song Festival, Chicago, Ill., 3 July 1983.

9. Rimvydas Šilbajoris, *Perfection of Exile: Fourteen Contemporary Lithuanian Writers* (Norman: University of Oklahoma Press, 1970), 22–23.

10. Various DPs told of trying to view their homeland from a neighboring noncommunist country.

BIBLIOGRAPHY

1. Archives and Historical Collections

American Friends Service Committee Archives, Philadelphia, Pa.
  Letters and reports from Europe, 1945–52.
Immigration History Research Center, St. Paul, Minn.
  Association of Ukrainian Political Prisoners (Munich, Germany) Papers.
  Association of Ukrainians in Great Britain Papers.
  Central Representation of Ukrainian Emigrants in Germany Papers.
  Displaced Persons Camps Newspaper Collection.
  John Panchuk Papers.
  Shevchenko Library and Museum (London) publications, 1946–67.
  United Ukrainian American Relief Committee Papers.
Lithuanian World Archives, Chicago.
Lutheran World Federation Service to Refugees Archives, Northfield, Minn.
National Archives, Washington, D.C.
United Nations Relief and Rehabilitation Administration Archives, New York.
William E. Wiener Oral History Library, American Jewish Committee, New York.

2. Interviews and Correspondence

NOTE: More than eighty interviews were conducted for this study. A large number were with persons who still have relatives in Communist countries and therefore did not wish their names to be published.

Bagdanavičius, Rev. Vytautas. Interview with author. Chicago, 24 July 1982.

Balinsky, Dr. B. I. Letters to author, 15 April 1982, 19 July 1982, 22 December 1983, 14 March 1984.

Cieslar, Jan. Interview with author. Seattle, 13 August 1981.

Friedman, Carl. Interview by Bea Stadtler, 1 December 1974. Transcript of tape recording, William E. Wiener Oral History Library of the American Jewish Committee, New York.

Gordon, Marek. Interview with author. Chicago, 20 March 1981.

Hering, Alfons, Interview with author. Stevens Point, Wis., 23 December 1982.

Hong, Prof. Howard V. Interview with author. St. Olaf College, Northfield, Minn., 28 December 1981.

Janavs, Dr. Visvaldis. Letter to author, 9 December 1983.

Kaplan, Ben. Interview with author. Guttenberg, N.J., 20 September 1981.

Landi, Monsignor Andrew P. Interview with author. Catholic Relief Services, New York, 18 September 1981.

MacCracken, Dr. James. Letter to author, 30 June 1983; telephone interview, 14 July 1983.

Masilionis, Juozas. Interview with author. Chicago, 24 July 1982.

Melaher, Joseph. Interview with author. Cleveland, 18 June 1982.

Panchuk, G. R. B. Interview with author. Toronto, Canada. 5 November 1983.

Pikre, Arnold F. Interview with author. Seattle, 15 August 1981.

Počs, Dr. Olgert. Interview with author. Illinois State University, Normal, Ill., 6 February 1981.

Ratti, Oscar. Interview with author. Catholic Relief Services, New York, 18 September 1981.

Revutsky, Prof. Valerian. Interview with author. Toronto, Canada. 5 November 1983.

Shulman, Prof. Sol. Interview with author. Illinois State University, Normal, Ill., 20 April 1981.

Sovik, Gertrude. Interview with author. Northfield, Minn., 28 December 1981.

Squadrilli, Alexander. Interview with author. Wilton, Conn., 21 September 1981.

Srole, Prof. Leo. Telephone interviews with author, 12 April 1983, 15 May 1983.

Straumanis, Prof. Alfreds. Letter to author, 30 October 1983; telephone interview with author, 17 November 1983.

Warach, Bernard. Interview with author. New York, 19 September 1981.

3. Publications from DP Camps

In the Name of the Lithuanian People. Wolfberg, Germany: Perkūnas. 1945.

Lithuanians of Dinkelsbühl Under UNRRA Care. Dinkelsbühl, Germany: Dinkelsbühl DP Camp, 1947.

Malinauskas, Professor, Teacher Mockus, and Teacher Zemaitis, comps. *14,000 Displaced Lithuanian School Children and Students Calling for Help*. Augsburg, Germany: P. Haas, 1947.

Narkeliūnaite, S., comp. *DP Baltic Camp at Seedorf*. Seedorf, Germany: UNRRA Team 295, 1946.

Tevzeme. (Latvian newspaper) Hanau, Germany, 1946.

4. Governmental and International Agency Reports

CANADA

G.D.A. Reid, "Report (respecting the suitability and desirability as immigrants of refugees of Polish, Ukrainian, and Baltic origin and refugees recently come from Yugoslavia, who are residing in Germany, Austria, Trieste and Italy)." Dr. V. J. Kaye Collection, MG 31 D69/v. 12, file 20, Public Archives of Canada.

INTER-GOVERNMENTAL COMMITTEE ON REFUGEES

Memorandum: From the American Resident Representative. N.p.: IGCR American Resident Representative, No. 1, 15 March 1946, through No. 22, 30 June 1947.

UNITED NATIONS RELIEF AND REHABILITATION ADMINISTRATION

Displaced Persons Operations: Report of Central Headquarters for Germany (Washington: UNRRA, 1946).

UNITED STATES

U.S. Army. *Displaced Persons.* Occupation Forces in Europe Series, 1945–46. Training Packet 53. Frankfurt am Main, Germany: U.S. Army, n.d.

U.S. Congress. House. Committee on the Judiciary. Subcommitttee on Immigration, Citizenship, and International Law. *Hearings on Alleged Nazi War Criminals.* Parts 1 and 2. 95th Cong., 1st sess., 1977. Serial no. 95–39.

————.Abraham G. Duker, "They Helped to Kill 434,329 Persons," included in Extension of Remarks of Hon. Arthur G. Klein, N.Y., 2 August 1948, "Many Among the DP's in the European Camps are Nazi Collaborationists," *Appendix to the Congressional Record.* 80th Cong., 2d Sess., 1948. Vol. 94, pt. 12, A4891-2.

————. *Proceedings of the National Resettlement Conference for Displaced Persons, April 5, 6, 7, 1949.* 81st Cong., 1st sess., 1949. H. Doc. 220.

U.S. Department of State. *American Policy in Occupied Areas.* 1947. Publication 2794.

————. *Directive Regarding the Military Government of Germany.* 11 July 1947. Publication 2913.

————. *The Displaced-Persons Problem: A Collection of Recent Official Statements.* 1947. Publication 2899.

————. Office of the U.S. High Commissioner for Germany. *Quarterly Reports.* 1950–51.

————. *Report of Earl G. Harrison.* Department of State *Bulletin.* 30 September 1945. Vol. 13., 456–63.

U.S. Displaced Persons Commission. *Semi-Annual Reports,* no. 1–6, Washington: GPO, 1949–51.

Memo to America: The DP Story—The Final Report of the United States Displaced Persons Commission. Washington: GPO, 1952.

U.S. Office of Military Government for Germany. *Weekly Information Bulletin,* nos. 1–125, 1945–47.

5. Published Memoirs, Letters, and Personal Experiences

Alexander, Earl. *The Alexander Memoirs, 1940–45.* New York: McGraw-Hill, 1961.

Anders, Władysław. *An Army in Exile: The Story of the Second Polish Corps.* London: Macmillan, 1949.

———. *Hitler's Defeat in Russia.* Chicago: Henry Regnery, 1953.

Arad, Yitzhak. *The Partisan: From the Valley of Death to Mount Zion.* New York: Holocaust Library, 1979.

Belsen. Israel: Irgun Sheerit Hapleita Me'haezor Habriti, 1957.

Boder, David P. *I Did Not Interview the Dead.* Urbana: University of Illinois Press, 1949.

Borowski, Tadeusz, *This Way for the Gas, Ladies and Gentlemen.* New York: Penguin, 1959; reprint, 1976.

Brockway, Fenner. *German Diary.* London: Victor Gollancz, 1946.

Clark, Mark W. *Calculated Risk.* New York: Harper and Brothers 1950.

Clay, Lucius D. *Decision in Germany.* Garden City, N.Y.: Doubleday, 1950.

———. *The Papers of General Lucius D. Clay: Germany, 1945–1949.* 2 vols. Edited by Jean Edward Smith. Bloomington: Indiana University Press, 1974.

Coffin, William Sloane. *Once to Every Man: A Memoir.* New York: Atheneum, 1977.

Deane, John R. *The Strange Alliance: The Story of Our Efforts at Wartime Co-operation With Russia.* New York: Viking, 1947.

Eisenhower, Dwight D. *Crusade in Europe.* New York: Doubleday, 1948.

———. *The Papers of Dwight David Eisenhower.* Vol. 6, *Occupation, 1945.* Edited by Alfred D. Chandler, Jr., and Louis Galambos. Baltimore: Johns Hopkins University press, 1978.

Gollancz, Victor. *In Darkest Germany.* Hinsdale, Ill.: Henry Regnery, 1947.

Hulme, Kathryn. *The Wild Place.* Boston: Little, Brown, 1953.

Maginnis, John J. *Military Government Journal: Normandy to Berlin.* Amherst: University of Massachusetts Press, 1971.

Morgan, Lt. Gen. Sir Frederick. *Peace and War: A Soldier's Life.* London: Hodder and Stoughton, 1961.

Panchuk, Bohdan. *Heroes of Their Day: The Reminiscences of Bohdan Panchuk.* Edited by Lubomyr Y. Luciuk. Toronto: Multicultural History Society, 1983.

Prcela, John, and Stanko Guldescu, eds. *Operation Slaughterhouse: Eyewitness Accounts of Postwar Massacres in Yugoslavia.* Philadelphia, Pa.: Dorrance, 1970.

Serbian Eastern Orthodox Diocese for the United States of America and Canada. *Martyrdom of the Serbs: Persecutions of the Serbian Orthodox Church and Massacre of the Serbian People.* Chicago: Palandech's Press, n.d.

Skrjabina, Elena. *After Leningrad—from the Caucasus to the Rhine: A Diary of Survival During World War II.* Carbondale: Southern Illinois University Press, 1978.

———. *The Allies on the Rhine—1945–1950.* Carbondale: Southern Illinois University Press, 1980.

Smith, Walter Bedell. *My Three Years in Moscow.* Philadelphia, Pa.: Lippincott, 1950.

Stone, I. F. *Underground to Palestine.* New York: Boni and Gaer, 1946.

6. Unpublished Dissertations, Reports, and Papers

Balinsky, Prof. B. I. "The UNRRA University in Munich, 1945–1947." Memoir, 15 April 1982.

Barley, Delbert. "Refugees in Germany: Relationships between Refugees and the Indigenous Population of a Rural Black Forest Community." Ph.D. diss., University of Pennsylvania, 1957.

Gobetz, Giles E. "Adjustment and Assimilation of Slovenian Refugees." Ph.D. diss., Ohio State University, 1962.

Hearst, Joseph Albert. "The Government of a Displaced Persons' Camp." Master's thesis, University of Washington, 1948.

Momryk, Myron. "Ukrainian Displaced Persons and the Canadian Government— 1946–1952." Paper presented at conference on "The D.P. Experience: Ukrainian Refugees After World War II," University of Toronto, Toronto, Canada, 3–6 November 1983.

Raymond, Edward A. "The Juridical Status of Persons Displaced from Soviet and Soviet-Dominated Territory." Ph.D. diss., American University, 1952.

Refugees Defense Committee, "Report." N.p. 1947.

7. Newspapers, Magazines, and Journals

NOTE: In addition to the separate articles cited in section 8, these publications provided information for this study.

The Child
International Refugee Organization Monthly Digest
Lithuanian Bulletin
New Statesman
New York Times
PCIRO News Bulletin
Polish Review
Public Health Nursing
Social Service Review
Stars and Stripes
Survey Graphic
Time
The Times (London)
Ukrainian Bulletin
UNRRA Review
UNRRA Team News

8. Articles

Adler-Rudel, S. "Jewish Literature in the DP Camps." *Jewish Spectator*, September 1947, 9, 16.

Althoff, Becky. "Observations on the Psychology of Children in a D.P. Camp." *Journal of Social Casework* 29 (January 1948): 17–22.

Andriewsky, Dmytro. "Soviets and the Emigration." *Ukrainian Quarterly* 11, no. 2 (Spring 1955): 127–30.

Arendt, Hannah. "The Stateless People." *Contemporary Jewish Record* 8, no. 2 (April 1945): 137–53.

Bahryany, Ivan. "Why I Do Not Want to Go 'Home.'" *Ukrainian Quarterly* 2, no. 3 (Spring 1946): 236–51.

Bernard, William S. "Refugee Asylum in the United States: How the Law was Changed to Admit Displaced Persons." *International Migration* 13, no. 1/2 (1975): 3–18.

Bernstein, David. "Europe's Jews: Summer, 1947." *Commentary* 4, no. 2 (August 1947): 101–109.

Blum-Dobkin, Toby. "The Landsberg Carnival: Purim in a Displaced Persons Center." *Purim: The Face and the Mask.* Yeshiva University Museum Catalogue (1979): 52–58.

Bracey, Bertha L. "Practical Problems of Repatriation and Relocation." *International Affairs* 21, no. 3 (July 1945): 295–305.

Chamberlin, William H. "Asylum for Europe's Uprooted." *Ukrainian Quarterly* 1, no. 4 (Summer 1945): 322–25.

Danys, Milda. "The Emigrant Experience: Contract Hiring of Displaced Persons in Canadian Domestic Employment, 1947–1950." *Lituanus* 29, no. 2 (Summer 1983): 40–51.

Dinnerstein, Leonard. "The U.S. Army and the Jews: Policies toward the Displaced Persons After World War II." *American Jewish History* 68, no. 3 (March 1979): 353–66.

Dushnyck, Walter. "The Importance of the Problem of Displaced Persons." *Ukrainian Quarterly* 2, no. 3 (Spring 1946): 285–88.

Epstein, Julius. "American Forced Repatriation." *Ukrainian Quarterly* 10, no. 4 (Autumn 1954): 354–65.

Feingold, Henry L. "Who Shall Bear Guilt for the Holocaust: The Human Dilemma." *American Jewish History* 68, no. 3 (March 1979): 261–82.

Fischer, George. "The New Soviet Emigration." *Russian Review* 8, no. 1 (January 1949): 6–19.

Frank, Gerold, "The Tragedy of the DP's." *New Republic* 114, no. 13 (1 April 1946): 436–38.

Friedman, Paul. "Can Freedom Be Taught?" *Journal of Social Casework* 29, no. 7 (July 1948): 247–55.

———. "The Road Back for the DP's." *Commentary* 6, no. 6 (December 1948): 502–10.

Genêt, "Letter From Aschaffenburg," *New Yorker,* 30 October 1948, 98–101.

———. "Letter From Wurzburg." *New Yorker,* 6 November 1948, 116–21.

Gottlieb, Amy Zahl. "Refugee Immigration: The Truman Directive." *Prologue* 13, no. 1 (Spring 1981): 5–17.

Gringauz, Samuel. "Jewish Destiny as the DP's See It." *Commentary* 4, no. 6 (December 1947): 501–509.

———. "Our New German Policy and the DP's." *Commentary* 5, no. 6 (June 1948): 508–14.

Harrison, Earl G. "The Last Hundred Thousand." *Survey Graphic,* December 1945, 469–73.

Jaunzems, I., and L. B. Brown. "A Social-Psychological Study of Latvian Immigrants in Canberra." *International Migration* 10, no. 1/2 (1972): 53–70.

Johansons, Andrejs. "Latvian Literature in Exile." *Slavonic Review* 30, no. 75 (June 1952): 472–75.

Kotoz, Vasili, "Stalin Thinks I'm Dead." *Saturday Evening Post,* 31 January 1948, 28, 57–58.

Krisciunas, Raymond G. "The Emigrant Experience: The Decision of Lithuanian Refugees to Emigrate, 1945–1950." *Lituanus* 29, no. 2 (Summer 1983): 30–39.

Kubiyovych, Volodymyr. "The Ukrainians Outside Ukraine." *Ukrainian Review* 5, no. 4 (Winter 1958): 71–75.

Lehiste, Ilse, "Three Estonian Writers and the Experience of Exile." *Lituanus* 18, no. 1 (Spring 1972): 15–31.

Lehrman, Hal. "Austria: Way-Station of Exodus—Pages from a Correspondent's Notebook." *Commentary* 2, no. 6 (December 1946): 565–72.

Manning, Clarence A. "The Significance of the Soviet Refugees" *Ukrainian Quarterly* 2, no. 1 (Autumn 1945): 14–24.

Martin, David. "Not 'Displaced Persons'—But Refugees." *Ukrainian Quarterly* 4, no. 2 (Spring 1948): 109–14.

Morgan, Edward P. "They Seek a Promised Land." *Colliers,* 4 May 1946, 66–67, 83–84.

Neuburger, Gottfried. "An Orthodox G.I. Fights a War." *Commentary* 8, no. 3 (March 1949): 265–72.

Papanek, Ernst. "They Are Not Expendable: The Homeless and Refugee Children of Germany." *Social Service Review* 20, no. 3 (September 1946): 312–19.

Pinson, Koppel S. "Jewish Life in Liberated Germany—A Study of the Jewish DP's." *Jewish Social Studies* 9, (April 1947): 101–26.

Popkin, Zelda. "Europe's Children." *Ladies' Home Journal,* August 1946, 168, 170–71.

Scott, John. "Interview With a Russian D.P." *Fortune* 39, no. 4 (April 1949): 81–84.

S. H. "Ukrainian Writers in Exile, 1945–1949." *Ukrainian Quarterly* 6, no. 1 (Winter 1950): 73–76.

Shils, Edward A. "Social and Psychological Aspects of Displacement and Repatriation." *Journal of Social Issues* 2, no. 3 (August 1946): 3–18.

Šilbajoris, Rimvydas. "The Experience of Exile in Lithuanian Literature." *Lituanus* 18, no. 1 (Spring 1972): 43–57.

Silenieks, Juris. "Latvian Literature in Exile: The Recycling of Signs." *Lituanus* 18, no. 1 (Spring 1972): 32–42.

Sobieski, Zygmunt. "Reminiscences from Lwow, 1939–1946." *Journal of Central European Affairs* 6, no. 4 (January 1947): 351–91.

Srole, Leo. Autobiographical article. *Harvard Class of 1933: Fiftieth Anniversary Report.* Cambridge, Mass.: Harvard Class of 1933, 520–25.

———. "Why the DPs Can't Wait." *Commentary* 3, no. 1 (January 1947): 13–21.

Tolstoy, Alexandra. "The Russian DPs." *Russian Review* 9, no. 1 (January 1950): 53–58.

"The Ukrainian Free University in Munich and the Harvard University Refugee Project." *Ukrainian Quarterly* 7, no. 3 (Summer 1951): 267–68.

Weinryb, Bernard D. "Jews in Central Europe." *Journal of Central European Affairs* 7, no. 1 (April 1946): 43–77.

Wylie, I. A. R. "Returning Europe's Kidnapped Children." *Ladies' Home Journal,* October 1946, 22–23, 254–57.

9. Secondary Studies

Andersons, Edgars, ed. *Cross Road Country—Latvia.* Waverly, Iowa: Latvju Gramata, 1953.

Bach, Julian, Jr. *America's Germany: An Account of the Occupation.* New York: Random House, 1946.

Bauer, Yehuda. *Flight and Rescue: BRICHAH.* New York: Random House, 1970.

———. *The Holocaust in Historical Perspective.* Seattle: University of Washington Press, 1978.

———. *The Jewish Emergence from Powerlessness.* Toronto: University of Toronto Press, 1979.

Bethell, Nicholas, *The Last Secret: Forcible Repatriation to Russia 1944–7.* London: Andre Deutsch, 1974.

Bouscaren, Anthony T. *International Migrations Since 1945.* New York: Frederick A. Praeger, 1963.

Corbett, David C. *Canada's Immigration Policy: A Critique.* Toronto: University of Toronto Press, 1957.

Dallin, David J., and Boris I. Nicolaevsky. *Forced Labor in Soviet Russia.* New Haven: Yale University Press, 1947.

The Dark Side of the Moon. London: Faber and Faber, 1946.

Davie, Maruice R. *Refugees in America: Report of the Committee for the Study of Recent Immigration from Europe.* New York: Harper and Brothers, 1947.

Davies, Norman. *God's Playground: A History of Poland.* New York: Columbia University Press, 1982.

Dedijer, Vladimir, Ivan Bozic, Sima Cirkovic, and Milorad Ekmecic. *History of Yugoslavia.* New York: McGraw-Hill, 1974.

Dinnerstein, Leonard. *America and the Survivors of the Holocaust.* New York: Columbia University Press, 1982.

Doroshenko, Dmytro. *A Survey of Ukrainian History.* Winnipeg, Canada: Humeniuk Foundation, 1975.

Elliott, Mark R. *Pawns of Yalta: Soviet Refugees and America's Role in Their Repatriation.* Urbana: University of Illinois Press, 1982.

The Encyclopedia of the Lutheran Church. 3 vols. Minneapolis, Minn.: Augsburg, 1965.

Epstein, Helen. *Children of the Holocaust: Conversations with Sons and Daughters of Survivors.* New York: Putnam's, 1979.

Epstein, Julius. *Operation Keelhaul: The Story of Forced Repatriation from 1944 to the Present.* Old Greenwich, Conn.: Devin-Adair, 1973.

Fischer, George. *Soviet Opposition to Stalin: A Case Study in World War II.* Cambridge, Mass.: Harvard University Press, 1952.

Flygtninge I Danmark 1945–1949. Copenhagen: I Kommission Hos Forlaget Fremad, 1950.

Frederiksen, Oliver J. *The American Military Occupation of Germany, 1945–1953.* Frankfurt am Main, Germany: U.S. Army, 1953.

Gerutis, Albertas, ed. *Lithuania 700 Years.* New York: Manyland Books, 1969.

Gimbel, John. *The American Occupation of Germany: Politics and the Military, 1945–1949.* Stanford, Calif.: Stanford University Press, 1968.

Grygier, Tadeusz. *Oppression: A Study in Social and Criminal Psychology.* Westport, Conn.: Greenwood Press, 1954; reprint, 1973.

Hirschmann, Ira A. *The Embers Still Burn: An Eye-Witness View of the Postwar Ferment in Europe and the Middle East and Our Disastrous Get-Soft-With-Germany Policy.* New York: Simon and Schuster, 1949.

Homze, Edward L. *Foreign Labor in Nazi Germany.* Princeton: Princeton University Press, 1967.

International Labour Office. *International Migration: 1945–1957.* Geneva, Switzerland: International Labour Office, 1957.

Jackson, J. Hampden. *Estonia.* London: George Allen and Unwin, 1941, 1948.

Kimche, Jon, and David Kimche. *The Secret Roads: The "Illegal" Migration of a People—1938–1948.* New York: Farrar, Straus and Cudahy, 1955.

Knauth, Percy. *Germany in Defeat.* New York: Knopf, 1946.

Kulischer, Eugene M. *Europe on the Move: War and Population Changes, 1917–47.* New York: Columbia University Press, 1948.

Levin, Nora. *The Holocaust: The Destruction of European Jewry, 1933–1945.* New York: Schocken Books, 1973.

Loftus, John. *The Belarus Secret.* New York: Knopf, 1982.

Macardle, Dorothy. *Children of Europe—A Study of the Children of Liberated Countries: Their War-Time Experiences, Their Reactions, and Their Needs, with a Note on Germany.* Boston: Beacon Press, 1951.

Milazzo, Matteo J. *The Chetnik Movement & the Yugoslav Resistance.* Baltimore: Johns Hopkins University Press, 1975.

Peterson, Edward N. *The American Occupation of Germany: Retreat to Victory.* Detroit: Wayne State University Press, 1977.

Proudfoot, Malcolm J. *European Refugees: 1939–1952—A Study in Forced Population Movement.* Evanston, Ill.: Northwestern University Press, 1956.

Putniņš, Aldis L. *Latvians in Australia: Alienation and Assimilation.* Canberra: Australian National University Press, 1981.

Roberts, Hew, ed. *Australia's Immigration Policy.* Nedlands: University of Western Australia Press, 1972.

Rothchild, Sylvia, ed. *Voices From the Holocaust.* New York: New American Library, 1981.

Šilbajoris, Rimvydas. *Perfection of Exile: Fourteen Contemporary Lithuanian Writers.* Norman: University of Oklahoma Press, 1970.

Swanstrom, Rt. Rev. Edward E. *Pilgrims of the Night: A Study of Expelled Peoples.* New York: Sheed and Ward, 1950.

Toland, John. *The Last 100 Days.* New York: Random House, 1965.

Tolstoy, Niolai. *Victims of Yalta.* London: Hodder and Stoughton, 1977.

Ukraine—A Concise Encyclopedia. Edited by Volodymyr Kubijovyč. 2 vols. Toronto, Canada: University of Toronto Press, 1963 (vol. 1); 1971 (vol. 2).

Vernant, Jacques. *The Refugee in the Post-War World.* New Haven: Yale University Press, 1953.

Willis, F. Roy. *The French in Germany—1945–1949.* Stanford, Calif.: Stanford University Press, 1962.

Woodbridge, George. *UNRRA: The History of the United Nations Relief and Rehabilitation Administration.* 3 vols. New York: Columbia University Press, 1950.

Ziemke, Earl F. *The U.S. Army in the Occupation of Germany, 1944–1946.* Washington: U.S. Army Center of Military History, 1975.

Zink, Harold. *The United States in Germany, 1944–1955.* Princeton: D. Van Nostrand, 1957.

INDEX OF DISPLACED PERSONS CAMPS

GENERAL INDEX